Josie and the Pussycats®

Volume Two

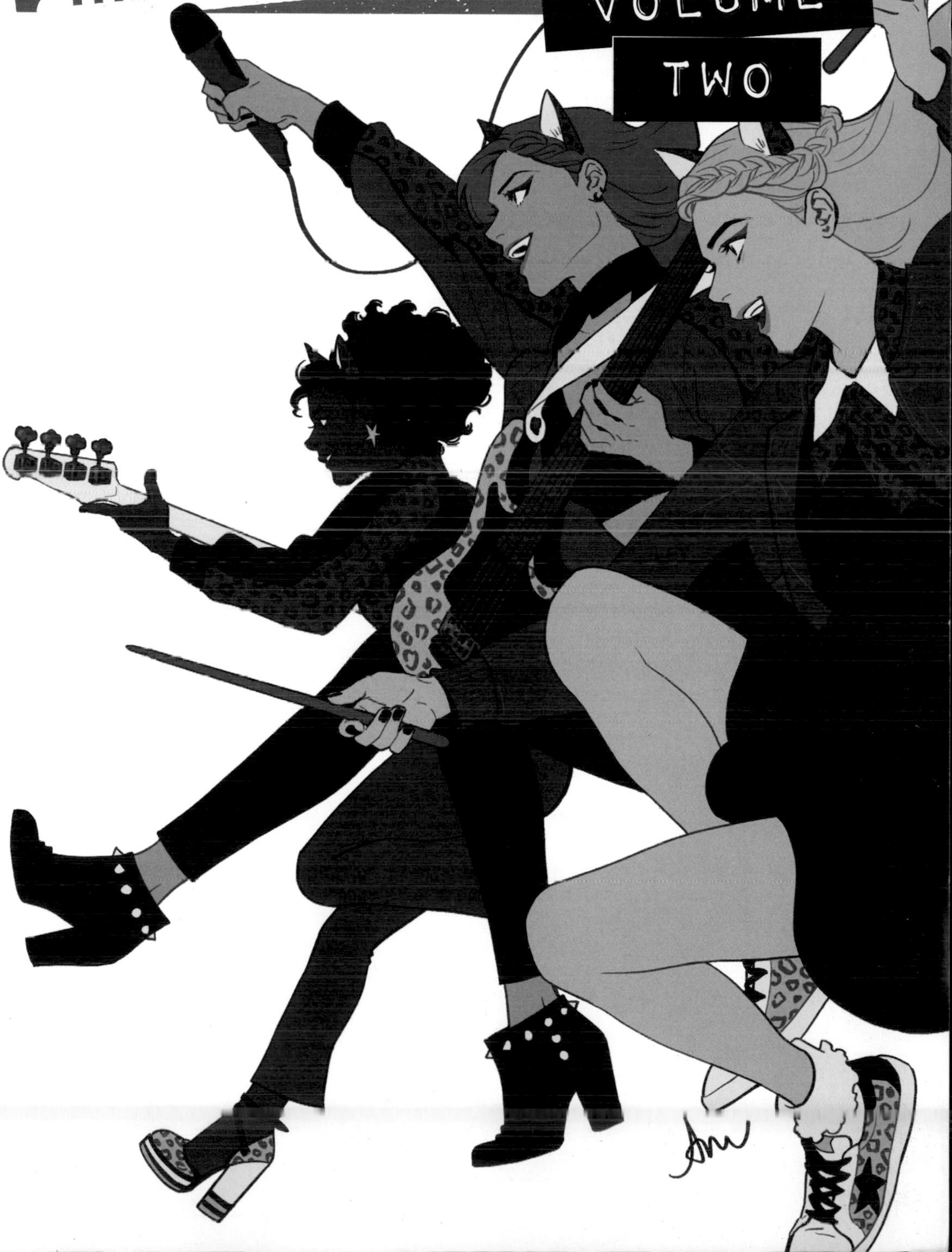

ART BY

AUDREY MOK
AND KELSEY SHANNON

STORY BY

MARGUERITE BENNETT
AND CAMERON DEORDIO

COLORING BY

KELLY FITZPATRICK
AND MATT HERMS

LETTERING BY

JACK MORELLI

EDITORS

ALEX SEGURA AND
MIKE PELLERITO

EDITOR-IN-CHIEF

VICTOR GORELICK

PUBLISHER

JON GOLDWATER

GRAPHIC DESIGN

KARI McLACHLAN

ASSOCIATE EDITOR

STEPHEN OSWALD

ASSISTANT EDITOR

JAMIE LEE ROTANTE

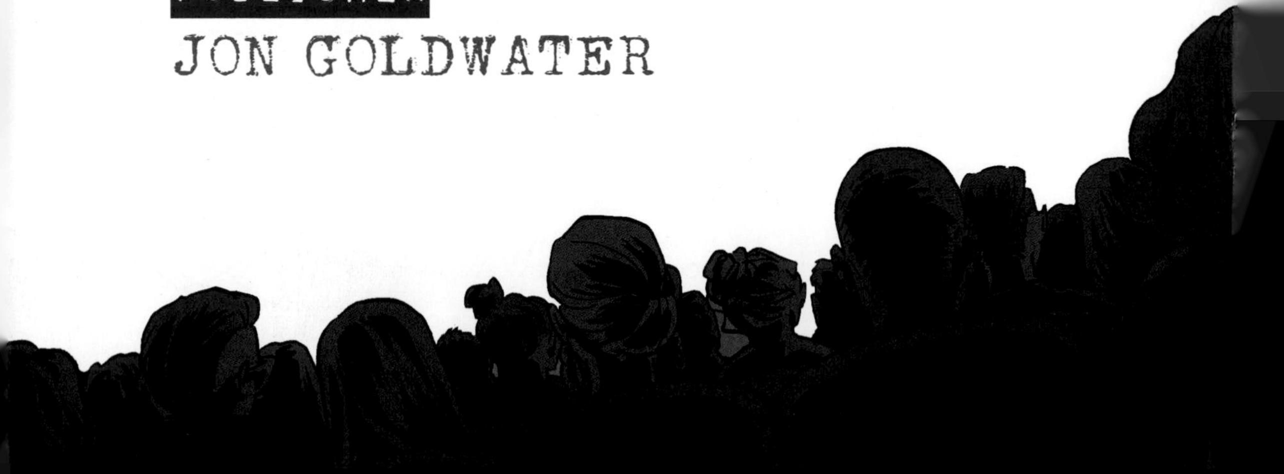

Josie AND THE PUSSYCATS

A ROCK BAND LIKE NO OTHER

Music comics are tough, that's the truth. As the writer or co-writer of titles like ARCHIE MEETS KISS and ARCHIE MEETS THE RAMONES, I knew that putting together comics that gave the impression of some kind of auditory experience was not easy. You have to use the tools you have available—imagery and words—to give the reader the impression of hearing something. It's doubly hard when the music you're asking them to hear doesn't even exist.

That was the big challenge I saw while mulling over a creative team for a new JOSIE AND THE PUSSYCATS series. We didn't have the added benefit of an identifiable, existing band coming in to give readers an idea of what they were hearing in their heads. Now, it was all imaginary; which meant the team that put this book together had to not only tell a great story, but get in the heads of the fans reading the book.

I lucked out, and struck gold out of the gate. I've known **Marguerite Bennett** for years, and seen her rise up the ranks to become one of the most acclaimed and respected writers in the business. The fact that she brought along her friend and super-talented co-writer **Cameron DeOrdio** was icing on the cake, giving the book a perfect balance of drama, action and humor while still being musically charged. The pitch they came up with was easy to visualize and I instantly wanted to read it. When we paired them with **Audrey Mok** as the interior artist—who has a knack for making even blades of grass seem gorgeous—and the amazing **Kelly Fitzpatrick** as colorist—an unsung talent who should be coloring everything. The first issue proved that *Josie & the Pussycats* was on our hands. Fun, heartfelt, honest and rocking, the book was something special. Fun, heartfelt, honest and rocking, the book was fun every step of the way, from reading the script to holding the finished issue in my hands. It was definitely one of the most enjoyable (and hey, let's face it—easy!) editorial gigs in my experience. When you've surrounded yourself with talented people, and you allow them to do their thing, the end result is always worth it.

Working on this book wasn't only fun, it was *important*. It's an off-the-wall yet emotionally resonant title that felt *current* and tapped-into modern day sensibilities in an interesting way. It's always a pleasure to get to work on a title that puts music at the forefront, but especially one that accomplishes so much in each story while exuding pure fun.

Hope you enjoy your quick tour with the band. I know I did.

Alex Segura
Editor, *Josie & the Pussycats*
Co-President, Archie Comics

ISSUE SIX

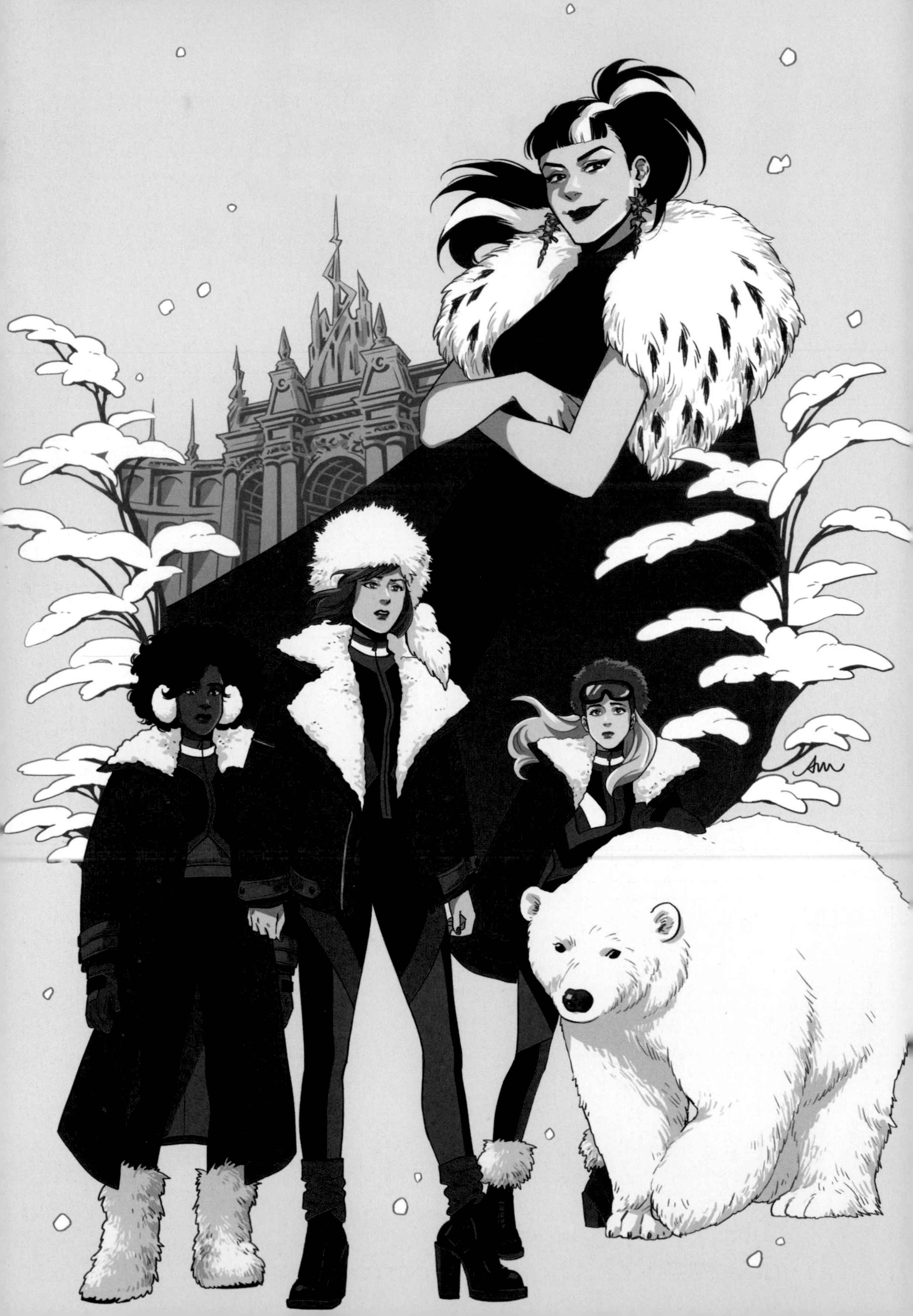

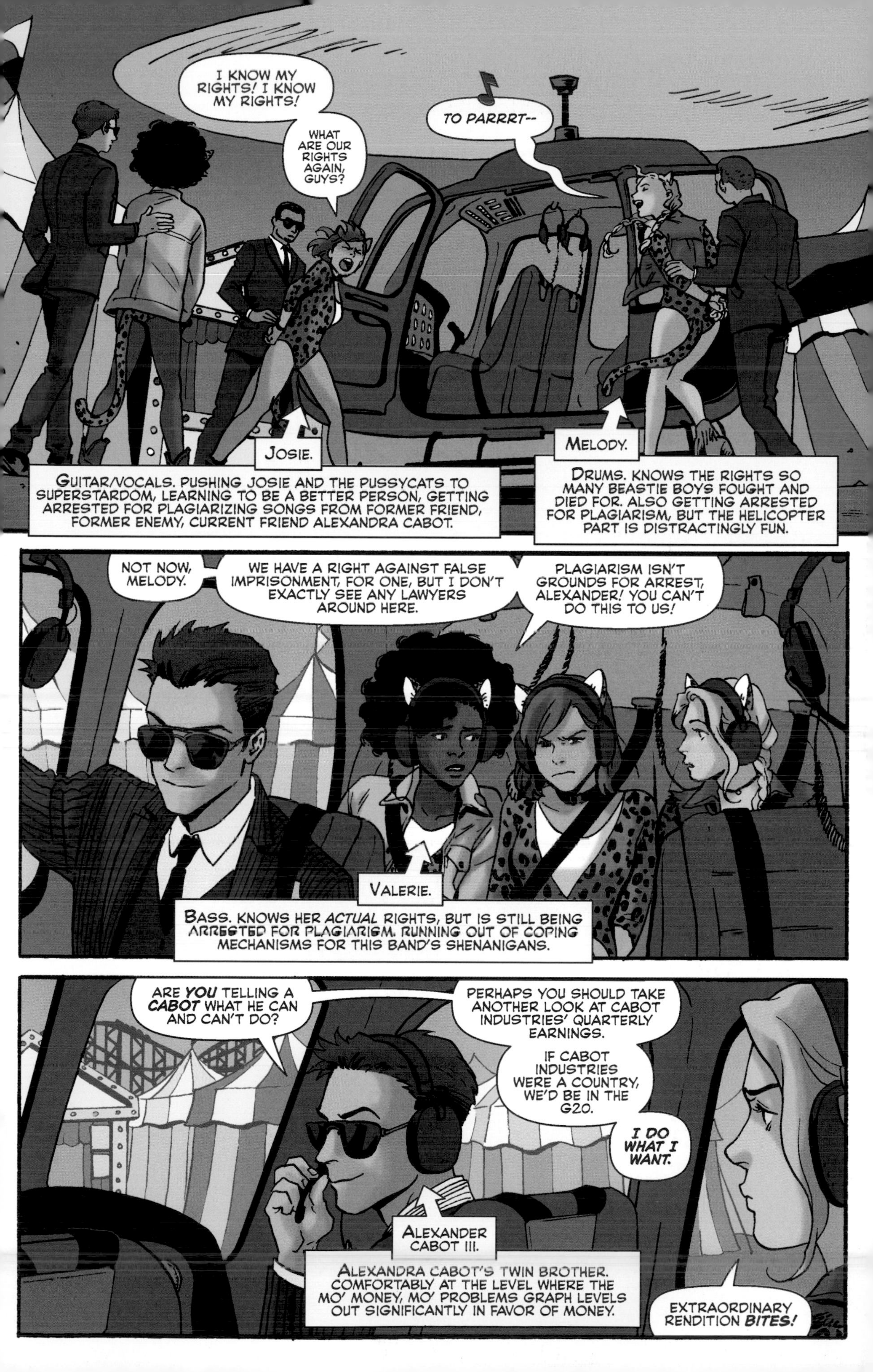
I KNOW MY RIGHTS! I KNOW MY RIGHTS!
WHAT ARE OUR RIGHTS AGAIN, GUYS?
TO PARRRT--
JOSIE.
GUITAR/VOCALS. PUSHING JOSIE AND THE PUSSYCATS TO SUPERSTARDOM, LEARNING TO BE A BETTER PERSON, GETTING ARRESTED FOR PLAGIARIZING SONGS FROM FORMER FRIEND, FORMER ENEMY, CURRENT FRIEND ALEXANDRA CABOT.
MELODY.
DRUMS. KNOWS THE RIGHTS SO MANY BEASTIE BOYS FOUGHT AND DIED FOR. ALSO GETTING ARRESTED FOR PLAGIARISM, BUT THE HELICOPTER PART IS DISTRACTINGLY FUN.
NOT NOW, MELODY.
WE HAVE A RIGHT AGAINST FALSE IMPRISONMENT, FOR ONE, BUT I DON'T EXACTLY SEE ANY LAWYERS AROUND HERE.
PLAGIARISM ISN'T GROUNDS FOR ARREST, ALEXANDER! YOU CAN'T DO THIS TO US!
VALERIE.
BASS. KNOWS HER *ACTUAL* RIGHTS, BUT IS STILL BEING ARRESTED FOR PLAGIARISM. RUNNING OUT OF COPING MECHANISMS FOR THIS BAND'S SHENANIGANS.
ARE ***YOU*** TELLING A ***CABOT*** WHAT HE CAN AND CAN'T DO?
PERHAPS YOU SHOULD TAKE ANOTHER LOOK AT CABOT INDUSTRIES' QUARTERLY EARNINGS.
IF CABOT INDUSTRIES WERE A COUNTRY, WE'D BE IN THE G20.
I DO WHAT I WANT.
ALEXANDER CABOT III.
ALEXANDRA CABOT'S TWIN BROTHER. COMFORTABLY AT THE LEVEL WHERE THE MO' MONEY, MO' PROBLEMS GRAPH LEVELS OUT SIGNIFICANTLY IN FAVOR OF MONEY.
EXTRAORDINARY RENDITION ***BITES!***

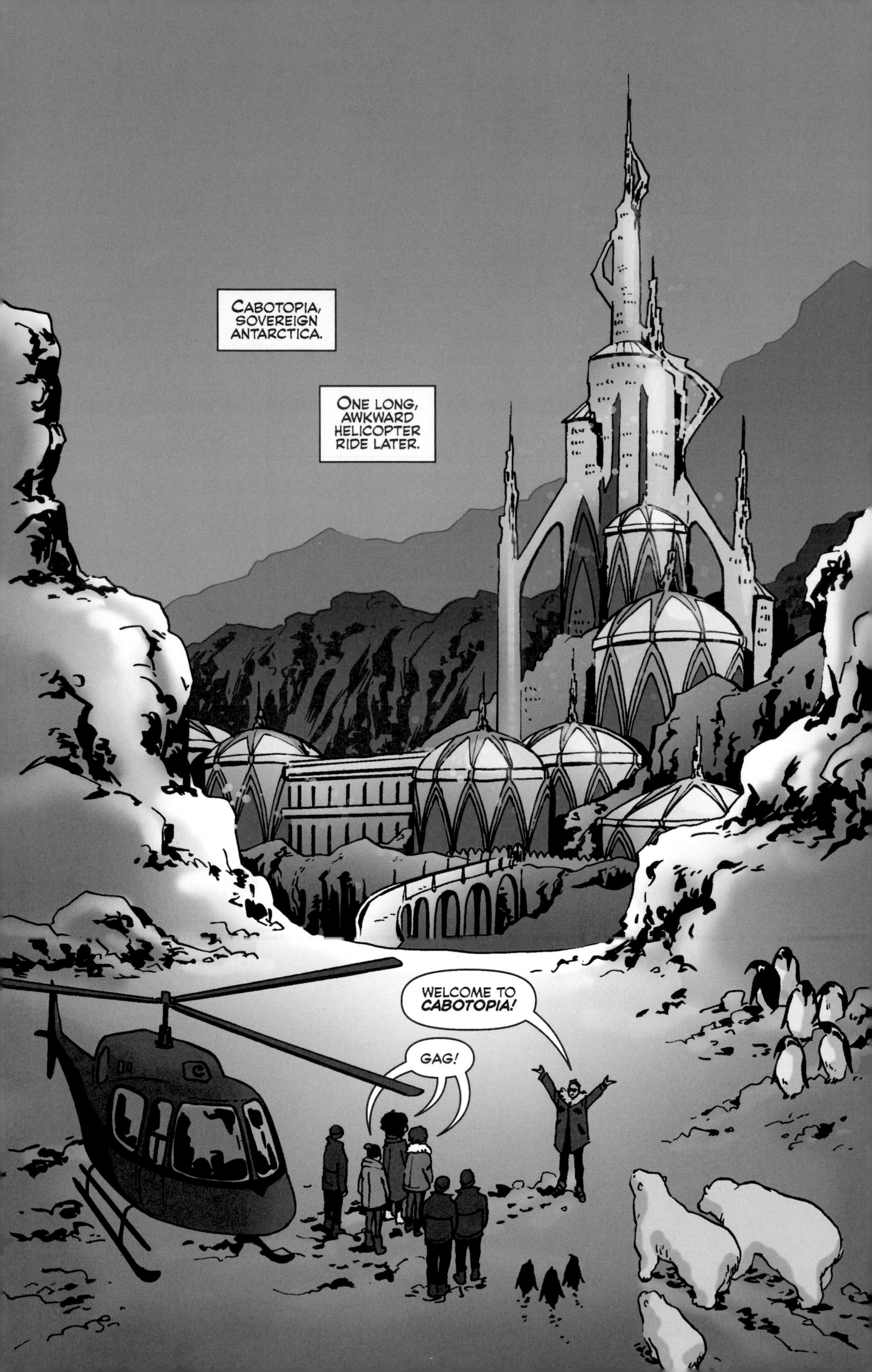
CABOTOPIA, SOVEREIGN ANTARCTICA.
ONE LONG, AWKWARD HELICOPTER RIDE LATER.
WELCOME TO *CABOTOPIA!*
GAG!

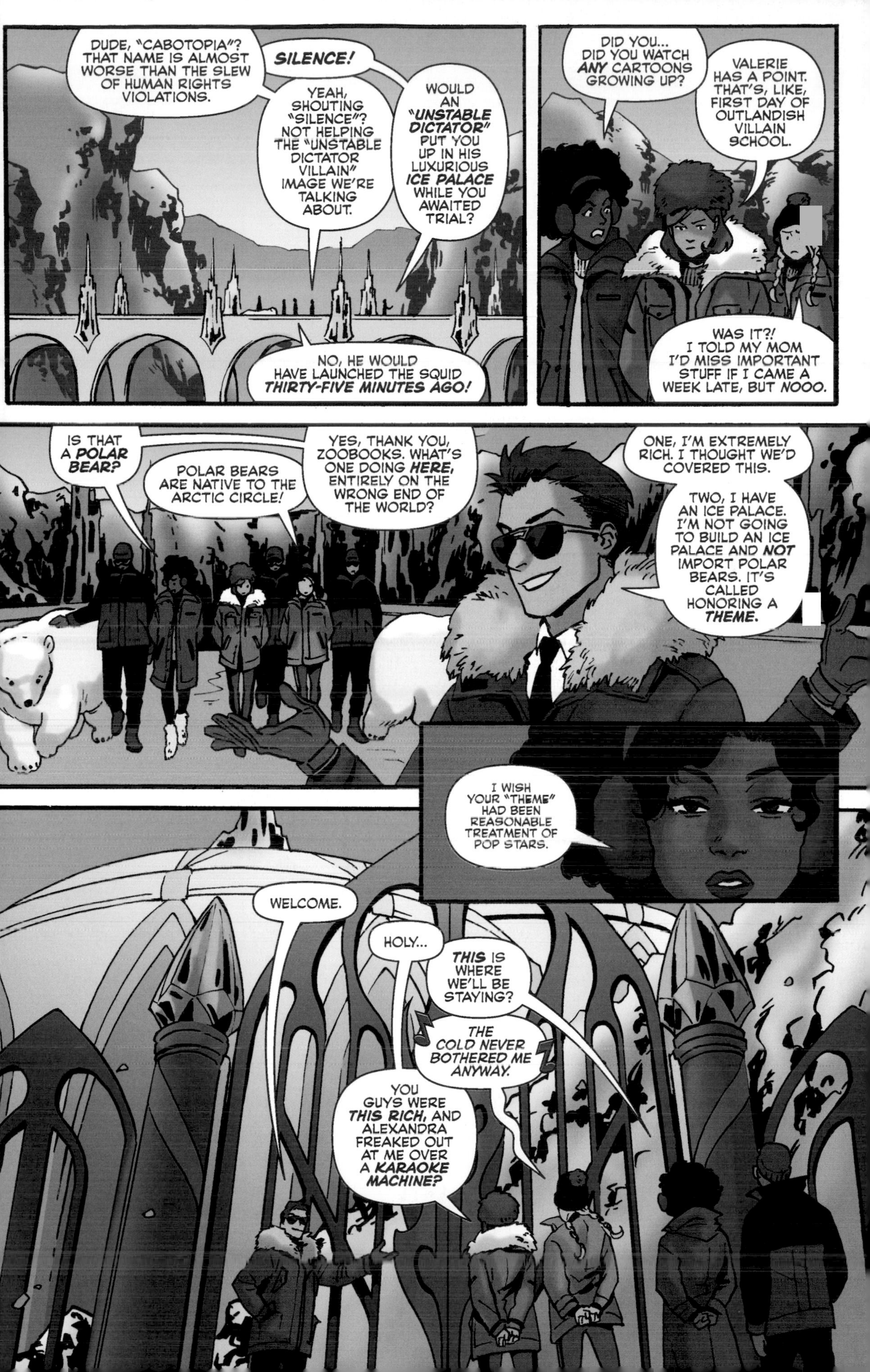
DUDE, "CABOTOPIA"? THAT NAME IS ALMOST WORSE THAN THE SLEW OF HUMAN RIGHTS VIOLATIONS.
SILENCE!
YEAH, SHOUTING "SILENCE"? NOT HELPING THE "UNSTABLE DICTATOR VILLAIN" IMAGE WE'RE TALKING ABOUT.
WOULD AN "UNSTABLE DICTATOR" PUT YOU UP IN HIS LUXURIOUS ICE PALACE WHILE YOU AWAITED TRIAL?
NO, HE WOULD HAVE LAUNCHED THE SQUID THIRTY-FIVE MINUTES AGO!
DID YOU... DID YOU WATCH ANY CARTOONS GROWING UP?
VALERIE HAS A POINT. THAT'S, LIKE, FIRST DAY OF OUTLANDISH VILLAIN SCHOOL.
WAS IT?! I TOLD MY MOM I'D MISS IMPORTANT STUFF IF I CAME A WEEK LATE, BUT NOOO.
IS THAT A POLAR BEAR?
POLAR BEARS ARE NATIVE TO THE ARCTIC CIRCLE!
YES, THANK YOU, ZOOBOOKS. WHAT'S ONE DOING HERE, ENTIRELY ON THE WRONG END OF THE WORLD?
ONE, I'M EXTREMELY RICH. I THOUGHT WE'D COVERED THIS.
TWO, I HAVE AN ICE PALACE. I'M NOT GOING TO BUILD AN ICE PALACE AND NOT IMPORT POLAR BEARS. IT'S CALLED HONORING A THEME.
I WISH YOUR "THEME" HAD BEEN REASONABLE TREATMENT OF POP STARS.
WELCOME.
HOLY...
THIS IS WHERE WE'LL BE STAYING?
THE COLD NEVER BOTHERED ME ANYWAY.
YOU GUYS WERE THIS RICH, AND ALEXANDRA FREAKED OUT AT ME OVER A KARAOKE MACHINE?

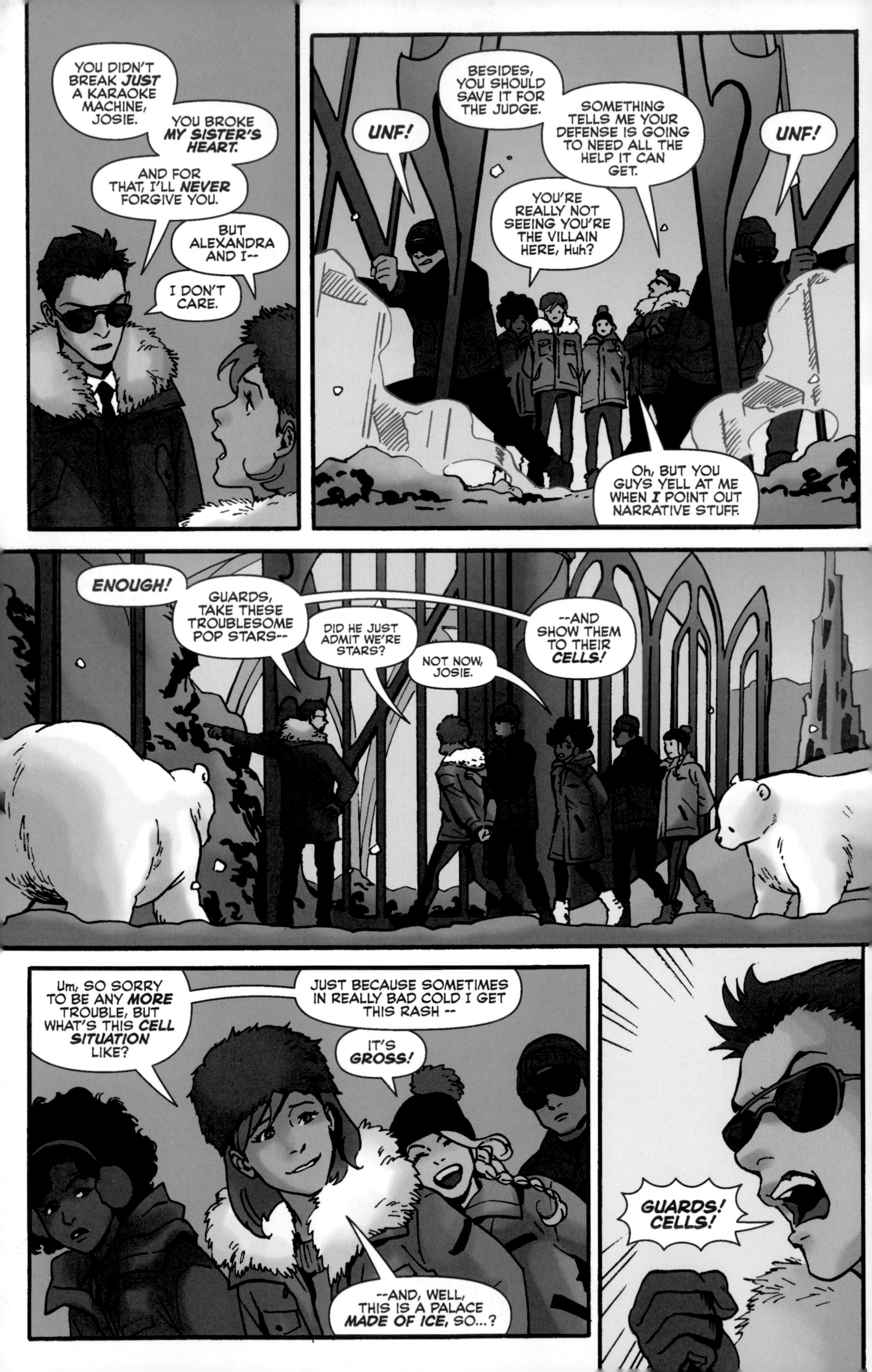

YOU DIDN'T BREAK JUST A KARAOKE MACHINE, JOSIE.
YOU BROKE MY SISTER'S HEART.
AND FOR THAT, I'LL NEVER FORGIVE YOU.
BUT ALEXANDRA AND I--
I DON'T CARE.
UNF!
BESIDES, YOU SHOULD SAVE IT FOR THE JUDGE.
SOMETHING TELLS ME YOUR DEFENSE IS GOING TO NEED ALL THE HELP IT CAN GET.
UNF!
YOU'RE REALLY NOT SEEING YOU'RE THE VILLAIN HERE, Huh?
Oh, BUT YOU GUYS YELL AT ME WHEN I POINT OUT NARRATIVE STUFF.
ENOUGH!
GUARDS, TAKE THESE TROUBLESOME POP STARS--
DID HE JUST ADMIT WE'RE STARS?
NOT NOW, JOSIE.
--AND SHOW THEM TO THEIR CELLS!
Um, SO SORRY TO BE ANY MORE TROUBLE, BUT WHAT'S THIS CELL SITUATION LIKE?
JUST BECAUSE SOMETIMES IN REALLY BAD COLD I GET THIS RASH --
IT'S GROSS!
--AND, WELL, THIS IS A PALACE MADE OF ICE, SO...?
GUARDS! CELLS!

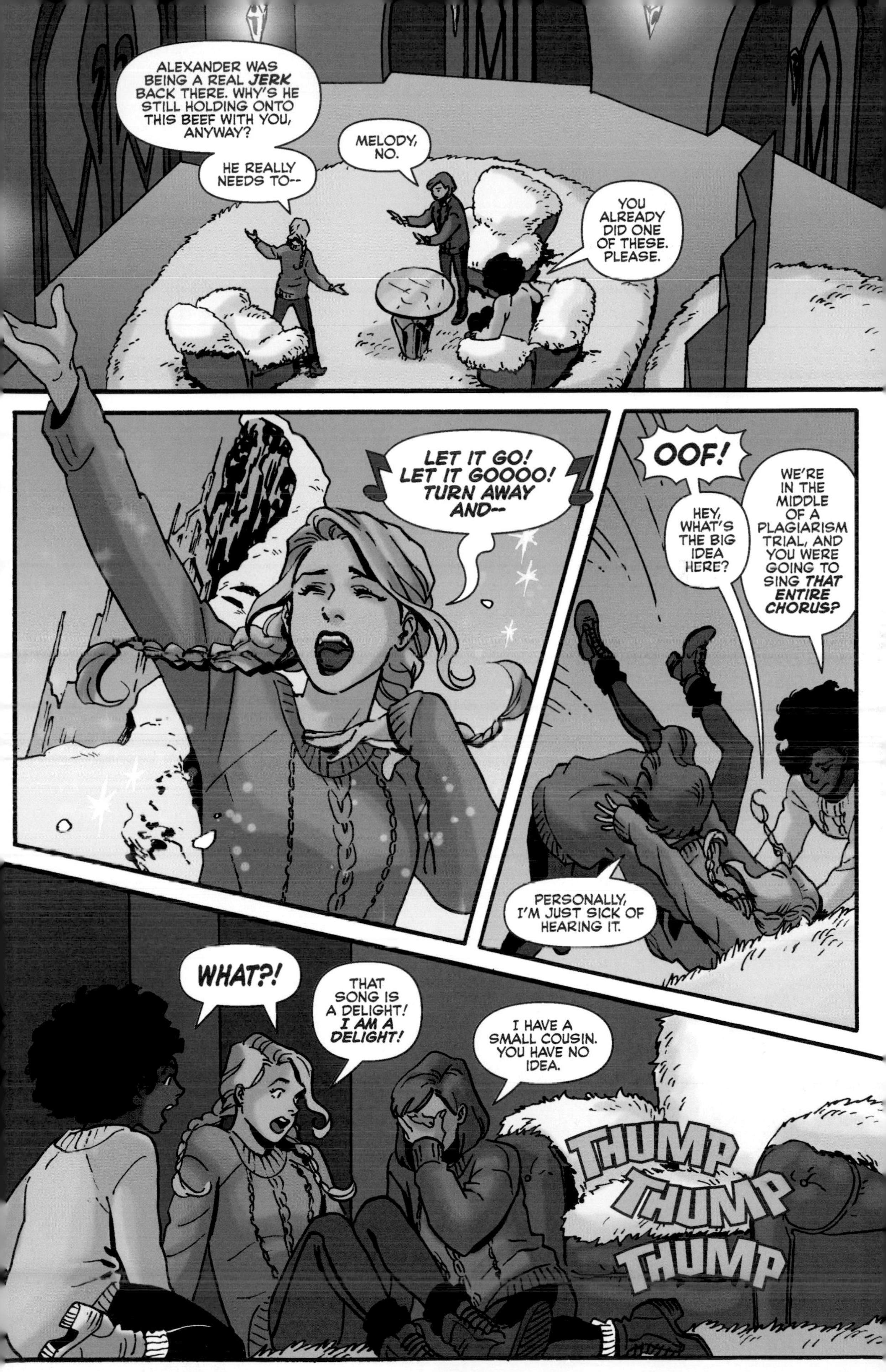
ALEXANDER WAS BEING A REAL JERK BACK THERE. WHY'S HE STILL HOLDING ONTO THIS BEEF WITH YOU, ANYWAY?
HE REALLY NEEDS TO--
MELODY, NO.
YOU ALREADY DID ONE OF THESE. PLEASE.
LET IT GO! LET IT GOOOO! TURN AWAY AND--
OOF!
HEY, WHAT'S THE BIG IDEA HERE?
WE'RE IN THE MIDDLE OF A PLAGIARISM TRIAL, AND YOU WERE GOING TO SING THAT ENTIRE CHORUS?
PERSONALLY, I'M JUST SICK OF HEARING IT.
WHAT?!
THAT SONG IS A DELIGHT! I AM A DELIGHT!
I HAVE A SMALL COUSIN. YOU HAVE NO IDEA.
THUMP
THUMP
THUMP

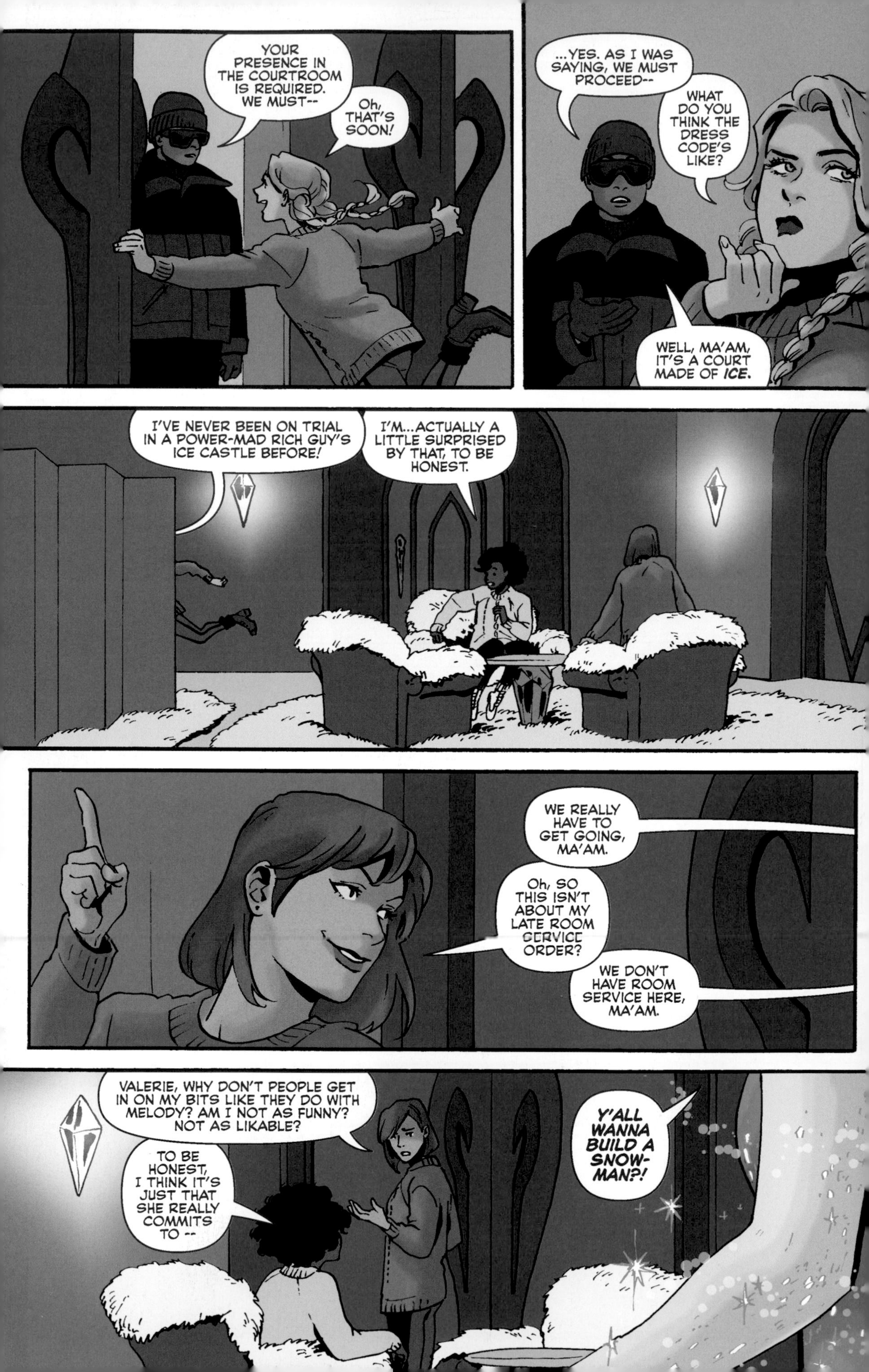
YOUR PRESENCE IN THE COURTROOM IS REQUIRED. WE MUST--
Oh, THAT'S SOON!
...YES. AS I WAS SAYING, WE MUST PROCEED--
WHAT DO YOU THINK THE DRESS CODE'S LIKE?
WELL, MA'AM, IT'S A COURT MADE OF ICE.
I'VE NEVER BEEN ON TRIAL IN A POWER-MAD RICH GUY'S ICE CASTLE BEFORE!
I'M...ACTUALLY A LITTLE SURPRISED BY THAT, TO BE HONEST.
WE REALLY HAVE TO GET GOING, MA'AM.
Oh, SO THIS ISN'T ABOUT MY LATE ROOM SERVICE ORDER?
WE DON'T HAVE ROOM SERVICE HERE, MA'AM.
VALERIE, WHY DON'T PEOPLE GET IN ON MY BITS LIKE THEY DO WITH MELODY? AM I NOT AS FUNNY? NOT AS LIKABLE?
TO BE HONEST, I THINK IT'S JUST THAT SHE REALLY COMMITS TO --
Y'ALL WANNA BUILD A SNOW-MAN?!

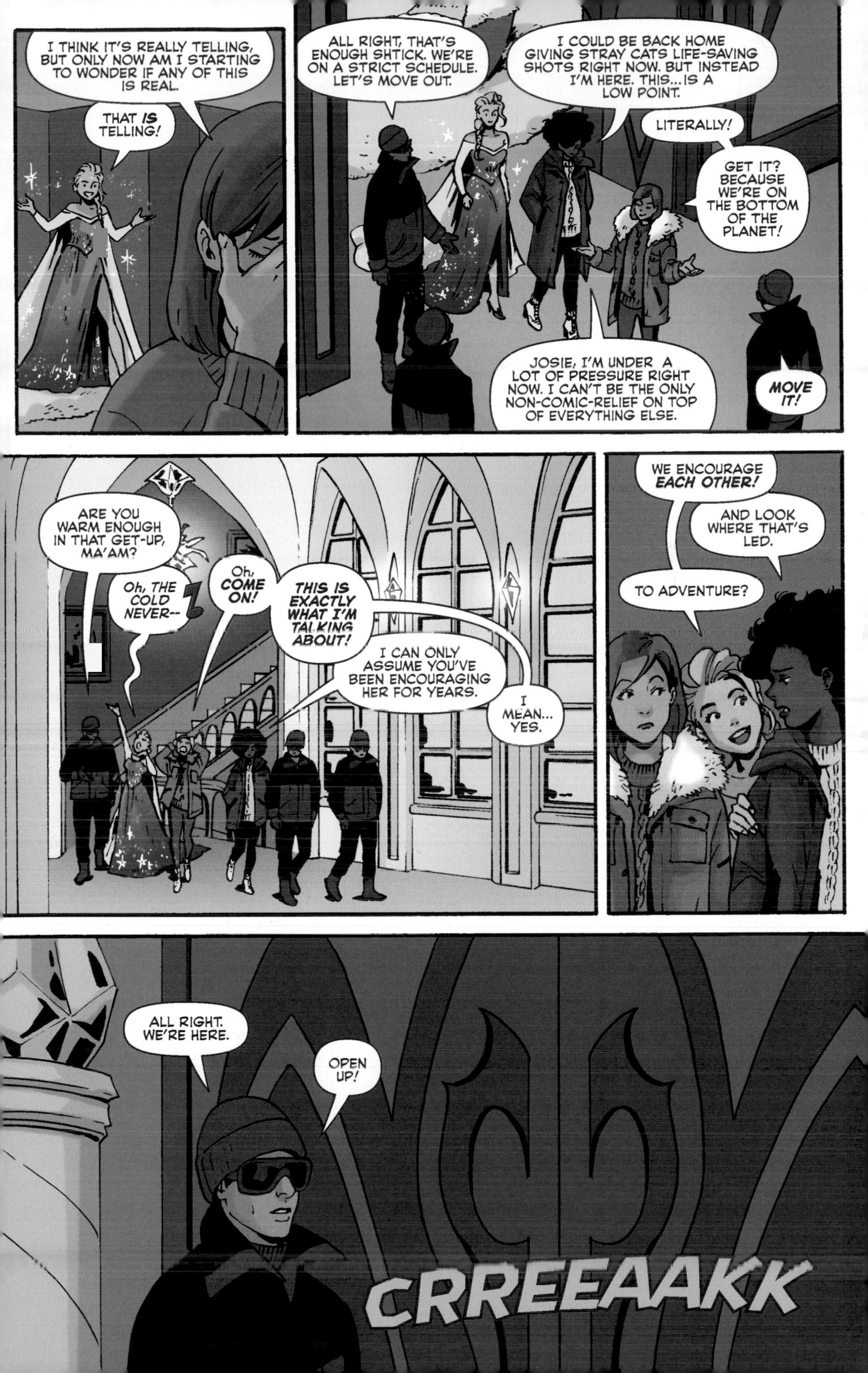
I THINK IT'S REALLY TELLING, BUT ONLY NOW AM I STARTING TO WONDER IF ANY OF THIS IS REAL.
THAT *IS* TELLING!
ALL RIGHT, THAT'S ENOUGH SHTICK. WE'RE ON A STRICT SCHEDULE. LET'S MOVE OUT.
I COULD BE BACK HOME GIVING STRAY CATS LIFE-SAVING SHOTS RIGHT NOW. BUT INSTEAD I'M HERE. THIS...IS A LOW POINT.
LITERALLY!
GET IT? BECAUSE WE'RE ON THE BOTTOM OF THE PLANET!
JOSIE, I'M UNDER A LOT OF PRESSURE RIGHT NOW. I CAN'T BE THE ONLY NON-COMIC-RELIEF ON TOP OF EVERYTHING ELSE.
MOVE IT!
ARE YOU WARM ENOUGH IN THAT GET-UP, MA'AM?
Oh, THE COLD NEVER--
Oh, *COME ON!*
THIS IS EXACTLY WHAT I'M TALKING ABOUT!
I CAN ONLY ASSUME YOU'VE BEEN ENCOURAGING HER FOR YEARS.
I MEAN... YES.
WE ENCOURAGE *EACH OTHER!*
AND LOOK WHERE THAT'S LED.
TO ADVENTURE?
ALL RIGHT. WE'RE HERE.
OPEN UP!
CRREEAAKK

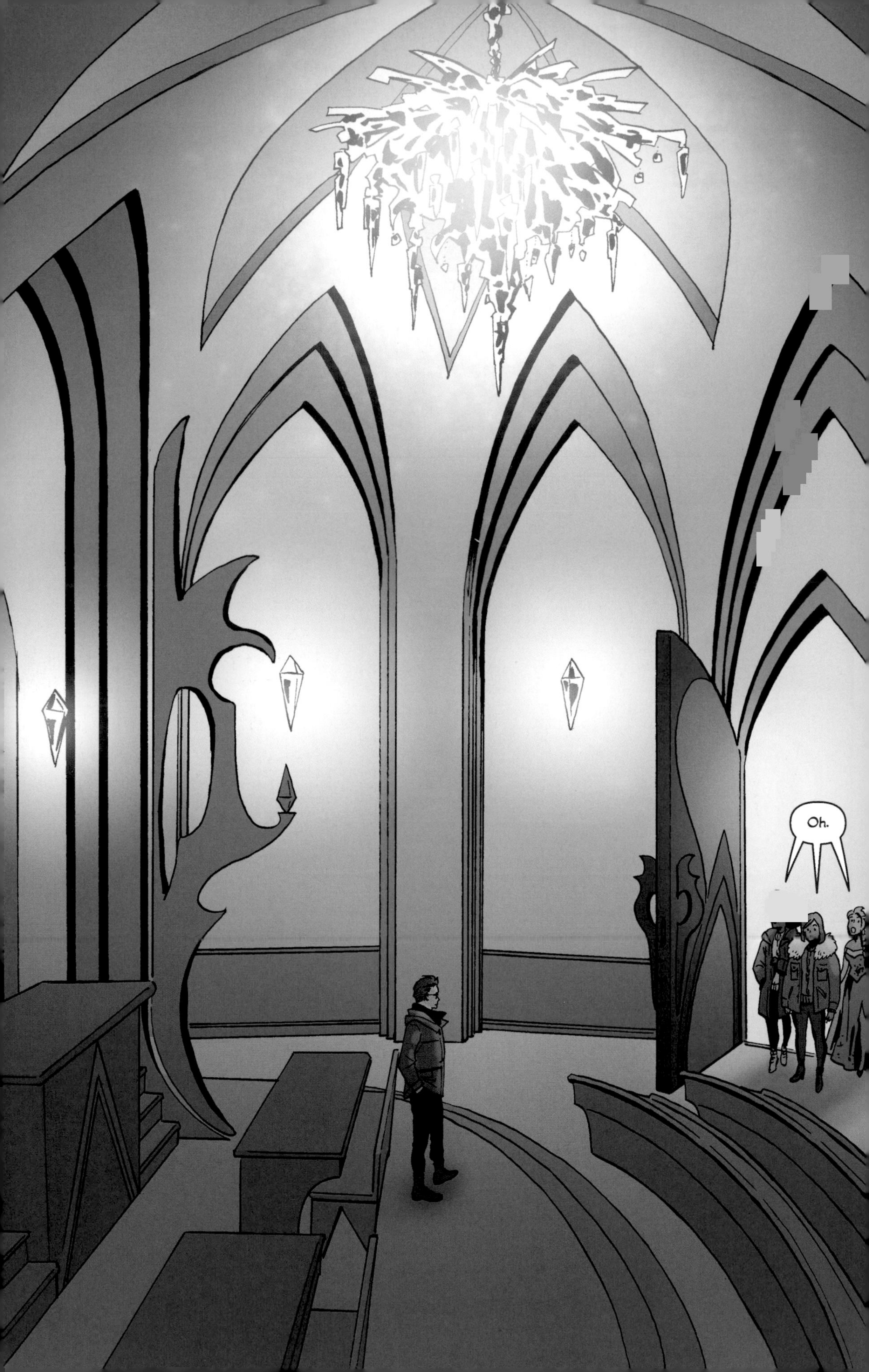
Oh.

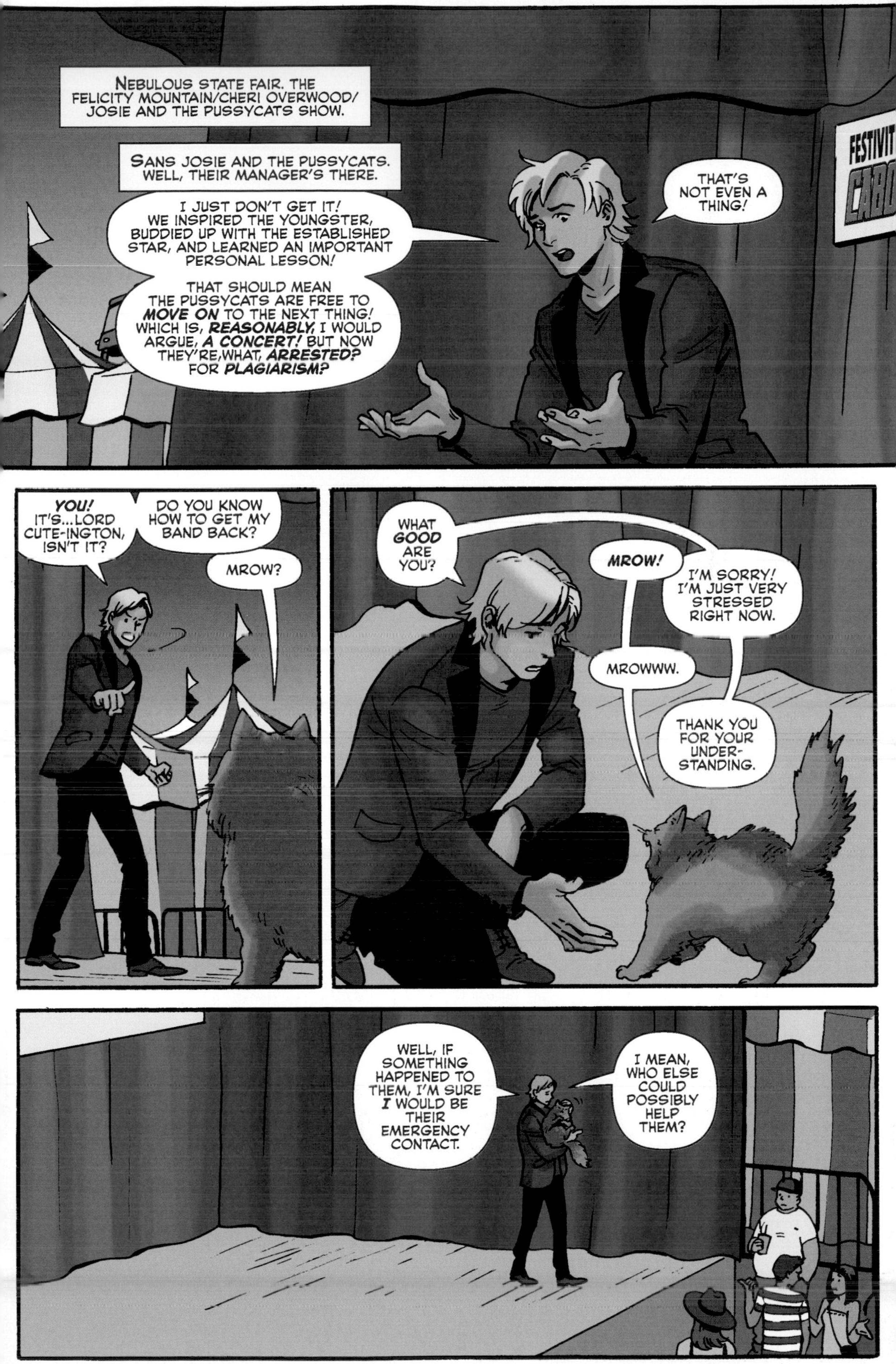
NEBULOUS STATE FAIR. THE FELICITY MOUNTAIN/CHERI OVERWOOD/ JOSIE AND THE PUSSYCATS SHOW.
SANS JOSIE AND THE PUSSYCATS. WELL, THEIR MANAGER'S THERE.
I JUST DON'T GET IT! WE INSPIRED THE YOUNGSTER, BUDDIED UP WITH THE ESTABLISHED STAR, AND LEARNED AN IMPORTANT PERSONAL LESSON!
THAT SHOULD MEAN THE PUSSYCATS ARE FREE TO MOVE ON TO THE NEXT THING! WHICH IS, REASONABLY, I WOULD ARGUE, A CONCERT! BUT NOW THEY'RE,WHAT, ARRESTED? FOR PLAGIARISM?
THAT'S NOT EVEN A THING!
FESTIVIT
YOU! IT'S...LORD CUTE-INGTON, ISN'T IT?
DO YOU KNOW HOW TO GET MY BAND BACK?
MROW?
WHAT GOOD ARE YOU?
MROW!
I'M SORRY! I'M JUST VERY STRESSED RIGHT NOW.
MROWWW.
THANK YOU FOR YOUR UNDER-STANDING.
WELL, IF SOMETHING HAPPENED TO THEM, I'M SURE I WOULD BE THEIR EMERGENCY CONTACT.
I MEAN, WHO ELSE COULD POSSIBLY HELP THEM?

ALEXANDRA'S BEDROOM, RIVERDALE.

THIS IS WHAT I GET FOR *FORGIVING SOMEONE!*

DADDY WAS RIGHT: ALL IT TAKES IS ONE ACT OF KINDNESS FOR SOMEONE TO LOSE ALL RESPECT.

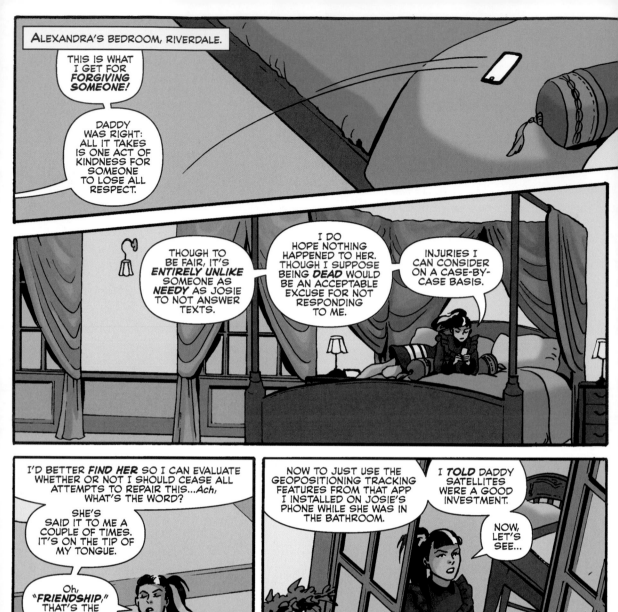

THOUGH TO BE FAIR, IT'S *ENTIRELY UNLIKE* SOMEONE AS *NEEDY* AS JOSIE TO NOT ANSWER TEXTS.

I DO HOPE NOTHING HAPPENED TO HER. THOUGH I SUPPOSE BEING *DEAD* WOULD BE AN ACCEPTABLE EXCUSE FOR NOT RESPONDING TO ME.

INJURIES I CAN CONSIDER ON A CASE-BY-CASE BASIS.

I'D BETTER *FIND HER* SO I CAN EVALUATE WHETHER OR NOT I SHOULD CEASE ALL ATTEMPTS TO REPAIR THIS...*Ach,* WHAT'S THE WORD?

SHE'S SAID IT TO ME A COUPLE OF TIMES. IT'S ON THE TIP OF MY TONGUE.

Oh, *"FRIENDSHIP,"* THAT'S THE ONE. *Hmph.*

NOW TO JUST USE THE GEOPOSITIONING TRACKING FEATURES FROM THAT APP I INSTALLED ON JOSIE'S PHONE WHILE SHE WAS IN THE BATHROOM.

I *TOLD* DADDY SATELLITES WERE A GOOD INVESTMENT.

NOW, LET'S SEE...

CABOTOPIA?!

ALEXANDER!

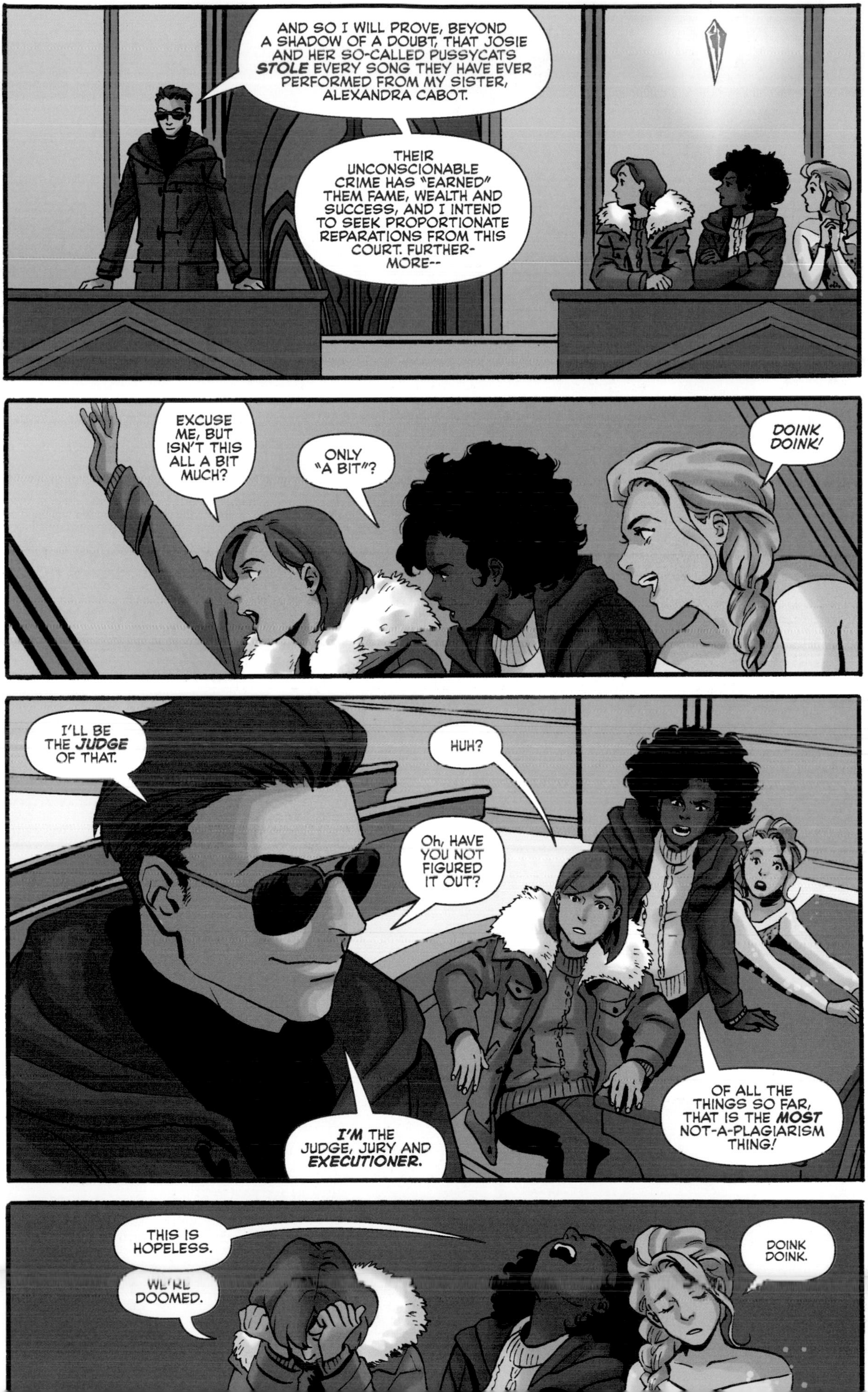
AND SO I WILL PROVE, BEYOND A SHADOW OF A DOUBT, THAT JOSIE AND HER SO-CALLED PUSSYCATS STOLE EVERY SONG THEY HAVE EVER PERFORMED FROM MY SISTER, ALEXANDRA CABOT.
THEIR UNCONSCIONABLE CRIME HAS "EARNED" THEM FAME, WEALTH AND SUCCESS, AND I INTEND TO SEEK PROPORTIONATE REPARATIONS FROM THIS COURT. FURTHER-MORE--
EXCUSE ME, BUT ISN'T THIS ALL A BIT MUCH?
ONLY "A BIT"?
DOINK DOINK!
I'LL BE THE JUDGE OF THAT.
HUH?
Oh, HAVE YOU NOT FIGURED IT OUT?
I'M THE JUDGE, JURY AND EXECUTIONER.
OF ALL THE THINGS SO FAR, THAT IS THE MOST NOT-A-PLAGIARISM THING!
THIS IS HOPELESS.
WE'RE DOOMED.
DOINK DOINK.

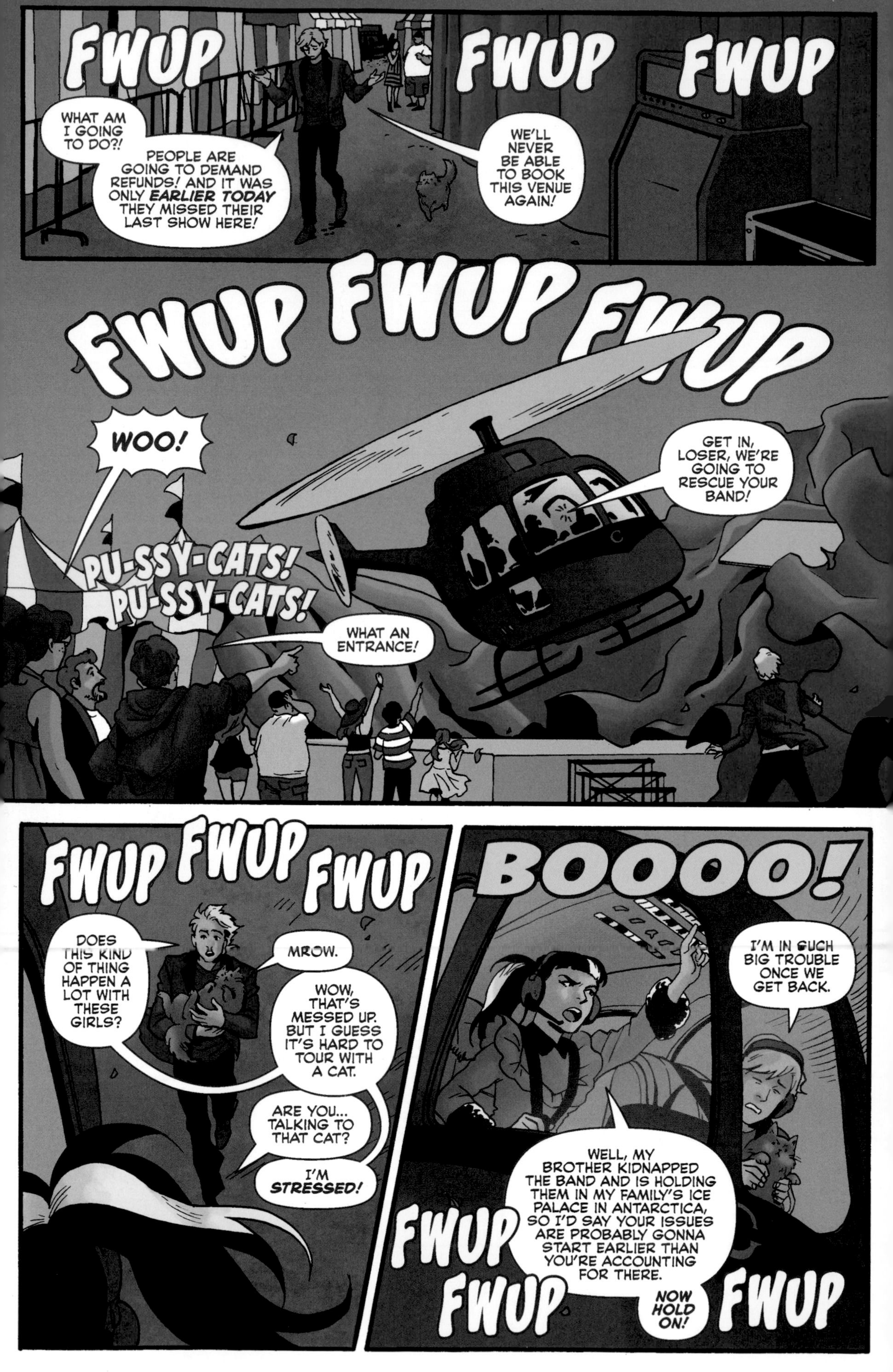

FWUP
WHAT AM I GOING TO DO?!
PEOPLE ARE GOING TO DEMAND REFUNDS! AND IT WAS ONLY EARLIER TODAY THEY MISSED THEIR LAST SHOW HERE!
FWUP
WE'LL NEVER BE ABLE TO BOOK THIS VENUE AGAIN!
FWUP
FWUP FWUP FWUP
WOO!
PU-SSY-CATS! PU-SSY-CATS!
GET IN, LOSER, WE'RE GOING TO RESCUE YOUR BAND!
WHAT AN ENTRANCE!
FWUP FWUP FWUP
DOES THIS KIND OF THING HAPPEN A LOT WITH THESE GIRLS?
MROW.
WOW, THAT'S MESSED UP. BUT I GUESS IT'S HARD TO TOUR WITH A CAT.
ARE YOU... TALKING TO THAT CAT?
I'M STRESSED!
BOOOOO!
I'M IN SUCH BIG TROUBLE ONCE WE GET BACK.
WELL, MY BROTHER KIDNAPPED THE BAND AND IS HOLDING THEM IN MY FAMILY'S ICE PALACE IN ANTARCTICA, SO I'D SAY YOUR ISSUES ARE PROBABLY GONNA START EARLIER THAN YOU'RE ACCOUNTING FOR THERE.
NOW HOLD ON!
FWUP FWUP FWUP

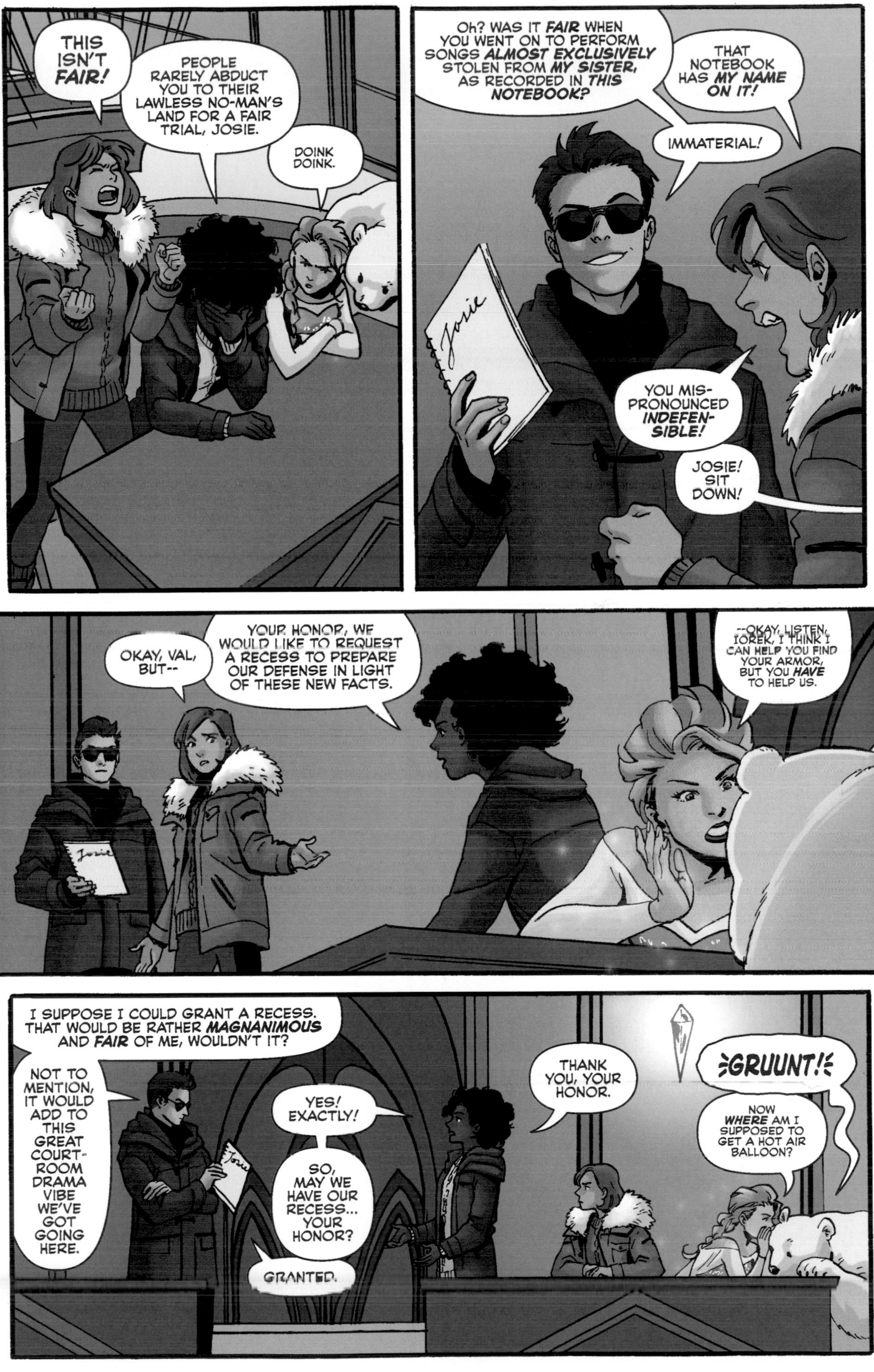
THIS ISN'T FAIR!
PEOPLE RARELY ABDUCT YOU TO THEIR LAWLESS NO-MAN'S LAND FOR A FAIR TRIAL, JOSIE.
DOINK DOINK.
Oh? WAS IT FAIR WHEN YOU WENT ON TO PERFORM SONGS ALMOST EXCLUSIVELY STOLEN FROM MY SISTER, AS RECORDED IN THIS NOTEBOOK?
THAT NOTEBOOK HAS MY NAME ON IT!
IMMATERIAL!
Josie
YOU MIS-PRONOUNCED INDEFEN-SIBLE!
JOSIE! SIT DOWN!
OKAY, VAL, BUT--
YOUR HONOR, WE WOULD LIKE TO REQUEST A RECESS TO PREPARE OUR DEFENSE IN LIGHT OF THESE NEW FACTS.
--OKAY, LISTEN, IOREK, I THINK I CAN HELP YOU FIND YOUR ARMOR, BUT YOU HAVE TO HELP US.
Josie
I SUPPOSE I COULD GRANT A RECESS. THAT WOULD BE RATHER MAGNANIMOUS AND FAIR OF ME, WOULDN'T IT?
NOT TO MENTION, IT WOULD ADD TO THIS GREAT COURT-ROOM DRAMA VIBE WE'VE GOT GOING HERE.
YES! EXACTLY!
SO, MAY WE HAVE OUR RECESS... YOUR HONOR?
GRANTED.
THANK YOU, YOUR HONOR.
GRUUNT!
NOW WHERE AM I SUPPOSED TO GET A HOT AIR BALLOON?
Josie

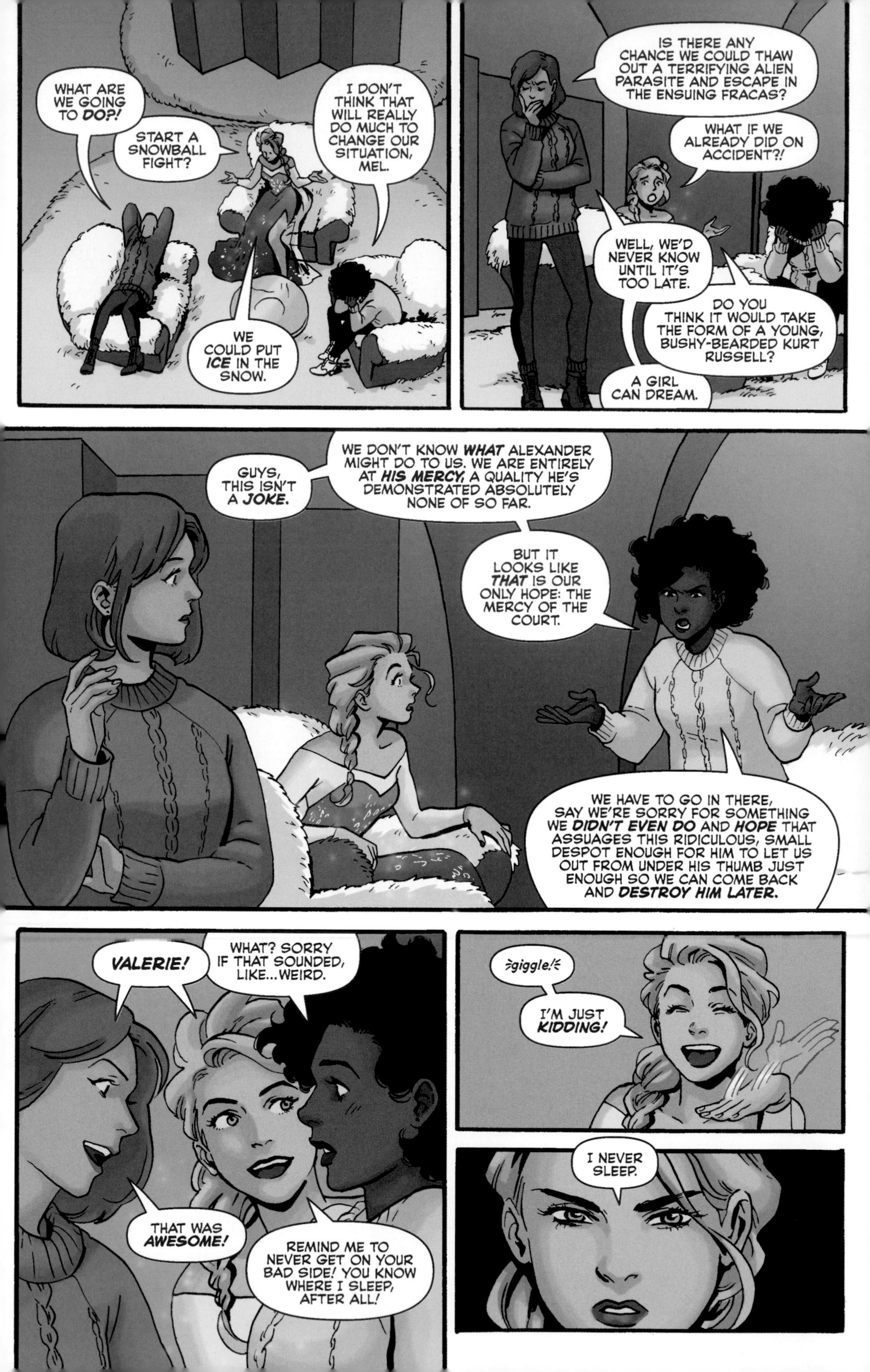
WHAT ARE WE GOING TO DO?!
START A SNOWBALL FIGHT?
I DON'T THINK THAT WILL REALLY DO MUCH TO CHANGE OUR SITUATION, MEL.
WE COULD PUT ICE IN THE SNOW.
IS THERE ANY CHANCE WE COULD THAW OUT A TERRIFYING ALIEN PARASITE AND ESCAPE IN THE ENSUING FRACAS?
WHAT IF WE ALREADY DID ON ACCIDENT?!
WELL, WE'D NEVER KNOW UNTIL IT'S TOO LATE.
DO YOU THINK IT WOULD TAKE THE FORM OF A YOUNG, BUSHY-BEARDED KURT RUSSELL?
A GIRL CAN DREAM.
GUYS, THIS ISN'T A JOKE.
WE DON'T KNOW WHAT ALEXANDER MIGHT DO TO US. WE ARE ENTIRELY AT HIS MERCY, A QUALITY HE'S DEMONSTRATED ABSOLUTELY NONE OF SO FAR.
BUT IT LOOKS LIKE THAT IS OUR ONLY HOPE: THE MERCY OF THE COURT.
WE HAVE TO GO IN THERE, SAY WE'RE SORRY FOR SOMETHING WE DIDN'T EVEN DO AND HOPE THAT ASSUAGES THIS RIDICULOUS, SMALL DESPOT ENOUGH FOR HIM TO LET US OUT FROM UNDER HIS THUMB JUST ENOUGH SO WE CAN COME BACK AND DESTROY HIM LATER.
VALERIE!
WHAT? SORRY IF THAT SOUNDED, LIKE...WEIRD.
THAT WAS AWESOME!
REMIND ME TO NEVER GET ON YOUR BAD SIDE! YOU KNOW WHERE I SLEEP, AFTER ALL!
giggle!
I'M JUST KIDDING!
I NEVER SLEEP.

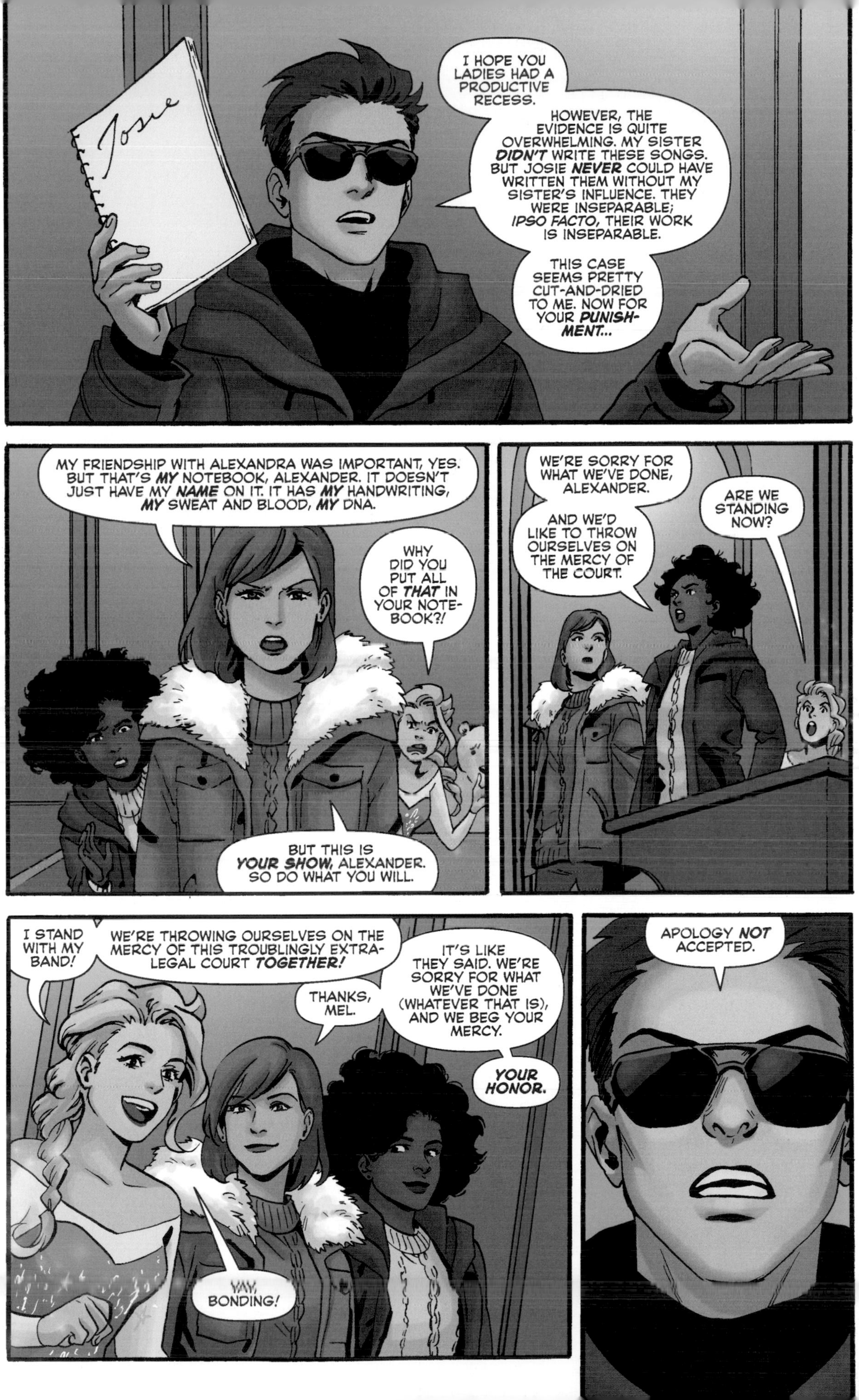

I HOPE YOU LADIES HAD A PRODUCTIVE RECESS.
HOWEVER, THE EVIDENCE IS QUITE OVERWHELMING. MY SISTER *DIDN'T* WRITE THESE SONGS. BUT JOSIE *NEVER* COULD HAVE WRITTEN THEM WITHOUT MY SISTER'S INFLUENCE. THEY WERE INSEPARABLE; *IPSO FACTO*, THEIR WORK IS INSEPARABLE.
THIS CASE SEEMS PRETTY CUT-AND-DRIED TO ME. NOW FOR YOUR *PUNISHMENT...*
MY FRIENDSHIP WITH ALEXANDRA WAS IMPORTANT, YES. BUT THAT'S *MY* NOTEBOOK, ALEXANDER. IT DOESN'T JUST HAVE MY *NAME* ON IT. IT HAS *MY* HANDWRITING, *MY* SWEAT AND BLOOD, *MY* DNA.
WHY DID YOU PUT ALL OF *THAT* IN YOUR NOTEBOOK?!
BUT THIS IS *YOUR SHOW*, ALEXANDER. SO DO WHAT YOU WILL.
WE'RE SORRY FOR WHAT WE'VE DONE, ALEXANDER.
AND WE'D LIKE TO THROW OURSELVES ON THE MERCY OF THE COURT.
ARE WE STANDING NOW?
I STAND WITH MY BAND!
WE'RE THROWING OURSELVES ON THE MERCY OF THIS TROUBLINGLY EXTRA-LEGAL COURT *TOGETHER!*
THANKS, MEL.
YAY, BONDING!
IT'S LIKE THEY SAID. WE'RE SORRY FOR WHAT WE'VE DONE (WHATEVER THAT IS), AND WE BEG YOUR MERCY.
YOUR HONOR.
APOLOGY *NOT* ACCEPTED.

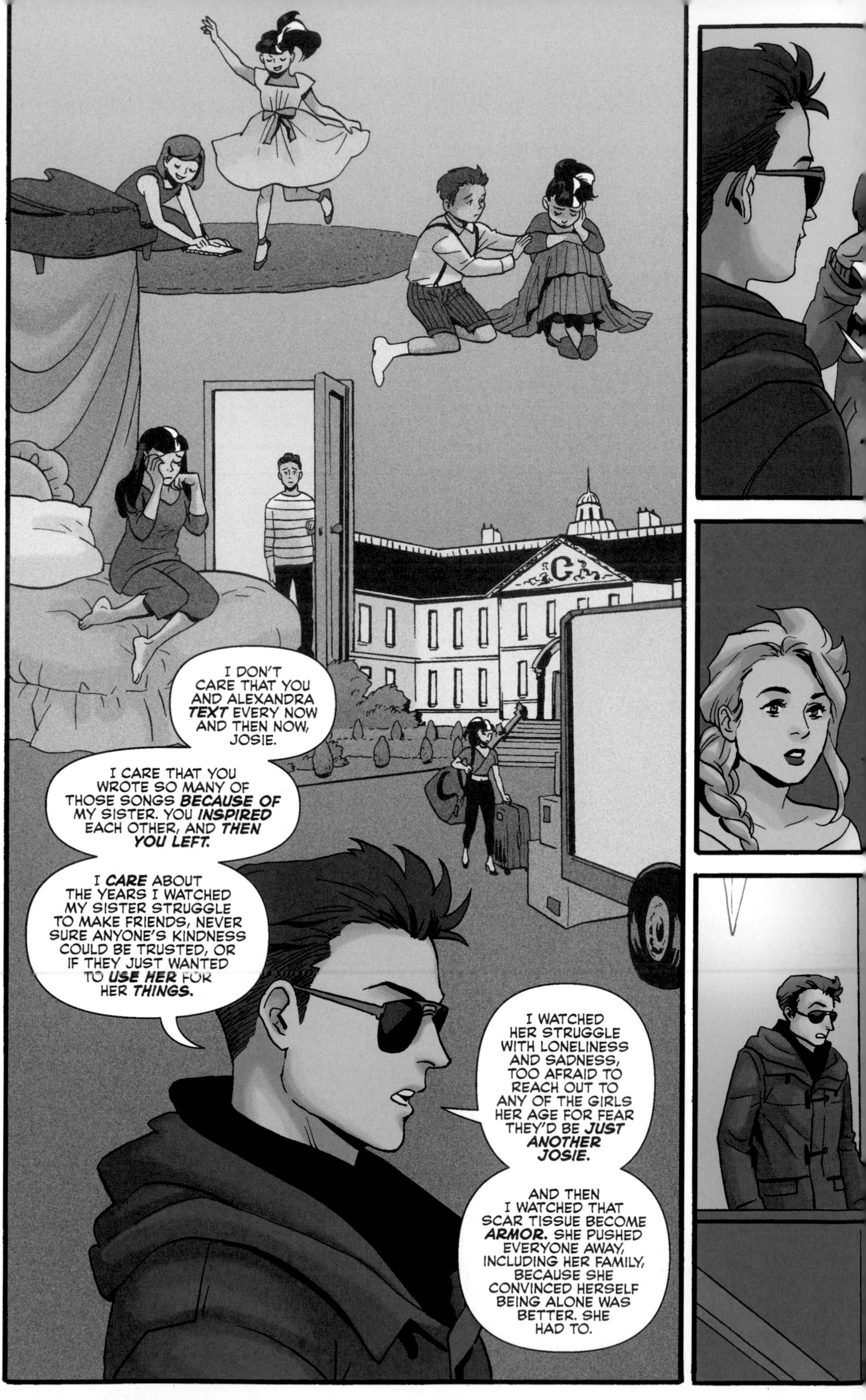

I DON'T CARE THAT YOU AND ALEXANDRA TEXT EVERY NOW AND THEN NOW, JOSIE.
I CARE THAT YOU WROTE SO MANY OF THOSE SONGS BECAUSE OF MY SISTER. YOU INSPIRED EACH OTHER, AND THEN YOU LEFT.
I CARE ABOUT THE YEARS I WATCHED MY SISTER STRUGGLE TO MAKE FRIENDS, NEVER SURE ANYONE'S KINDNESS COULD BE TRUSTED, OR IF THEY JUST WANTED TO USE HER FOR HER THINGS.
I WATCHED HER STRUGGLE WITH LONELINESS AND SADNESS, TOO AFRAID TO REACH OUT TO ANY OF THE GIRLS HER AGE FOR FEAR THEY'D BE JUST ANOTHER JOSIE.
AND THEN I WATCHED THAT SCAR TISSUE BECOME ARMOR. SHE PUSHED EVERYONE AWAY, INCLUDING HER FAMILY, BECAUSE SHE CONVINCED HERSELF BEING ALONE WAS BETTER. SHE HAD TO.

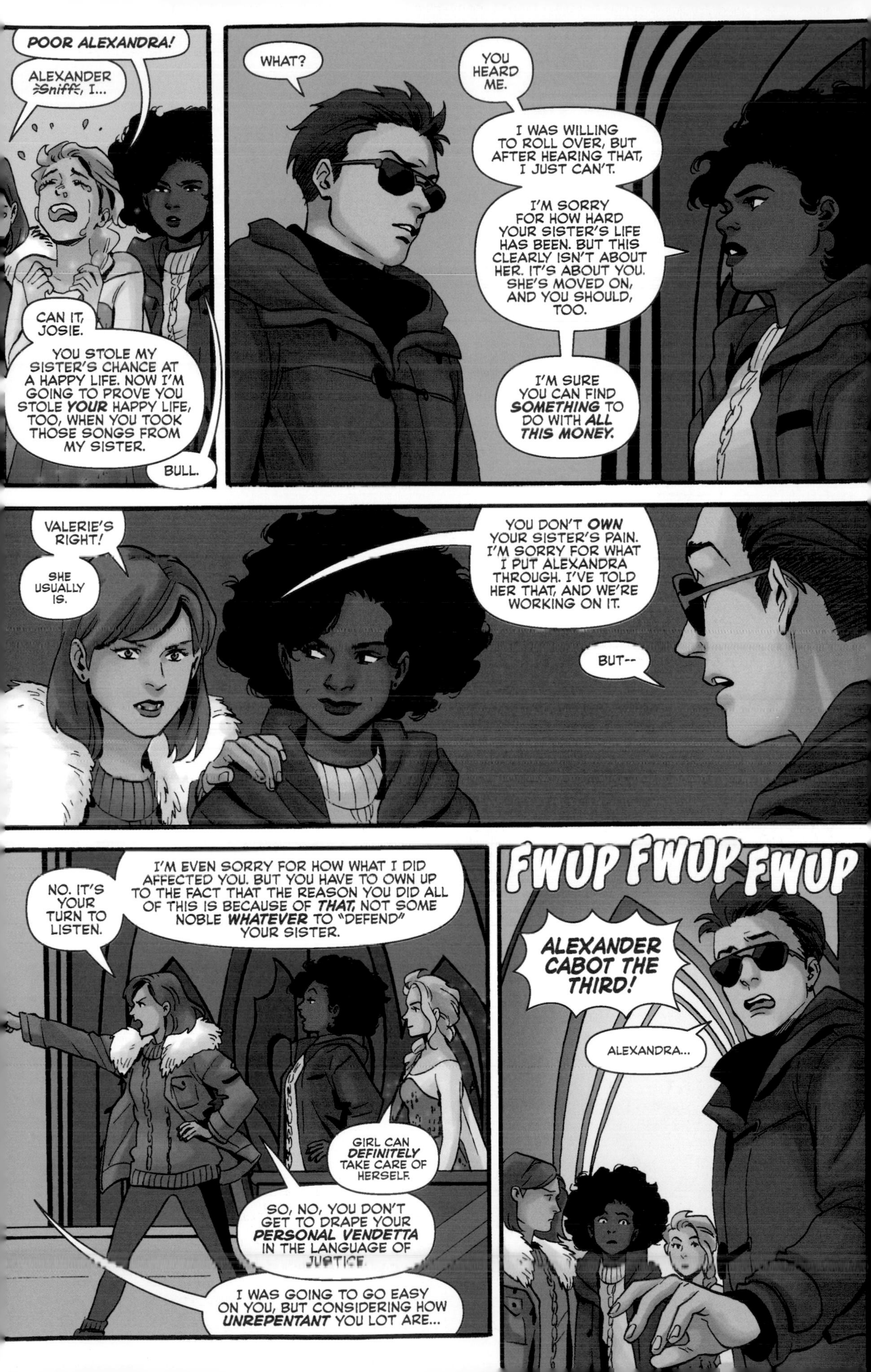
POOR ALEXANDRA!
ALEXANDER *Sniff*, I...
CAN IT, JOSIE.
YOU STOLE MY SISTER'S CHANCE AT A HAPPY LIFE. NOW I'M GOING TO PROVE YOU STOLE YOUR HAPPY LIFE, TOO, WHEN YOU TOOK THOSE SONGS FROM MY SISTER.
BULL.
WHAT?
YOU HEARD ME.
I WAS WILLING TO ROLL OVER, BUT AFTER HEARING THAT, I JUST CAN'T.
I'M SORRY FOR HOW HARD YOUR SISTER'S LIFE HAS BEEN. BUT THIS CLEARLY ISN'T ABOUT HER. IT'S ABOUT YOU. SHE'S MOVED ON, AND YOU SHOULD, TOO.
I'M SURE YOU CAN FIND SOMETHING TO DO WITH ALL THIS MONEY.
VALERIE'S RIGHT!
SHE USUALLY IS.
YOU DON'T OWN YOUR SISTER'S PAIN. I'M SORRY FOR WHAT I PUT ALEXANDRA THROUGH. I'VE TOLD HER THAT, AND WE'RE WORKING ON IT.
BUT--
NO. IT'S YOUR TURN TO LISTEN.
I'M EVEN SORRY FOR HOW WHAT I DID AFFECTED YOU. BUT YOU HAVE TO OWN UP TO THE FACT THAT THE REASON YOU DID ALL OF THIS IS BECAUSE OF THAT, NOT SOME NOBLE WHATEVER TO "DEFEND" YOUR SISTER.
GIRL CAN DEFINITELY TAKE CARE OF HERSELF.
SO, NO, YOU DON'T GET TO DRAPE YOUR PERSONAL VENDETTA IN THE LANGUAGE OF JUSTICE.
I WAS GOING TO GO EASY ON YOU, BUT CONSIDERING HOW UNREPENTANT YOU LOT ARE...
FWUP FWUP FWUP
ALEXANDER CABOT THE THIRD!
ALEXANDRA...

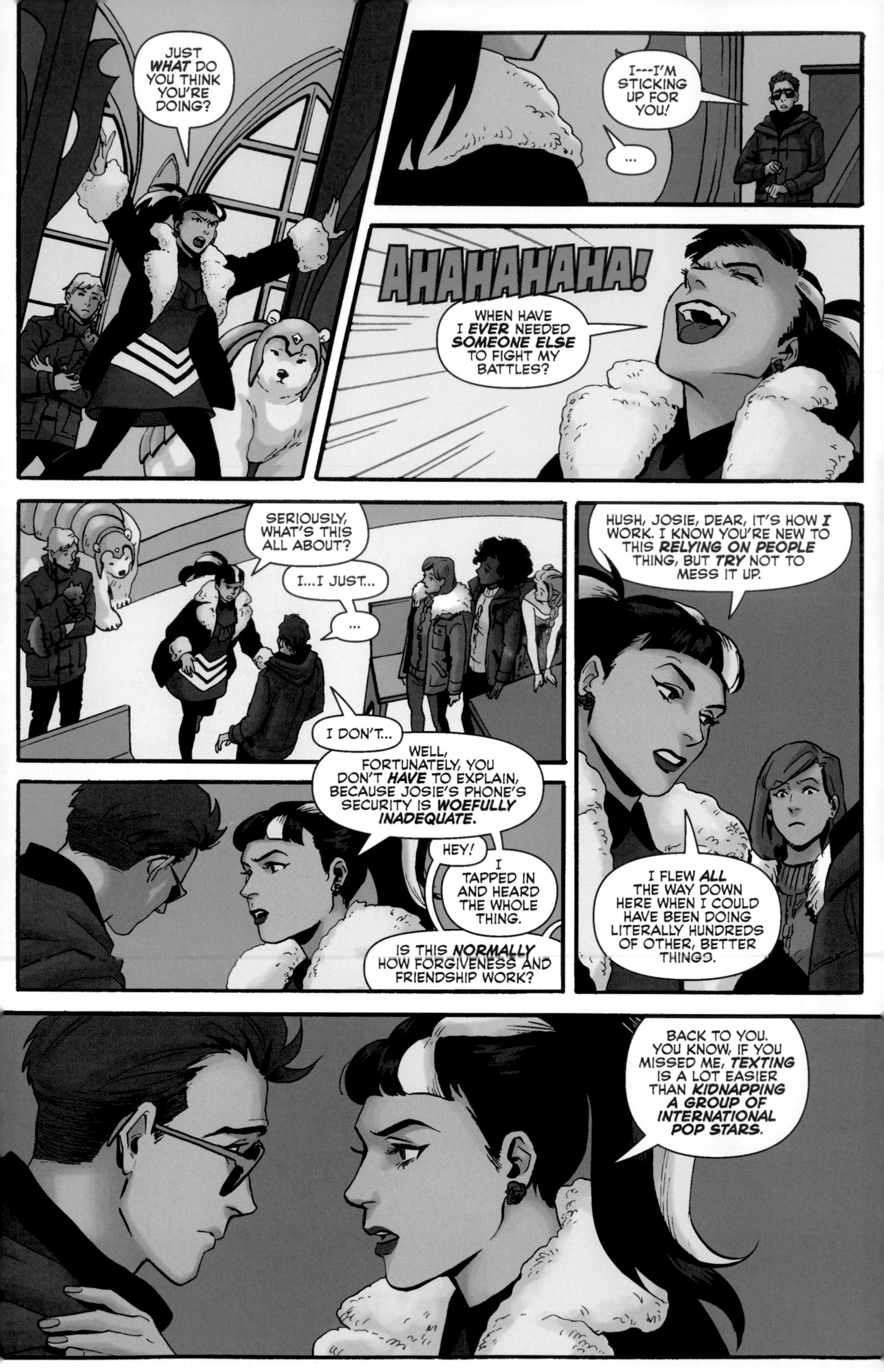

JUST WHAT DO YOU THINK YOU'RE DOING?
I---I'M STICKING UP FOR YOU!
...
AHAHAHAHA!
WHEN HAVE I EVER NEEDED SOMEONE ELSE TO FIGHT MY BATTLES?
SERIOUSLY, WHAT'S THIS ALL ABOUT?
I...I JUST...
...
I DON'T...
WELL, FORTUNATELY, YOU DON'T HAVE TO EXPLAIN, BECAUSE JOSIE'S PHONE'S SECURITY IS WOEFULLY INADEQUATE.
HEY!
I TAPPED IN AND HEARD THE WHOLE THING.
IS THIS NORMALLY HOW FORGIVENESS AND FRIENDSHIP WORK?
HUSH, JOSIE, DEAR, IT'S HOW I WORK. I KNOW YOU'RE NEW TO THIS RELYING ON PEOPLE THING, BUT TRY NOT TO MESS IT UP.
I FLEW ALL THE WAY DOWN HERE WHEN I COULD HAVE BEEN DOING LITERALLY HUNDREDS OF OTHER, BETTER THINGS.
BACK TO YOU. YOU KNOW, IF YOU MISSED ME, TEXTING IS A LOT EASIER THAN KIDNAPPING A GROUP OF INTERNATIONAL POP STARS.

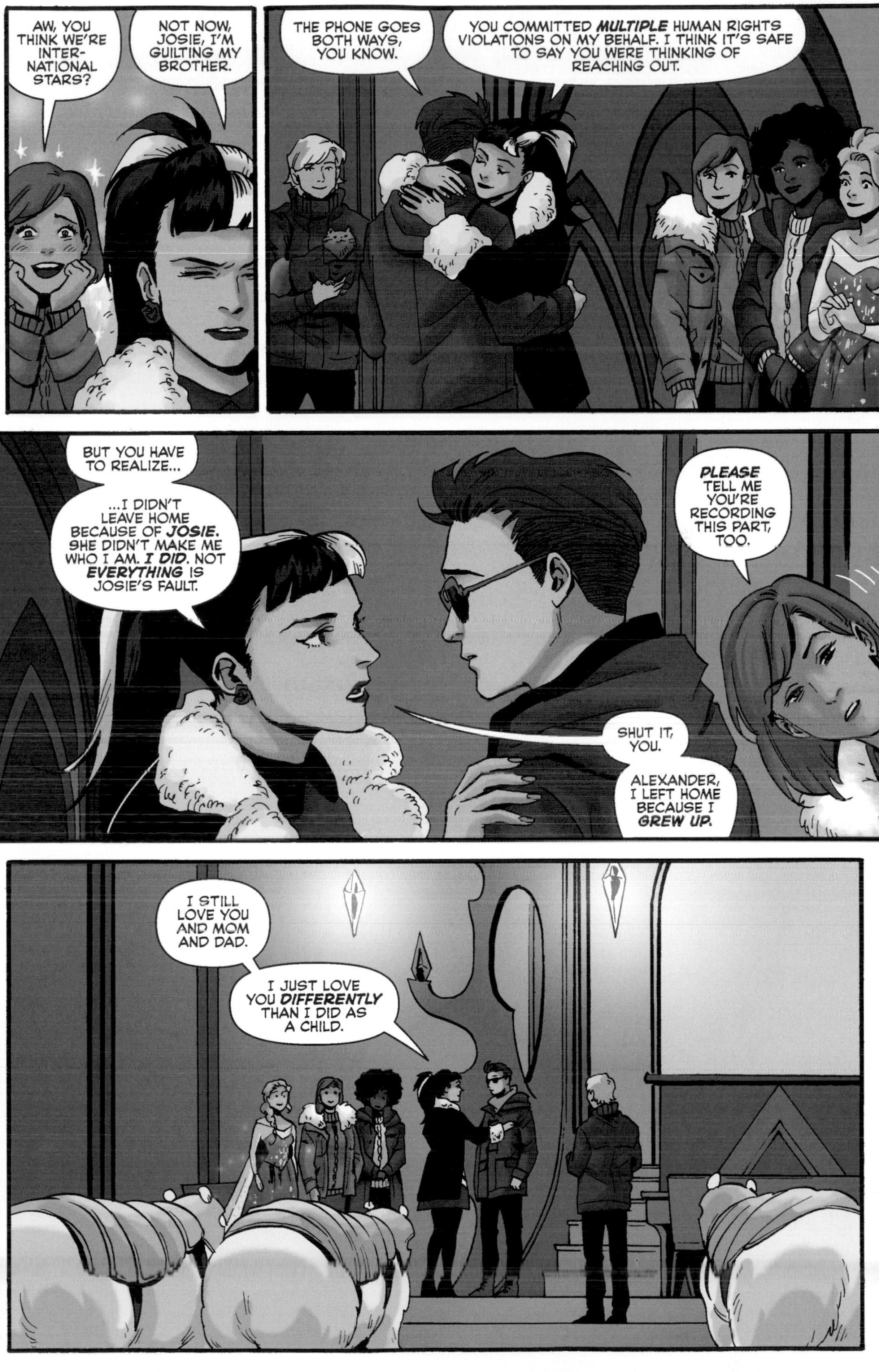
AW, YOU THINK WE'RE INTER-NATIONAL STARS?
NOT NOW, JOSIE, I'M GUILTING MY BROTHER.
THE PHONE GOES BOTH WAYS, YOU KNOW.
YOU COMMITTED MULTIPLE HUMAN RIGHTS VIOLATIONS ON MY BEHALF. I THINK IT'S SAFE TO SAY YOU WERE THINKING OF REACHING OUT.
BUT YOU HAVE TO REALIZE...
...I DIDN'T LEAVE HOME BECAUSE OF JOSIE. SHE DIDN'T MAKE ME WHO I AM. I DID. NOT EVERYTHING IS JOSIE'S FAULT.
PLEASE TELL ME YOU'RE RECORDING THIS PART, TOO.
SHUT IT, YOU.
ALEXANDER, I LEFT HOME BECAUSE I GREW UP.
I STILL LOVE YOU AND MOM AND DAD.
I JUST LOVE YOU DIFFERENTLY THAN I DID AS A CHILD.

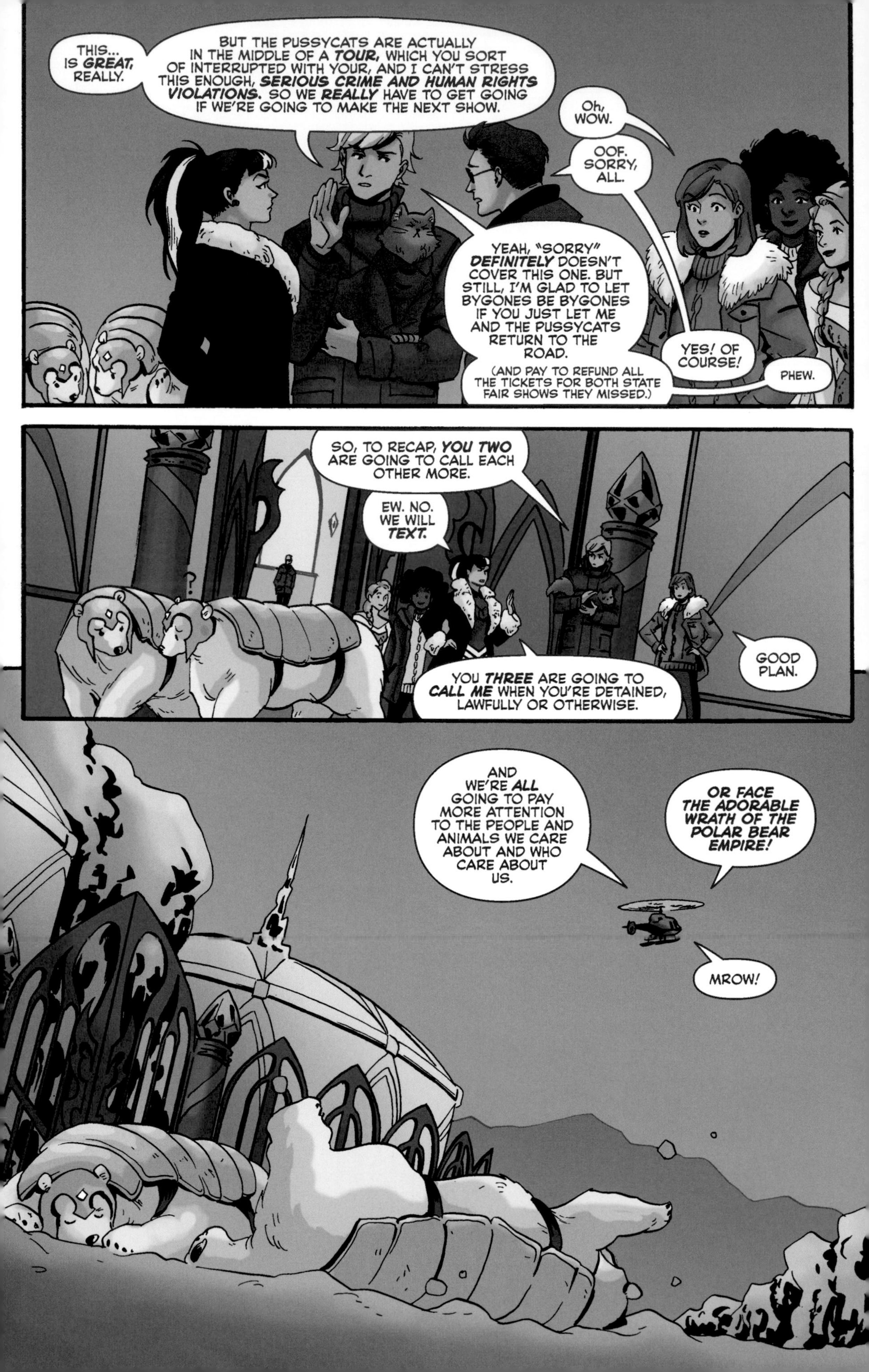
THIS... IS GREAT, REALLY.
BUT THE PUSSYCATS ARE ACTUALLY IN THE MIDDLE OF A TOUR, WHICH YOU SORT OF INTERRUPTED WITH YOUR, AND I CAN'T STRESS THIS ENOUGH, SERIOUS CRIME AND HUMAN RIGHTS VIOLATIONS. SO WE REALLY HAVE TO GET GOING IF WE'RE GOING TO MAKE THE NEXT SHOW.
Oh, WOW.
OOF. SORRY, ALL.
YEAH, "SORRY" DEFINITELY DOESN'T COVER THIS ONE. BUT STILL, I'M GLAD TO LET BYGONES BE BYGONES IF YOU JUST LET ME AND THE PUSSYCATS RETURN TO THE ROAD.
(AND PAY TO REFUND ALL THE TICKETS FOR BOTH STATE FAIR SHOWS THEY MISSED.)
YES! OF COURSE!
PHEW.
SO, TO RECAP, YOU TWO ARE GOING TO CALL EACH OTHER MORE.
EW. NO. WE WILL TEXT.
?
YOU THREE ARE GOING TO CALL ME WHEN YOU'RE DETAINED, LAWFULLY OR OTHERWISE.
GOOD PLAN.
AND WE'RE ALL GOING TO PAY MORE ATTENTION TO THE PEOPLE AND ANIMALS WE CARE ABOUT AND WHO CARE ABOUT US.
OR FACE THE ADORABLE WRATH OF THE POLAR BEAR EMPIRE!
MROW!

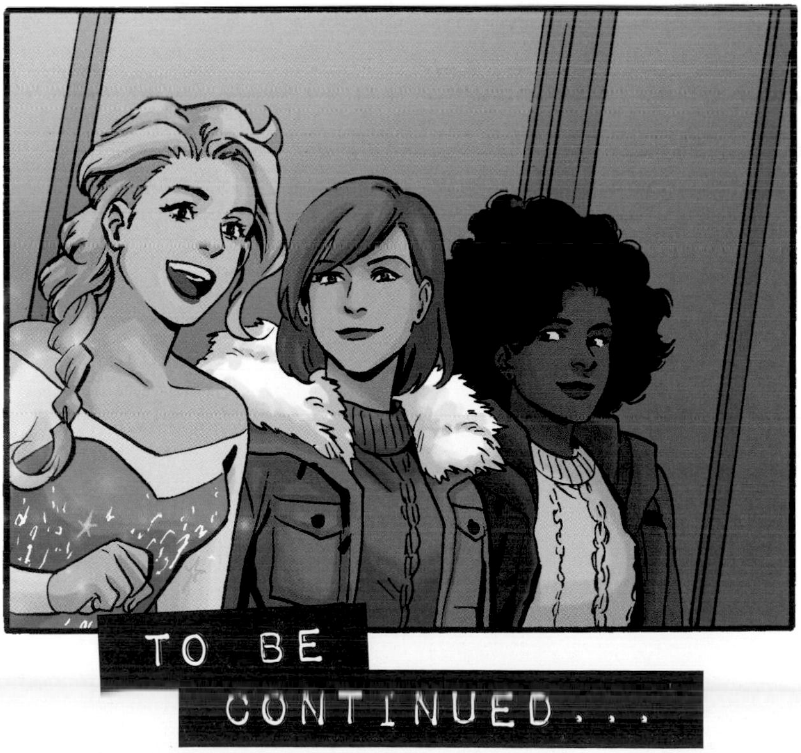
TO BE
CONTINUED...

ISSUE SEVEN

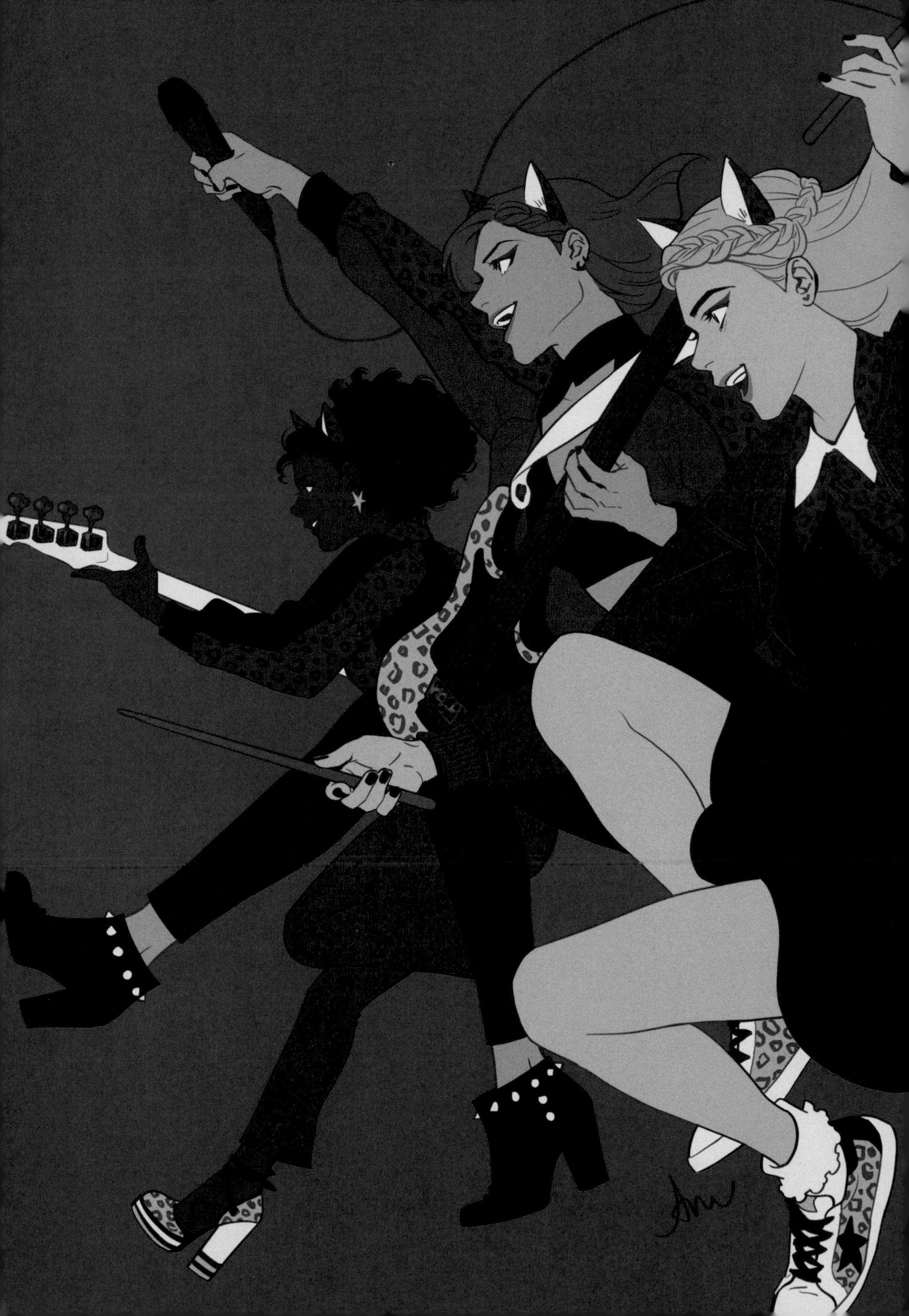

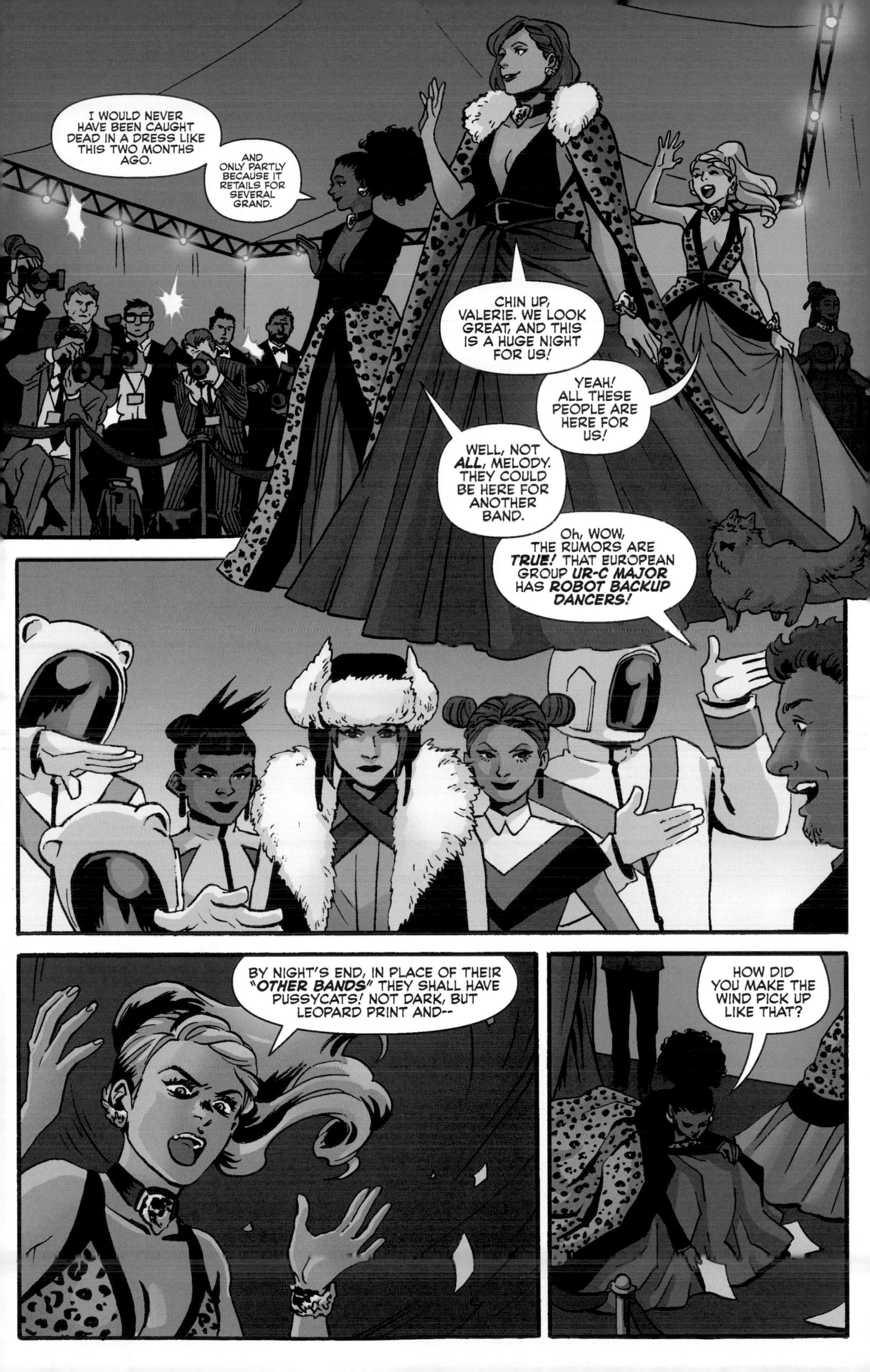
I WOULD NEVER HAVE BEEN CAUGHT DEAD IN A DRESS LIKE THIS TWO MONTHS AGO.
AND ONLY PARTLY BECAUSE IT RETAILS FOR SEVERAL GRAND.
CHIN UP, VALERIE. WE LOOK GREAT, AND THIS IS A HUGE NIGHT FOR US!
YEAH! ALL THESE PEOPLE ARE HERE FOR US!
WELL, NOT ALL, MELODY. THEY COULD BE HERE FOR ANOTHER BAND.
Oh, WOW, THE RUMORS ARE TRUE! THAT EUROPEAN GROUP UR-C MAJOR HAS ROBOT BACKUP DANCERS!
BY NIGHT'S END, IN PLACE OF THEIR "OTHER BANDS" THEY SHALL HAVE PUSSYCATS! NOT DARK, BUT LEOPARD PRINT AND--
HOW DID YOU MAKE THE WIND PICK UP LIKE THAT?

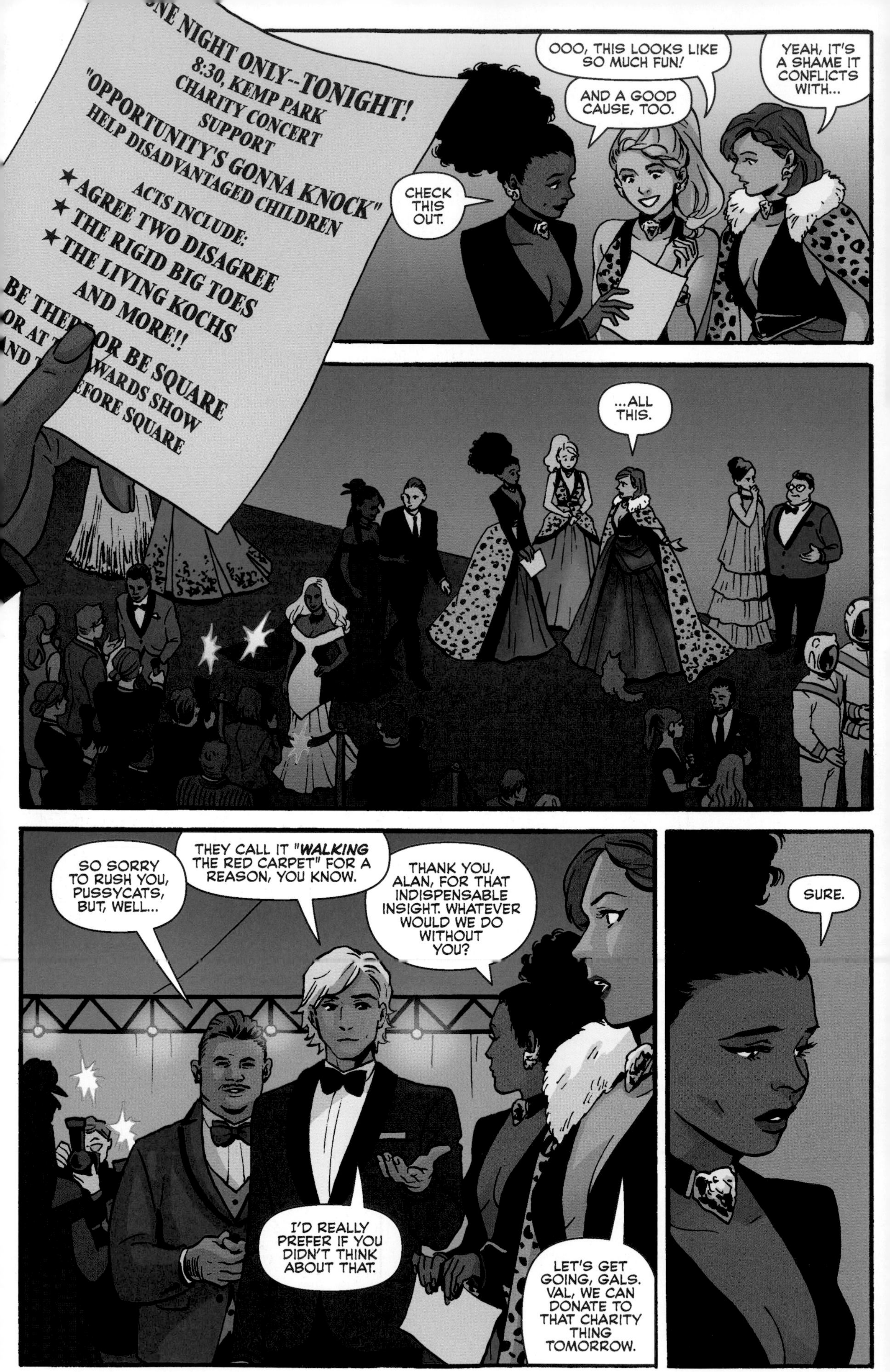
ONE NIGHT ONLY--TONIGHT!
8:30, KEMP PARK
CHARITY CONCERT
SUPPORT
"OPPORTUNITY'S GONNA KNOCK"
HELP DISADVANTAGED CHILDREN
ACTS INCLUDE:
★ AGREE TWO DISAGREE
★ THE RIGID BIG TOES
★ THE LIVING KOCHS
AND MORE!!
BE THERE OR BE SQUARE
CHECK THIS OUT.
OOO, THIS LOOKS LIKE SO MUCH FUN!
AND A GOOD CAUSE, TOO.
YEAH, IT'S A SHAME IT CONFLICTS WITH...
...ALL THIS.
SO SORRY TO RUSH YOU, PUSSYCATS, BUT, WELL...
THEY CALL IT "WALKING THE RED CARPET" FOR A REASON, YOU KNOW.
THANK YOU, ALAN, FOR THAT INDISPENSABLE INSIGHT. WHATEVER WOULD WE DO WITHOUT YOU?
I'D REALLY PREFER IF YOU DIDN'T THINK ABOUT THAT.
LET'S GET GOING, GALS. VAL, WE CAN DONATE TO THAT CHARITY THING TOMORROW.
SURE.

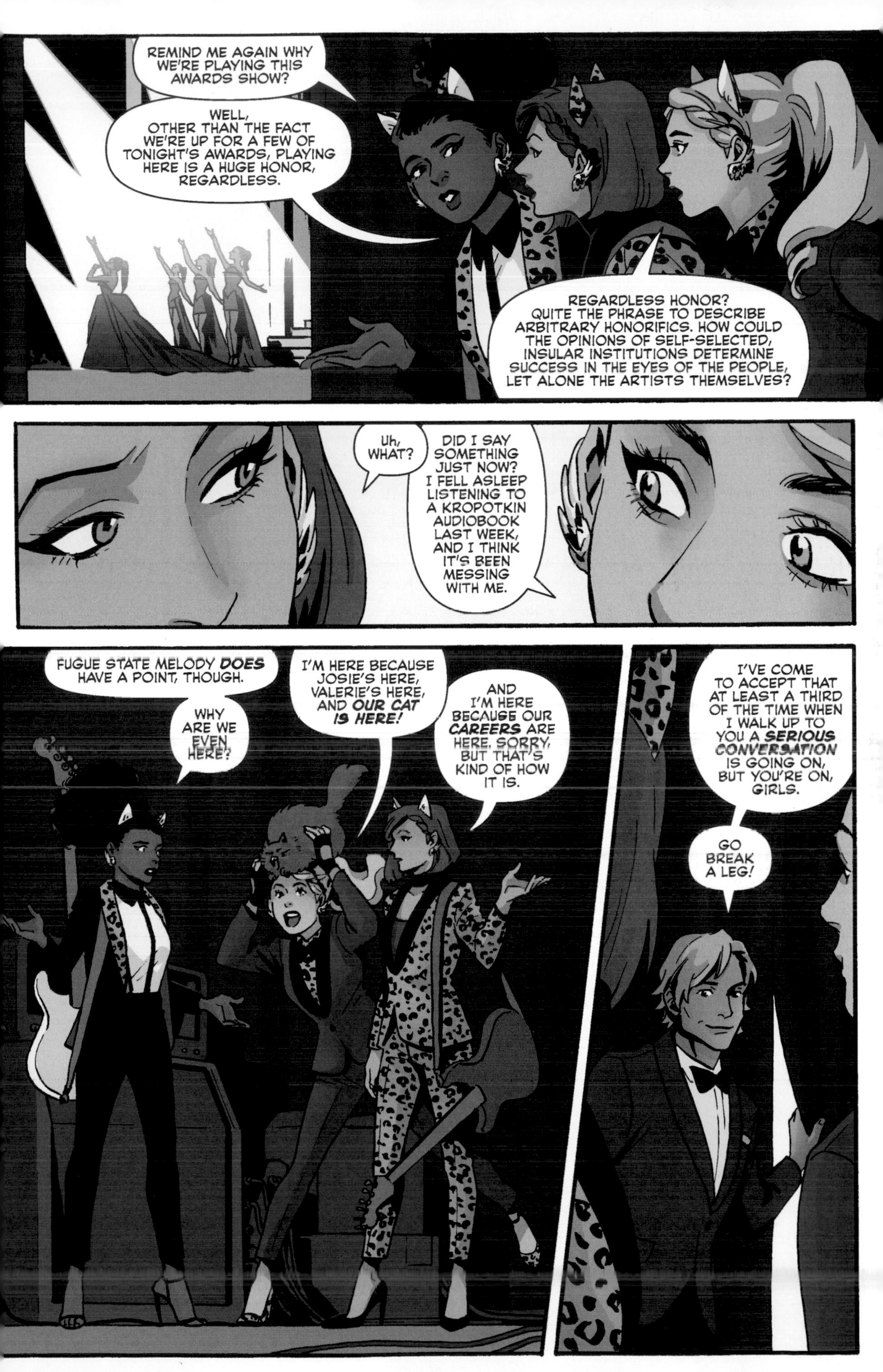
REMIND ME AGAIN WHY WE'RE PLAYING THIS AWARDS SHOW?
WELL, OTHER THAN THE FACT WE'RE UP FOR A FEW OF TONIGHT'S AWARDS, PLAYING HERE IS A HUGE HONOR, REGARDLESS.
REGARDLESS HONOR? QUITE THE PHRASE TO DESCRIBE ARBITRARY HONORIFICS. HOW COULD THE OPINIONS OF SELF-SELECTED, INSULAR INSTITUTIONS DETERMINE SUCCESS IN THE EYES OF THE PEOPLE, LET ALONE THE ARTISTS THEMSELVES?
Uh, WHAT?
DID I SAY SOMETHING JUST NOW? I FELL ASLEEP LISTENING TO A KROPOTKIN AUDIOBOOK LAST WEEK, AND I THINK IT'S BEEN MESSING WITH ME.
FUGUE STATE MELODY DOES HAVE A POINT, THOUGH.
WHY ARE WE EVEN HERE?
I'M HERE BECAUSE JOSIE'S HERE, VALERIE'S HERE, AND OUR CAT IS HERE!
AND I'M HERE BECAUSE OUR CAREERS ARE HERE. SORRY, BUT THAT'S KIND OF HOW IT IS.
I'VE COME TO ACCEPT THAT AT LEAST A THIRD OF THE TIME WHEN I WALK UP TO YOU A SERIOUS CONVERSATION IS GOING ON, BUT YOU'RE ON, GIRLS.
GO BREAK A LEG!

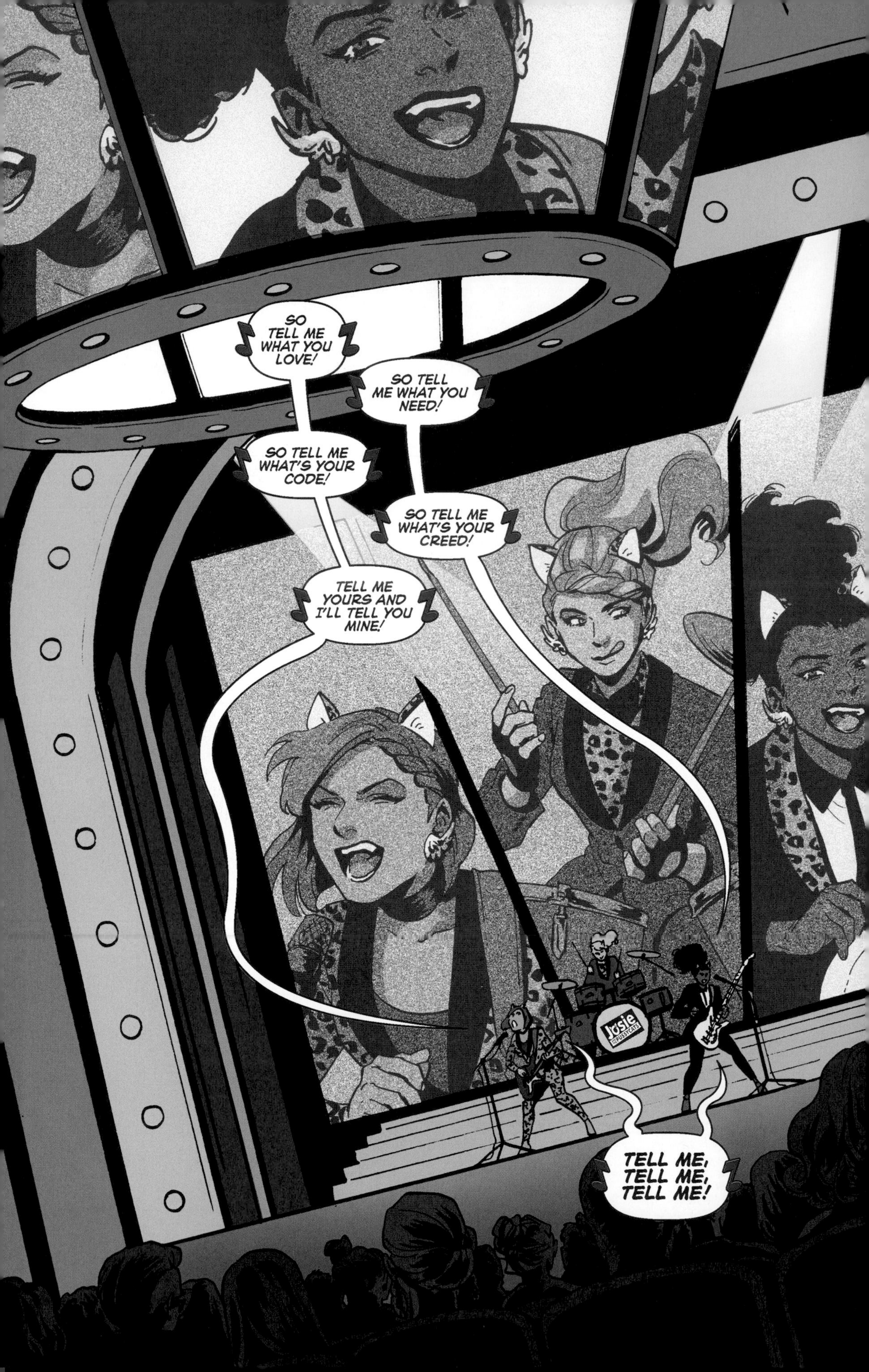
SO TELL ME WHAT YOU LOVE!
SO TELL ME WHAT YOU NEED!
SO TELL ME WHAT'S YOUR CODE!
SO TELL ME WHAT'S YOUR CREED!
TELL ME YOURS AND I'LL TELL YOU MINE!
TELL ME, TELL ME, TELL ME!
JOSIE AND THE PUSSYCATS

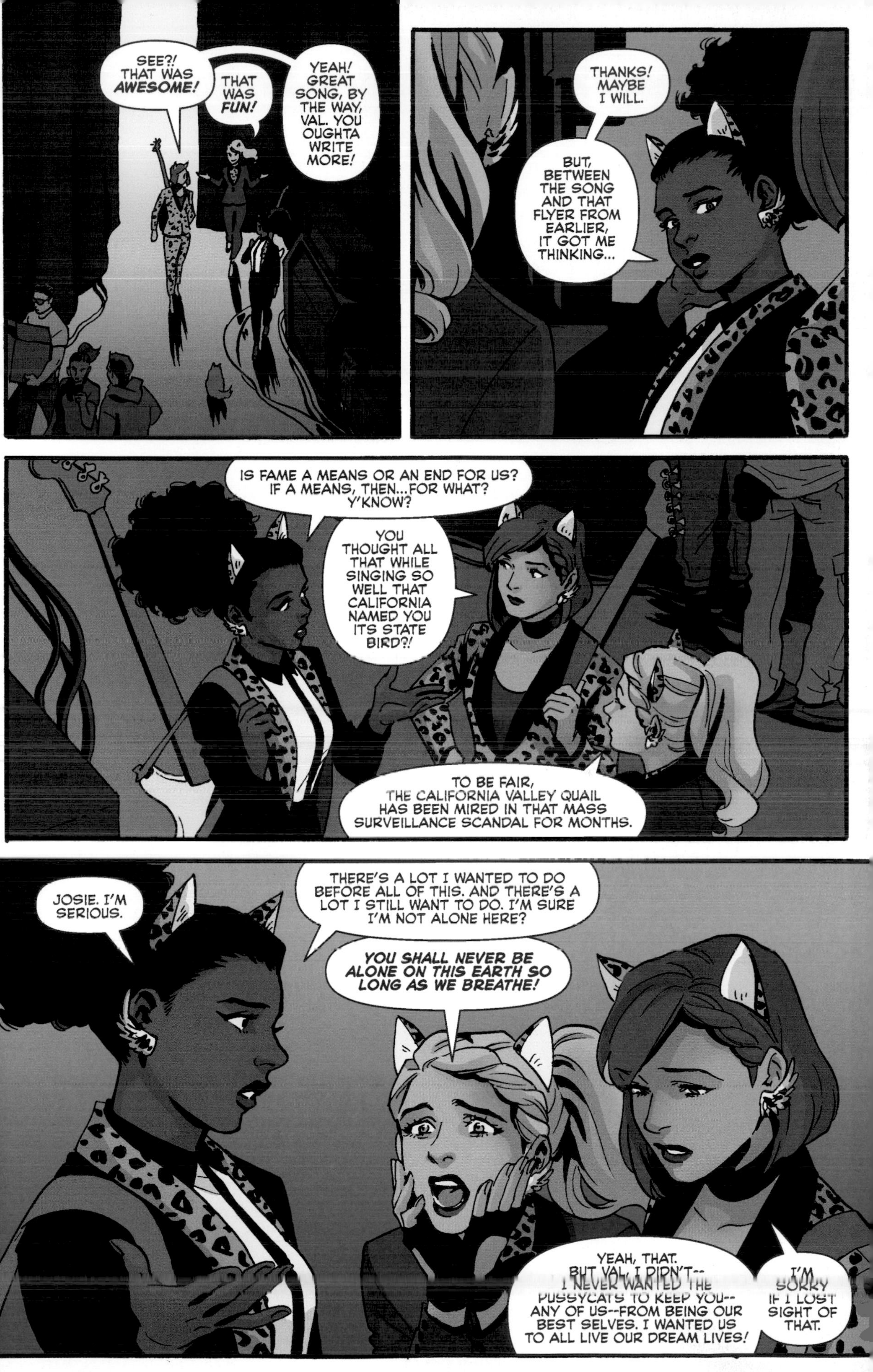
SEE?! THAT WAS AWESOME!
THAT WAS FUN!
YEAH! GREAT SONG, BY THE WAY, VAL. YOU OUGHTA WRITE MORE!
THANKS! MAYBE I WILL.
BUT, BETWEEN THE SONG AND THAT FLYER FROM EARLIER, IT GOT ME THINKING...
IS FAME A MEANS OR AN END FOR US? IF A MEANS, THEN...FOR WHAT? Y'KNOW?
YOU THOUGHT ALL THAT WHILE SINGING SO WELL THAT CALIFORNIA NAMED YOU ITS STATE BIRD?!
TO BE FAIR, THE CALIFORNIA VALLEY QUAIL HAS BEEN MIRED IN THAT MASS SURVEILLANCE SCANDAL FOR MONTHS.
JOSIE. I'M SERIOUS.
THERE'S A LOT I WANTED TO DO BEFORE ALL OF THIS. AND THERE'S A LOT I STILL WANT TO DO. I'M SURE I'M NOT ALONE HERE?
YOU SHALL NEVER BE ALONE ON THIS EARTH SO LONG AS WE BREATHE!
YEAH, THAT. BUT VAL, I DIDN'T-- I NEVER WANTED THE PUSSYCATS TO KEEP YOU-- ANY OF US--FROM BEING OUR BEST SELVES. I WANTED US TO ALL LIVE OUR DREAM LIVES!
I'M SORRY IF I LOST SIGHT OF THAT.

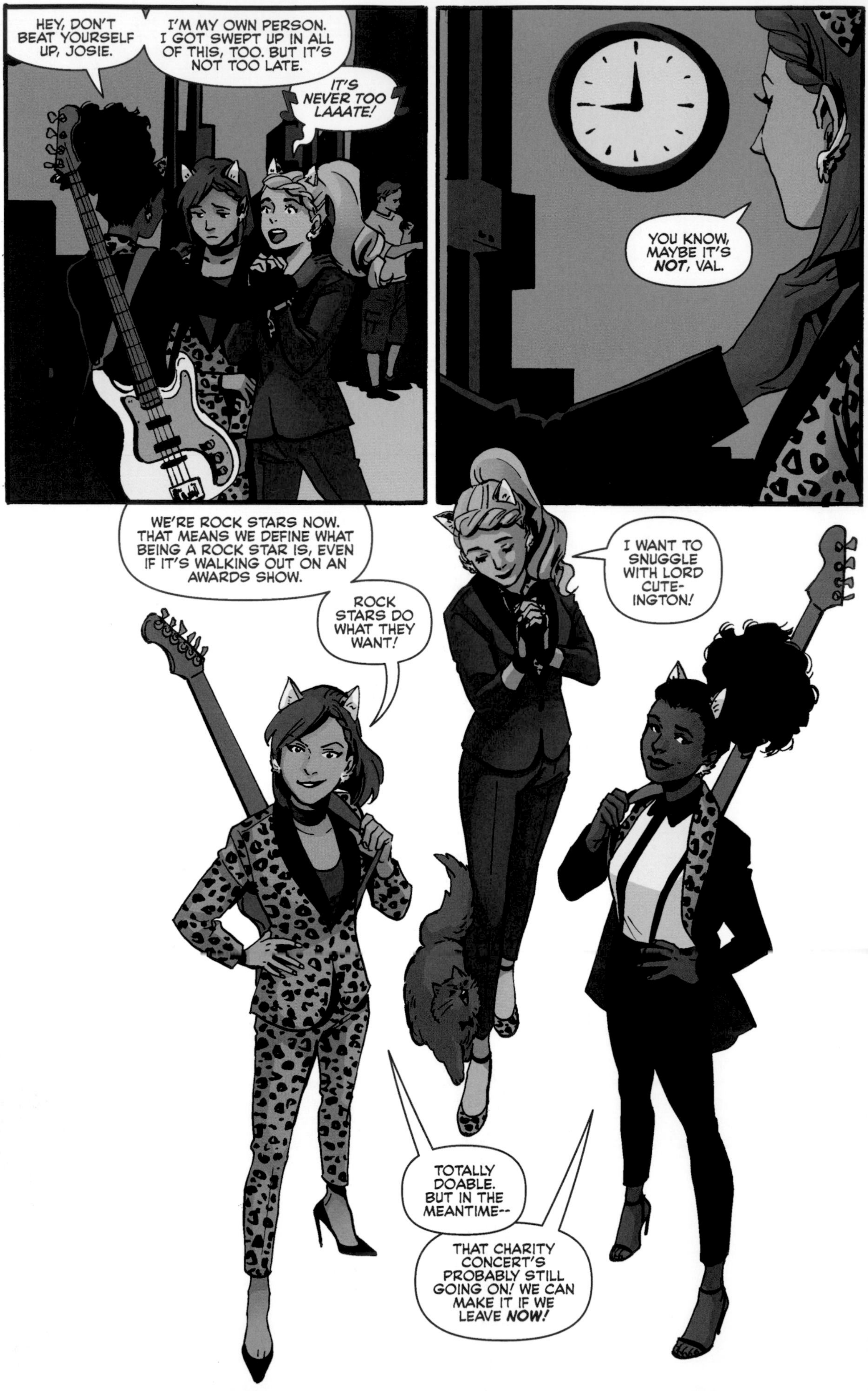
HEY, DON'T BEAT YOURSELF UP, JOSIE.
I'M MY OWN PERSON. I GOT SWEPT UP IN ALL OF THIS, TOO. BUT IT'S NOT TOO LATE.
IT'S NEVER TOO LAAATE!
YOU KNOW, MAYBE IT'S NOT, VAL.
WE'RE ROCK STARS NOW. THAT MEANS WE DEFINE WHAT BEING A ROCK STAR IS, EVEN IF IT'S WALKING OUT ON AN AWARDS SHOW.
ROCK STARS DO WHAT THEY WANT!
I WANT TO SNUGGLE WITH LORD CUTE-INGTON!
TOTALLY DOABLE. BUT IN THE MEANTIME--
THAT CHARITY CONCERT'S PROBABLY STILL GOING ON! WE CAN MAKE IT IF WE LEAVE NOW!

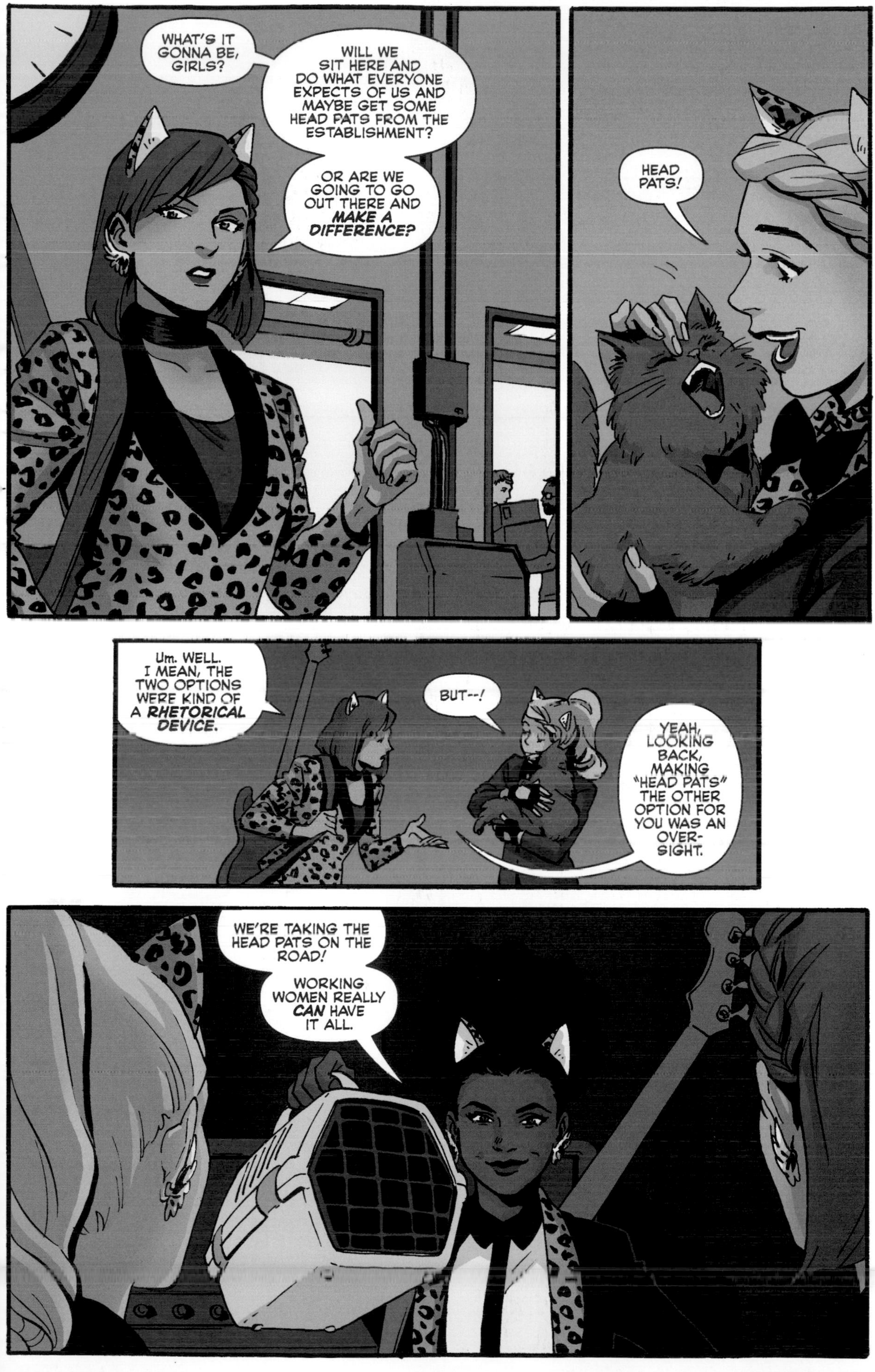
WHAT'S IT GONNA BE, GIRLS?
WILL WE SIT HERE AND DO WHAT EVERYONE EXPECTS OF US AND MAYBE GET SOME HEAD PATS FROM THE ESTABLISHMENT?
OR ARE WE GOING TO GO OUT THERE AND *MAKE A DIFFERENCE?*
HEAD PATS!
Um. WELL. I MEAN, THE TWO OPTIONS WERE KIND OF A *RHETORICAL DEVICE.*
BUT--!
YEAH, LOOKING BACK, MAKING "HEAD PATS" THE OTHER OPTION FOR YOU WAS AN OVER-SIGHT.
WE'RE TAKING THE HEAD PATS ON THE ROAD!
WORKING WOMEN REALLY *CAN* HAVE IT ALL.

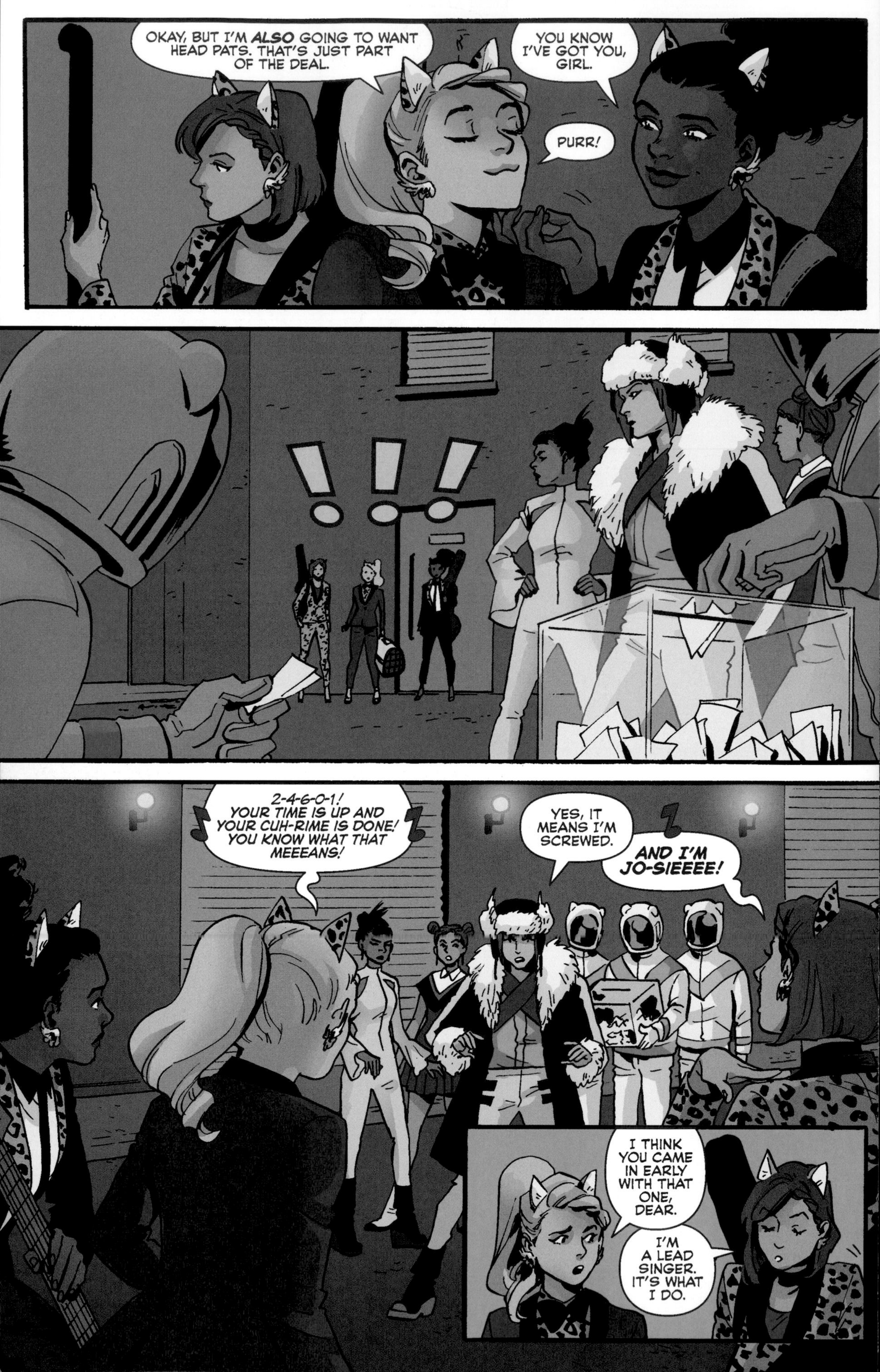
OKAY, BUT I'M ALSO GOING TO WANT HEAD PATS. THAT'S JUST PART OF THE DEAL.
YOU KNOW I'VE GOT YOU, GIRL.
PURR!
2-4-6-0-1! YOUR TIME IS UP AND YOUR CUH-RIME IS DONE! YOU KNOW WHAT THAT MEEEANS!
YES, IT MEANS I'M SCREWED.
AND I'M JO-SIEEEE!
I THINK YOU CAME IN EARLY WITH THAT ONE, DEAR.
I'M A LEAD SINGER. IT'S WHAT I DO.

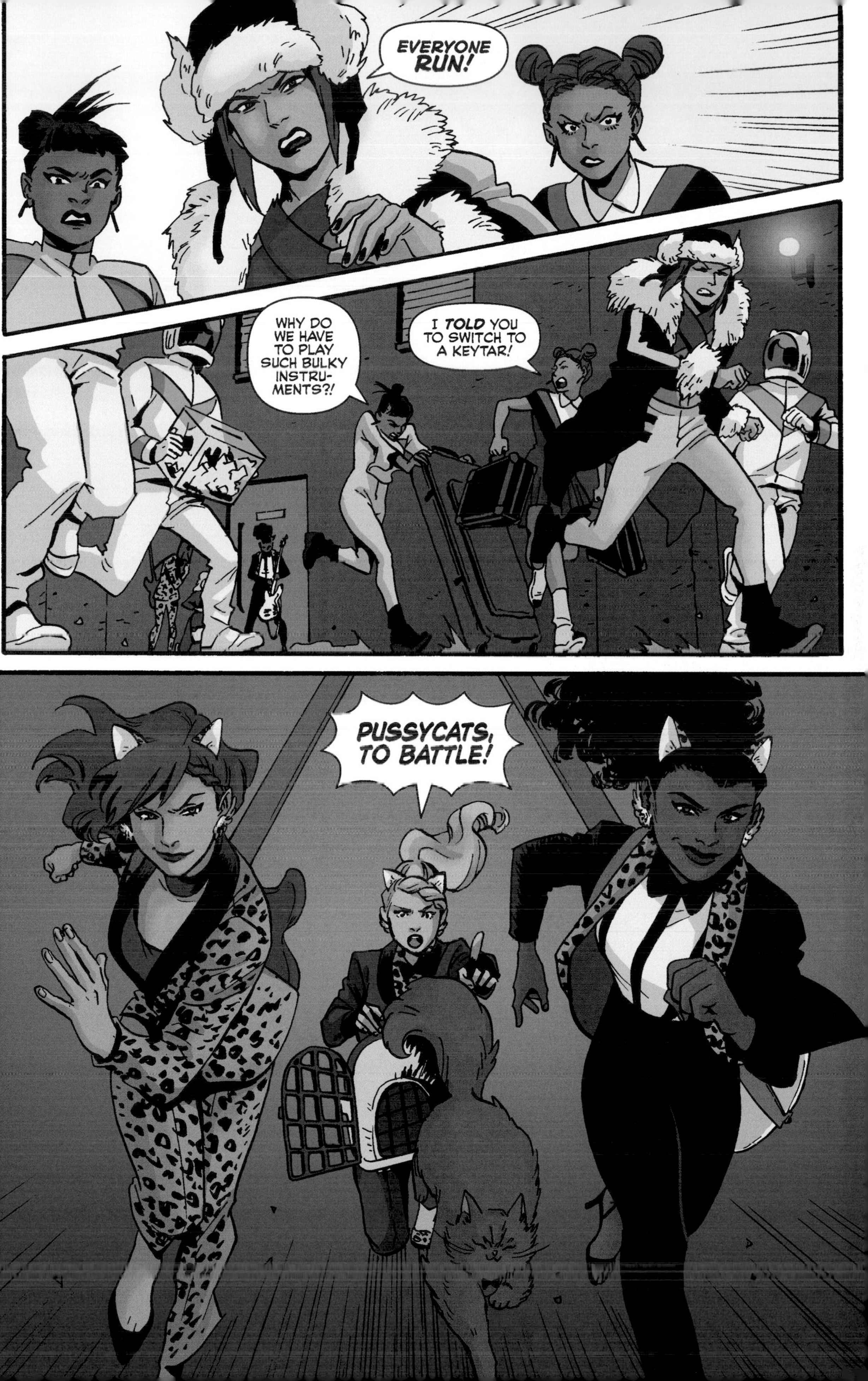
EVERYONE RUN!
WHY DO WE HAVE TO PLAY SUCH BULKY INSTRU-MENTS?!
I TOLD YOU TO SWITCH TO A KEYTAR!
PUSSYCATS, TO BATTLE!

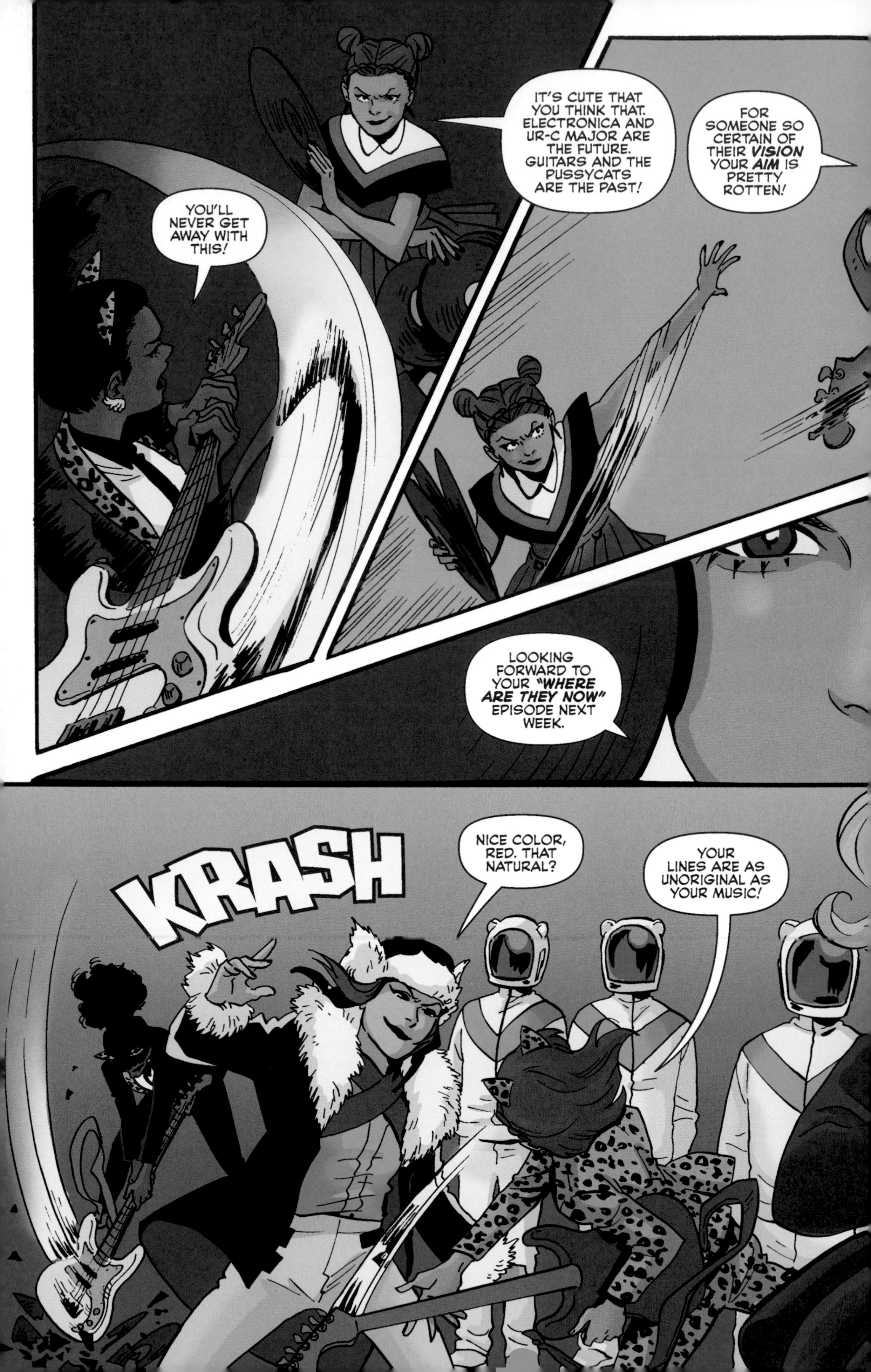
YOU'LL NEVER GET AWAY WITH THIS!
IT'S CUTE THAT YOU THINK THAT. ELECTRONICA AND UR-C MAJOR ARE THE FUTURE. GUITARS AND THE PUSSYCATS ARE THE PAST!
FOR SOMEONE SO CERTAIN OF THEIR *VISION* YOUR *AIM* IS PRETTY ROTTEN!
LOOKING FORWARD TO YOUR ***"WHERE ARE THEY NOW"*** EPISODE NEXT WEEK.
KRASH
NICE COLOR, RED. THAT NATURAL?
YOUR LINES ARE AS UNORIGINAL AS YOUR MUSIC!

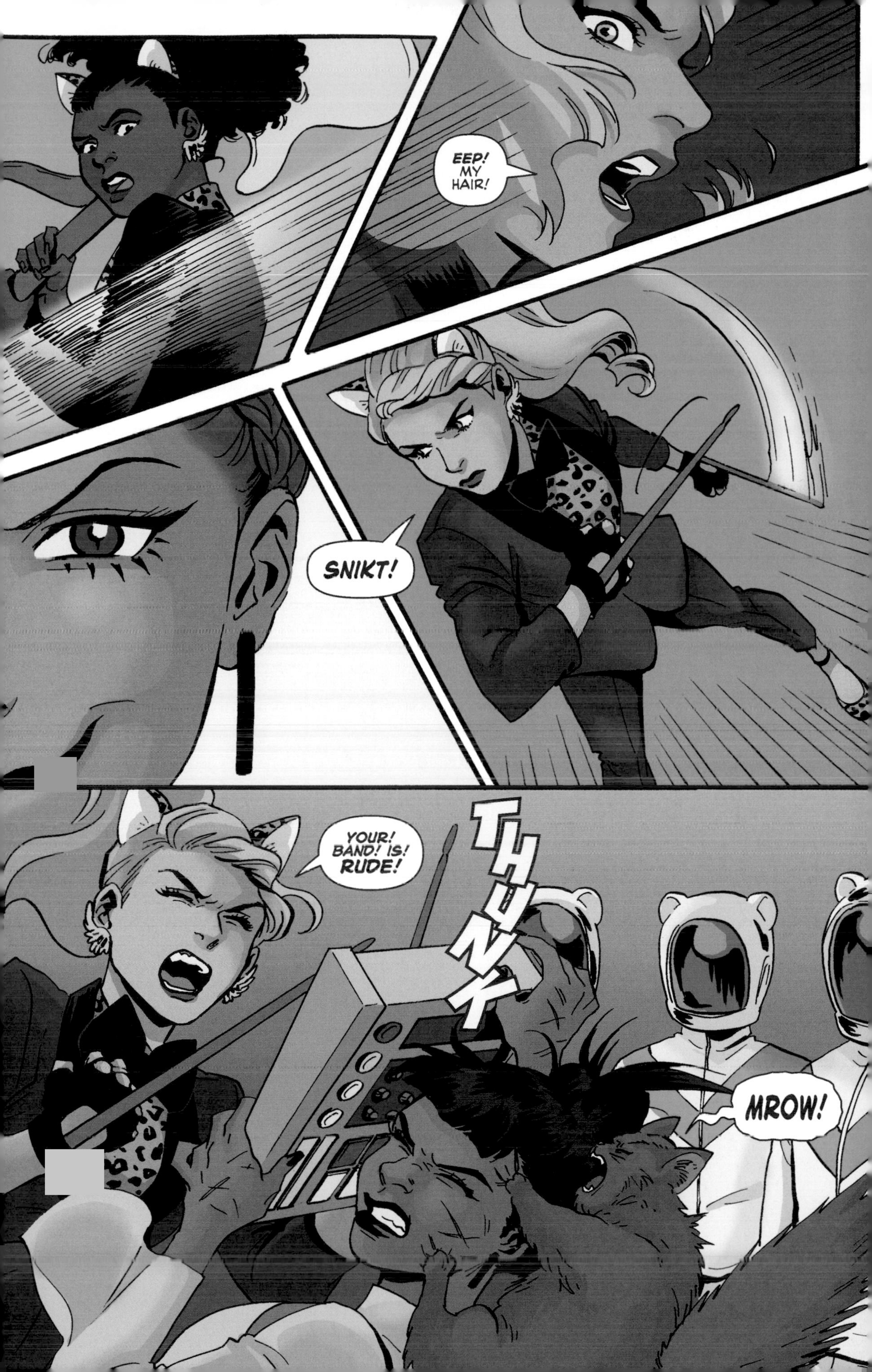
EEP! MY HAIR!
SNIKT!
YOUR! BAND! IS! RUDE!
THUNK
MROW!

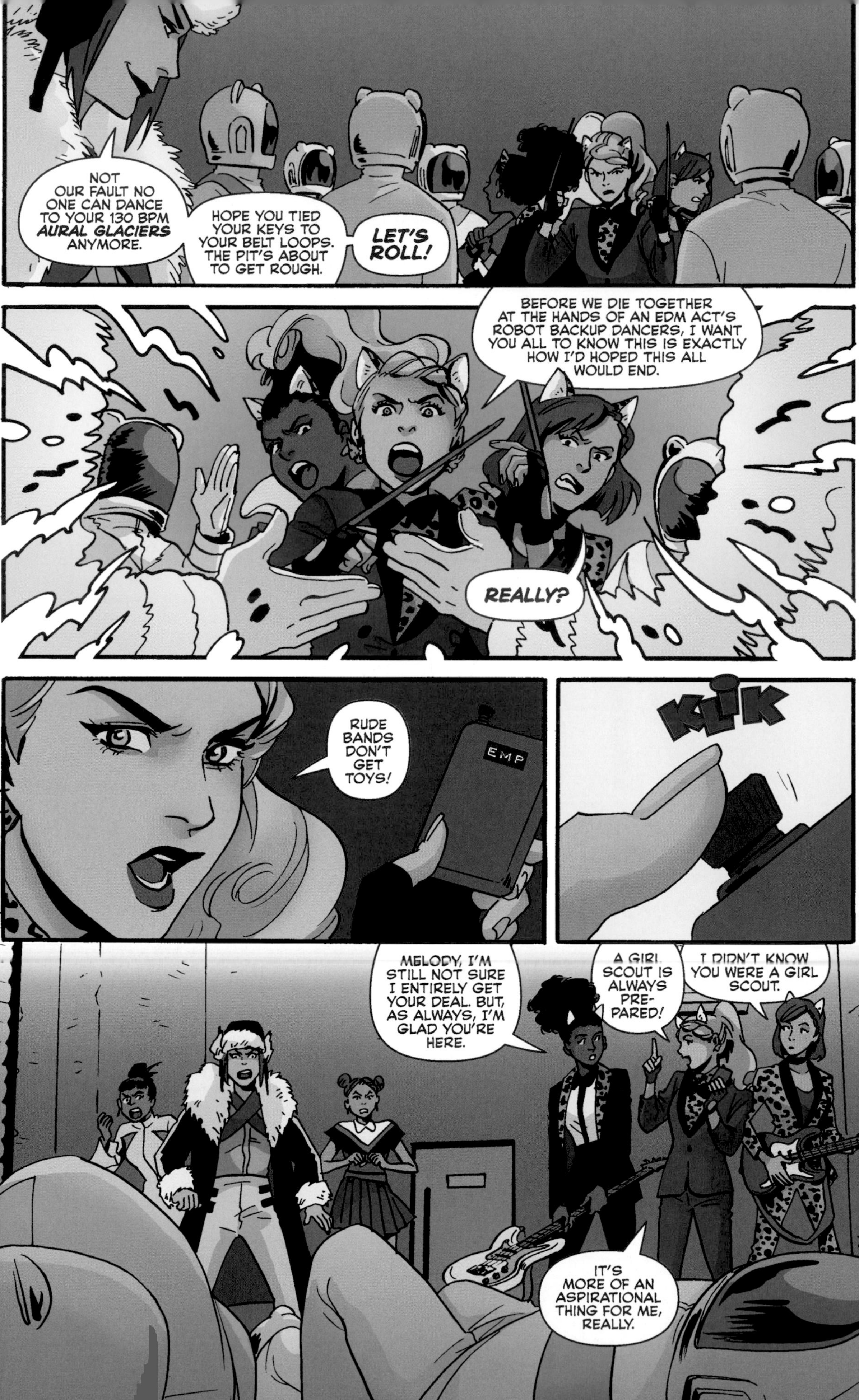
NOT OUR FAULT NO ONE CAN DANCE TO YOUR 130 BPM *AURAL GLACIERS* ANYMORE.
HOPE YOU TIED YOUR KEYS TO YOUR BELT LOOPS. THE PIT'S ABOUT TO GET ROUGH.
LET'S ROLL!
BEFORE WE DIE TOGETHER AT THE HANDS OF AN EDM ACT'S ROBOT BACKUP DANCERS, I WANT YOU ALL TO KNOW THIS IS EXACTLY HOW I'D HOPED THIS ALL WOULD END.
REALLY?
RUDE BANDS DON'T GET TOYS!
EMP
KLIK
MELODY, I'M STILL NOT SURE I ENTIRELY GET YOUR DEAL. BUT, AS ALWAYS, I'M GLAD YOU'RE HERE.
A GIRL SCOUT IS ALWAYS PRE-PARED!
I DIDN'T KNOW YOU WERE A GIRL SCOUT.
IT'S MORE OF AN ASPIRATIONAL THING FOR ME, REALLY.

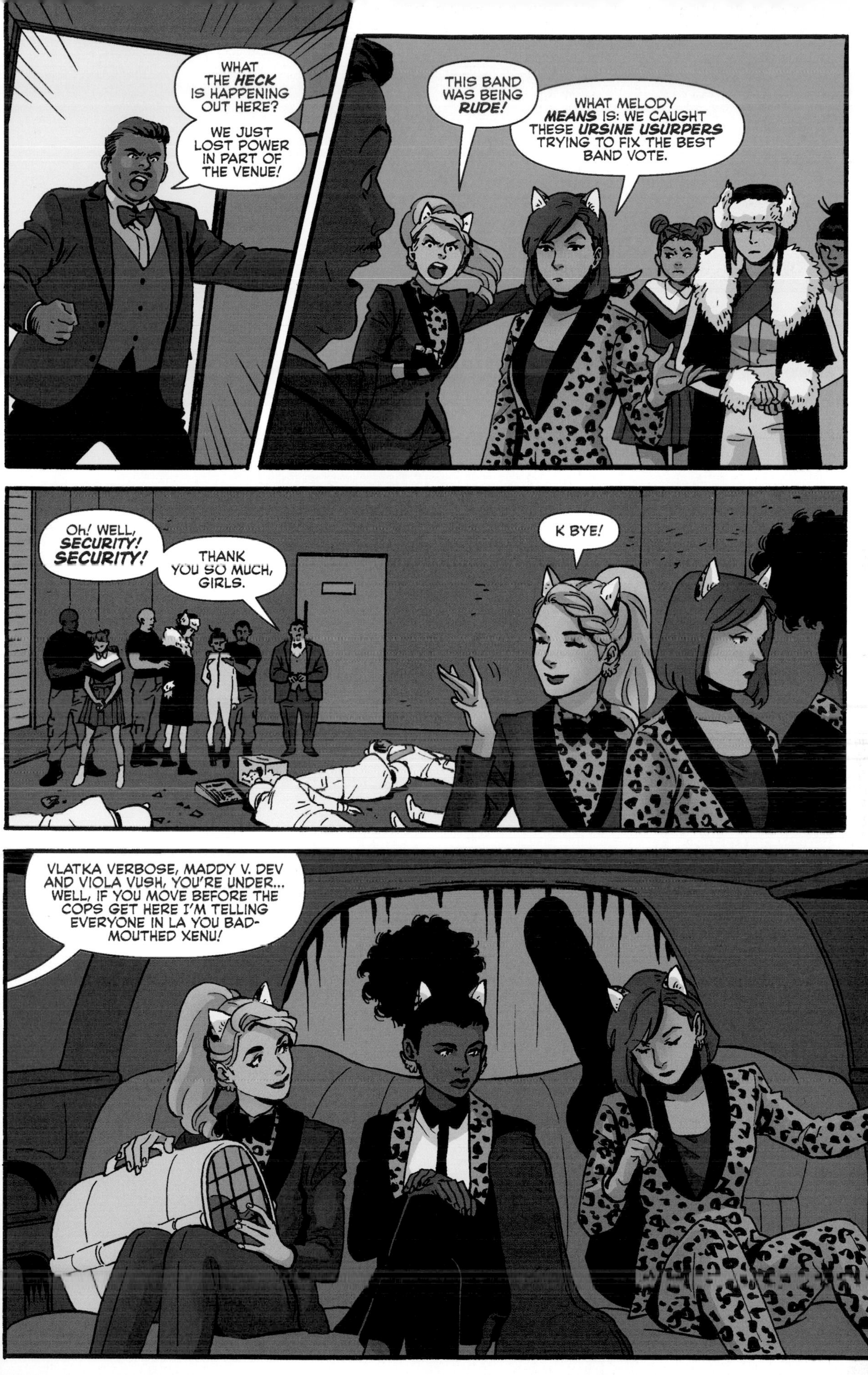
WHAT THE **HECK** IS HAPPENING OUT HERE?
WE JUST LOST POWER IN PART OF THE VENUE!
THIS BAND WAS BEING **RUDE!**
WHAT MELODY **MEANS** IS: WE CAUGHT THESE **URSINE USURPERS** TRYING TO FIX THE BEST BAND VOTE.
Oh! WELL, **SECURITY! SECURITY!**
THANK YOU SO MUCH, GIRLS.
K BYE!
VLATKA VERBOSE, MADDY V. DEV AND VIOLA VUSH, YOU'RE UNDER... WELL, IF YOU MOVE BEFORE THE COPS GET HERE I'M TELLING EVERYONE IN LA YOU BAD-MOUTHED XENU!

AND AFTER A QUICK BREAK, WE'LL HAVE THE RESULTS FOR THIS YEAR'S BEST BAND!

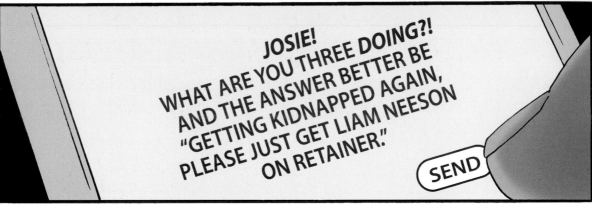

JOSIE! WHAT ARE YOU THREE DOING?! AND THE ANSWER BETTER BE "GETTING KIDNAPPED AGAIN, PLEASE JUST GET LIAM NEESON ON RETAINER."

SEND

THIS IS BAD.

THIS IS *SO* BAD.

SHOULD I CALL HER?

...

NO, SHE HATES TALKING ON THE PHONE.

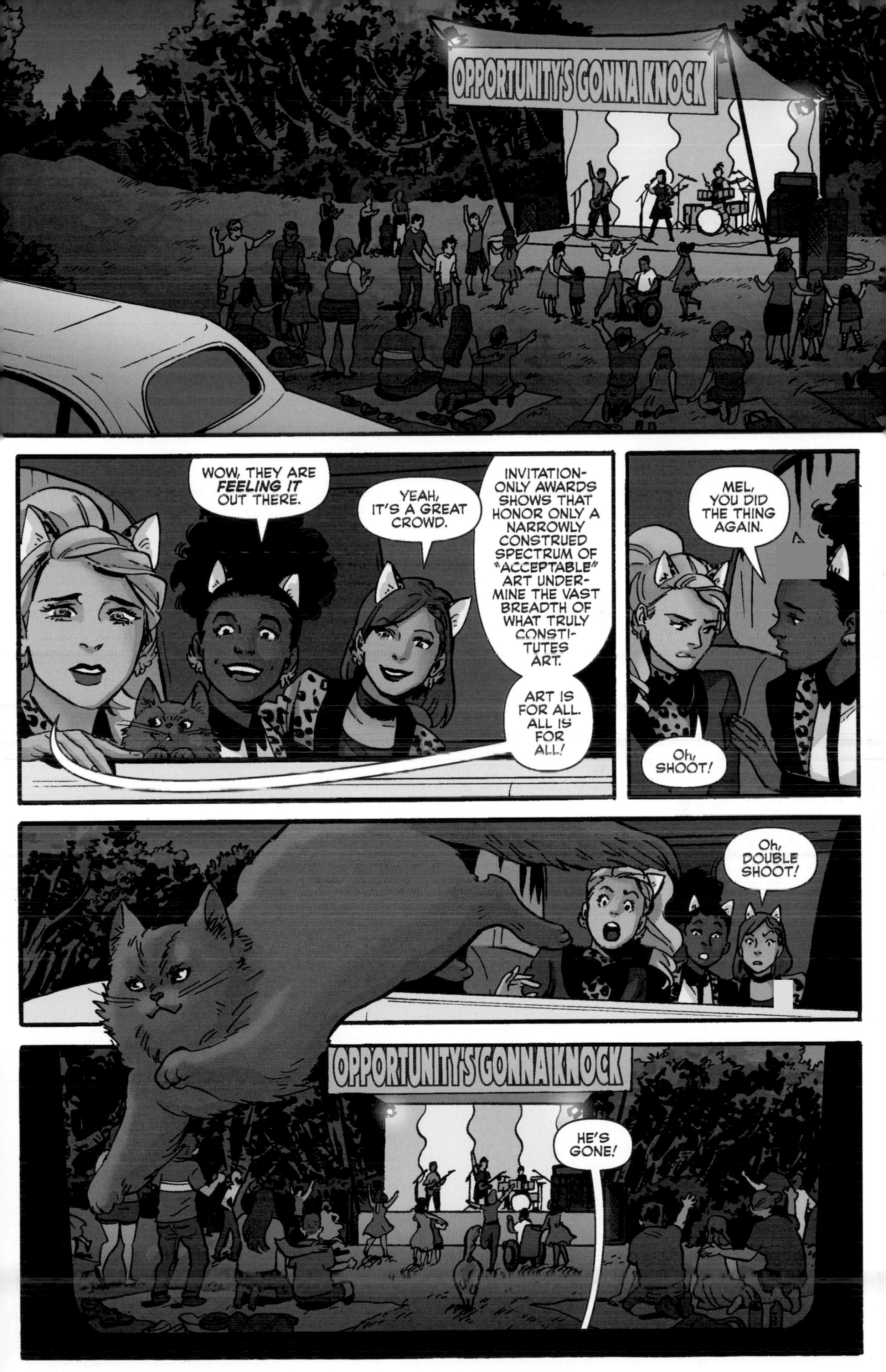
OPPORTUNITY'S GONNA KNOCK
WOW, THEY ARE FEELING IT OUT THERE.
YEAH, IT'S A GREAT CROWD.
INVITATION-ONLY AWARDS SHOWS THAT HONOR ONLY A NARROWLY CONSTRUED SPECTRUM OF "ACCEPTABLE" ART UNDERMINE THE VAST BREADTH OF WHAT TRULY CONSTITUTES ART.
ART IS FOR ALL. ALL IS FOR ALL!
MEL, YOU DID THE THING AGAIN.
Oh, SHOOT!
Oh, DOUBLE SHOOT!
OPPORTUNITY'S GONNA KNOCK
HE'S GONE!

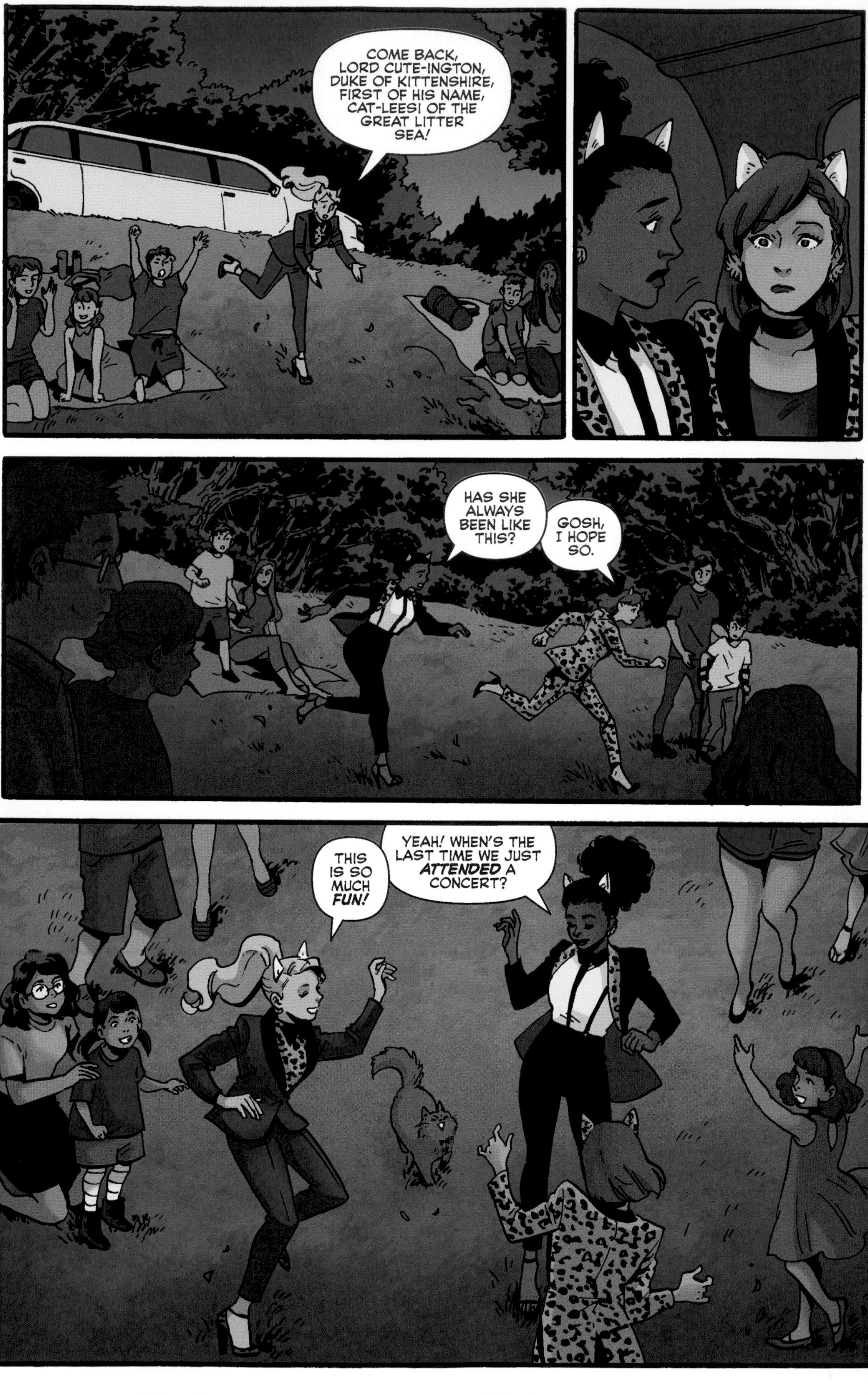
COME BACK, LORD CUTE-INGTON, DUKE OF KITTENSHIRE, FIRST OF HIS NAME, CAT-LEESI OF THE GREAT LITTER SEA!
HAS SHE ALWAYS BEEN LIKE THIS?
GOSH, I HOPE SO.
THIS IS SO MUCH *FUN!*
YEAH! WHEN'S THE LAST TIME WE JUST *ATTENDED* A CONCERT?

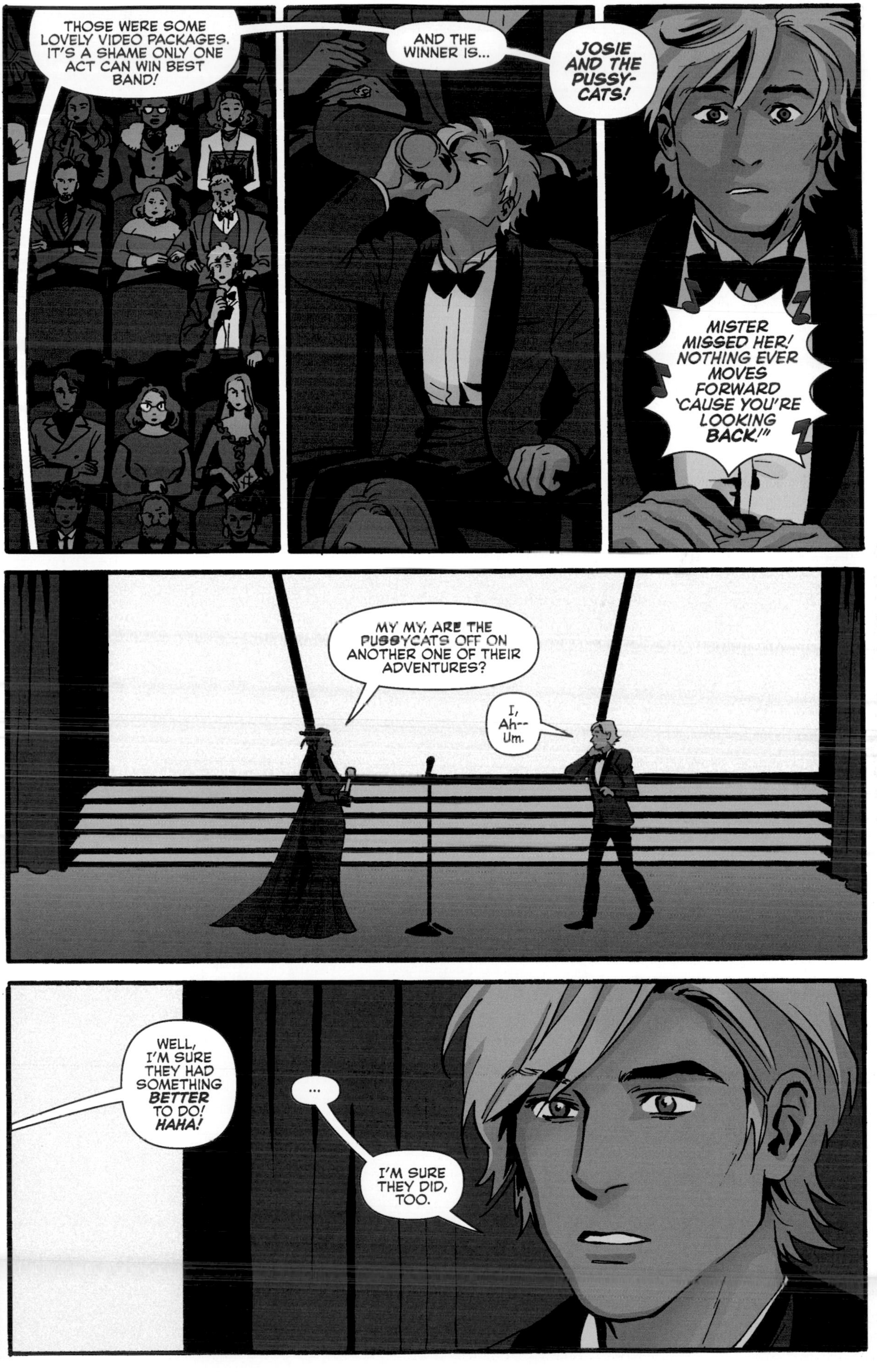
THOSE WERE SOME LOVELY VIDEO PACKAGES. IT'S A SHAME ONLY ONE ACT CAN WIN BEST BAND!
AND THE WINNER IS...
JOSIE AND THE PUSSY-CATS!
MISTER MISSED HER! NOTHING EVER MOVES FORWARD 'CAUSE YOU'RE LOOKING BACK!"
MY MY, ARE THE PUSSYCATS OFF ON ANOTHER ONE OF THEIR ADVENTURES?
I, Ah-- Um.
WELL, I'M SURE THEY HAD SOMETHING BETTER TO DO! HAHA!
...
I'M SURE THEY DID, TOO.

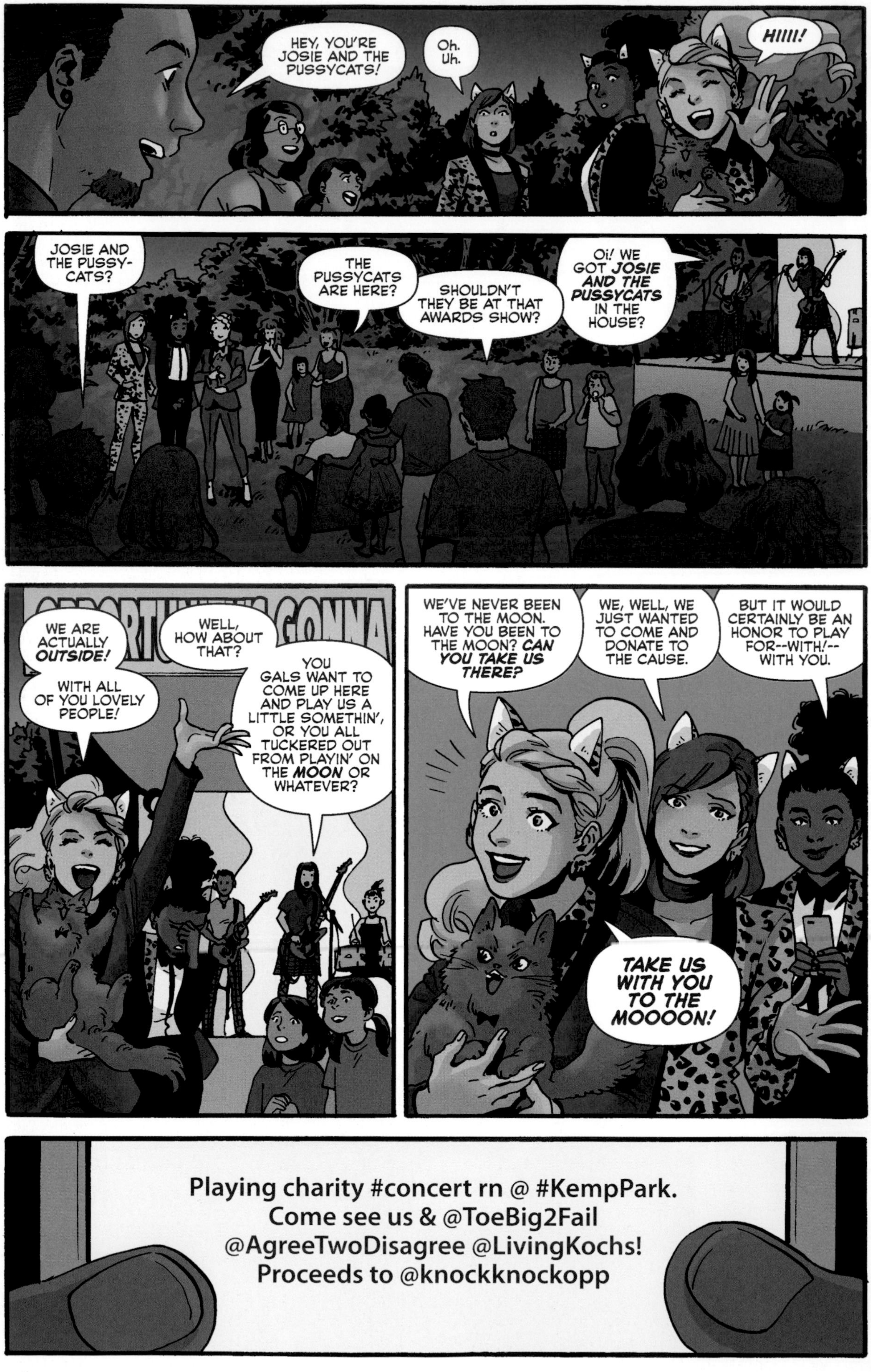
HEY, YOU'RE JOSIE AND THE PUSSYCATS!
Oh. Uh.
HIIII!
JOSIE AND THE PUSSY-CATS?
THE PUSSYCATS ARE HERE?
SHOULDN'T THEY BE AT THAT AWARDS SHOW?
Oi! WE GOT JOSIE AND THE PUSSYCATS IN THE HOUSE?
WE ARE ACTUALLY OUTSIDE!
WITH ALL OF YOU LOVELY PEOPLE!
WELL, HOW ABOUT THAT?
YOU GALS WANT TO COME UP HERE AND PLAY US A LITTLE SOMETHIN', OR YOU ALL TUCKERED OUT FROM PLAYIN' ON THE MOON OR WHATEVER?
WE'VE NEVER BEEN TO THE MOON. HAVE YOU BEEN TO THE MOON? CAN YOU TAKE US THERE?
WE, WELL, WE JUST WANTED TO COME AND DONATE TO THE CAUSE.
BUT IT WOULD CERTAINLY BE AN HONOR TO PLAY FOR--WITH!--WITH YOU.
TAKE US WITH YOU TO THE MOOOON!
Playing charity #concert rn @ #KempPark.
Come see us & @ToeBig2Fail
@AgreeTwoDisagree @LivingKochs!
Proceeds to @knockknockopp

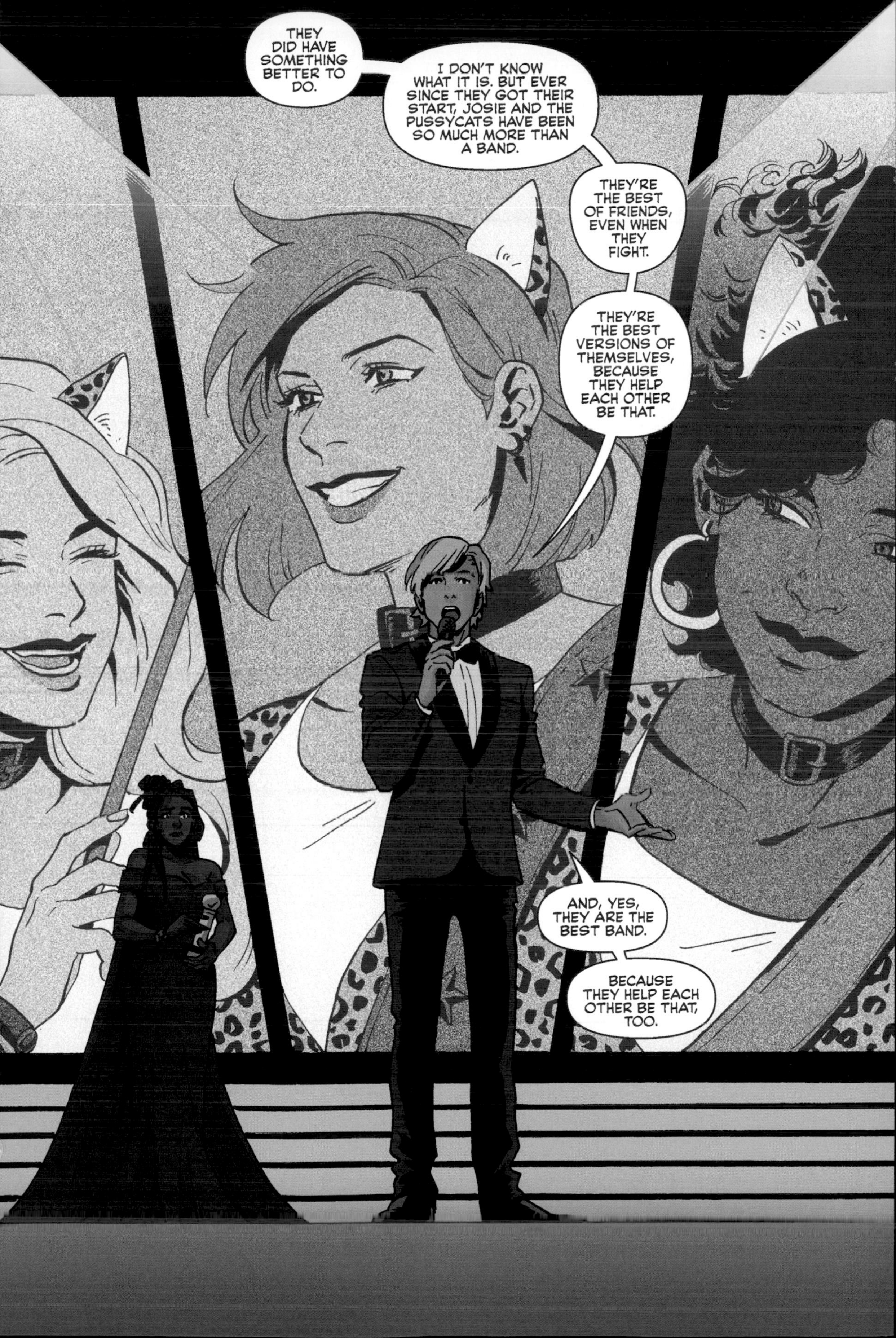
THEY DID HAVE SOMETHING BETTER TO DO.
I DON'T KNOW WHAT IT IS. BUT EVER SINCE THEY GOT THEIR START, JOSIE AND THE PUSSYCATS HAVE BEEN SO MUCH MORE THAN A BAND.
THEY'RE THE BEST OF FRIENDS, EVEN WHEN THEY FIGHT.
THEY'RE THE BEST VERSIONS OF THEMSELVES, BECAUSE THEY HELP EACH OTHER BE THAT.
AND, YES, THEY ARE THE BEST BAND.
BECAUSE THEY HELP EACH OTHER BE THAT, TOO.

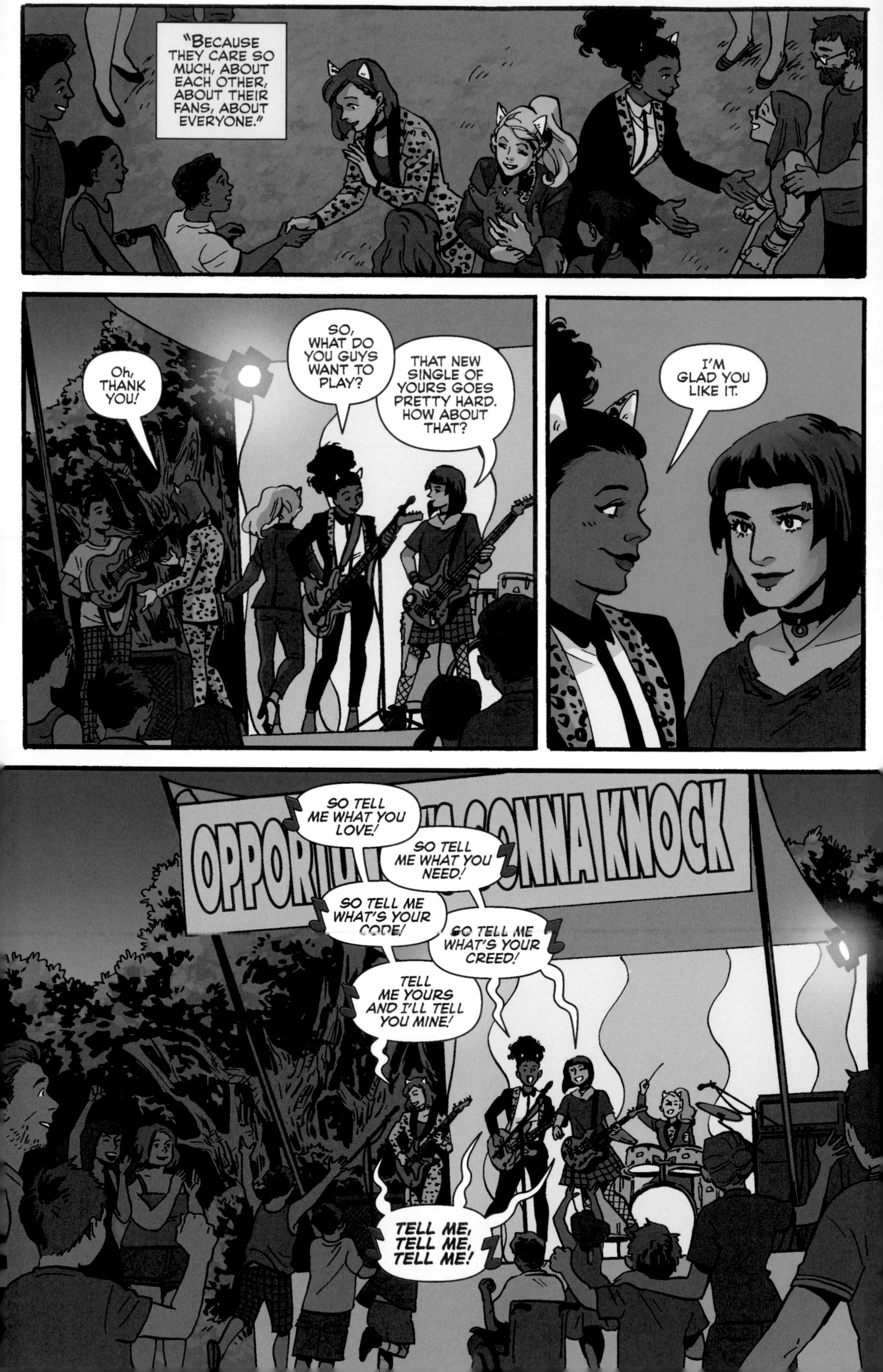
"BECAUSE THEY CARE SO MUCH, ABOUT EACH OTHER, ABOUT THEIR FANS, ABOUT EVERYONE."
Oh, THANK YOU!
SO, WHAT DO YOU GUYS WANT TO PLAY?
THAT NEW SINGLE OF YOURS GOES PRETTY HARD. HOW ABOUT THAT?
I'M GLAD YOU LIKE IT.
SO TELL ME WHAT YOU LOVE!
SO TELL ME WHAT YOU NEED!
SO TELL ME WHAT'S YOUR CODE!
SO TELL ME WHAT'S YOUR CREED!
TELL ME YOURS AND I'LL TELL YOU MINE!
TELL ME, TELL ME, TELL ME!

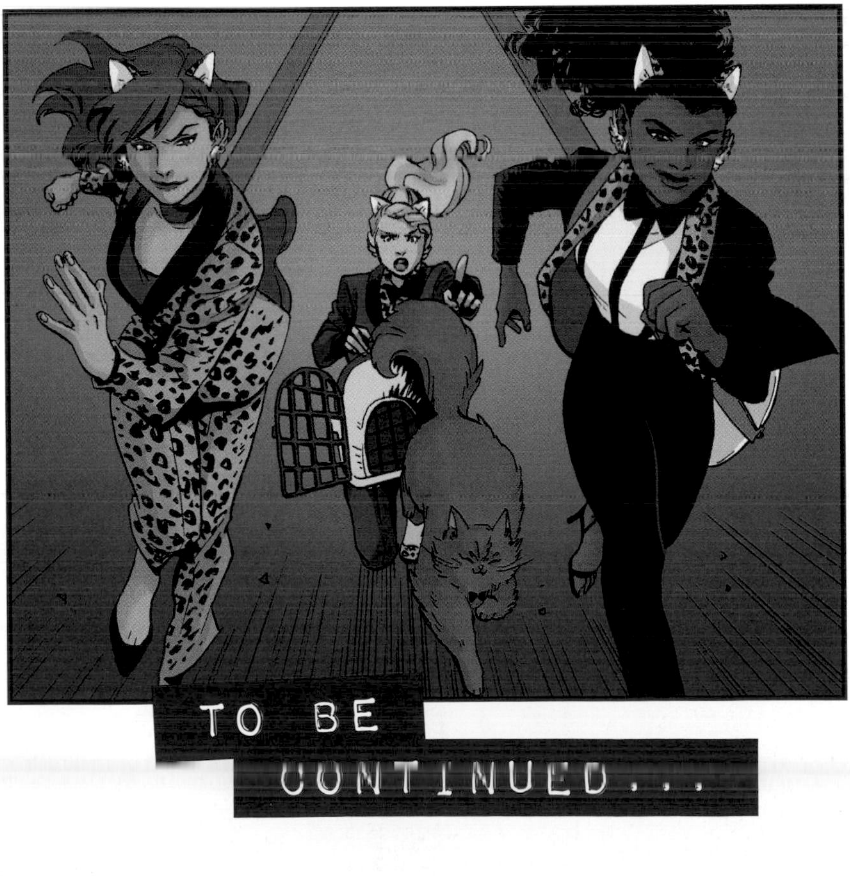
TO BE
CONTINUED...

ISSUE EIGHT

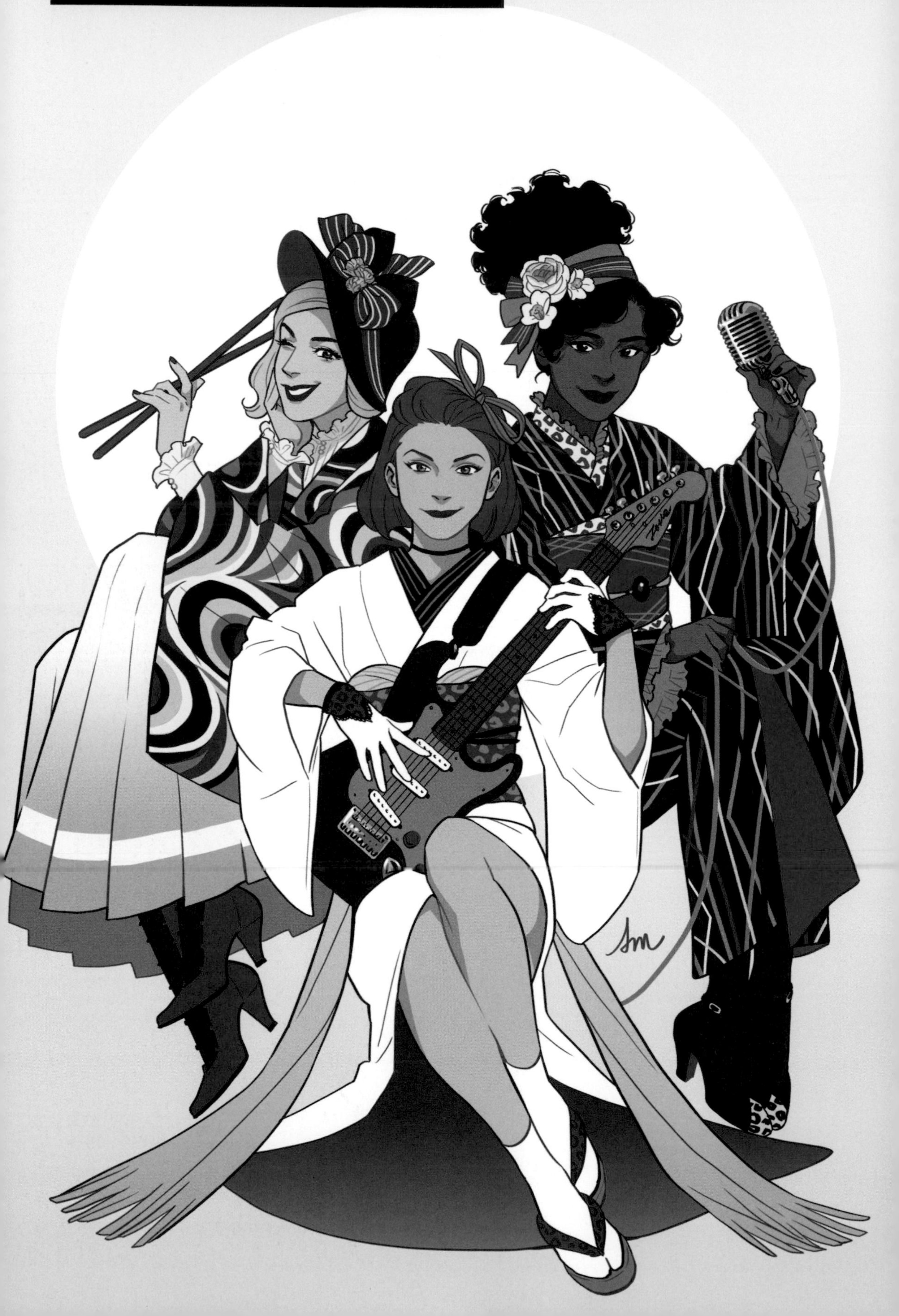

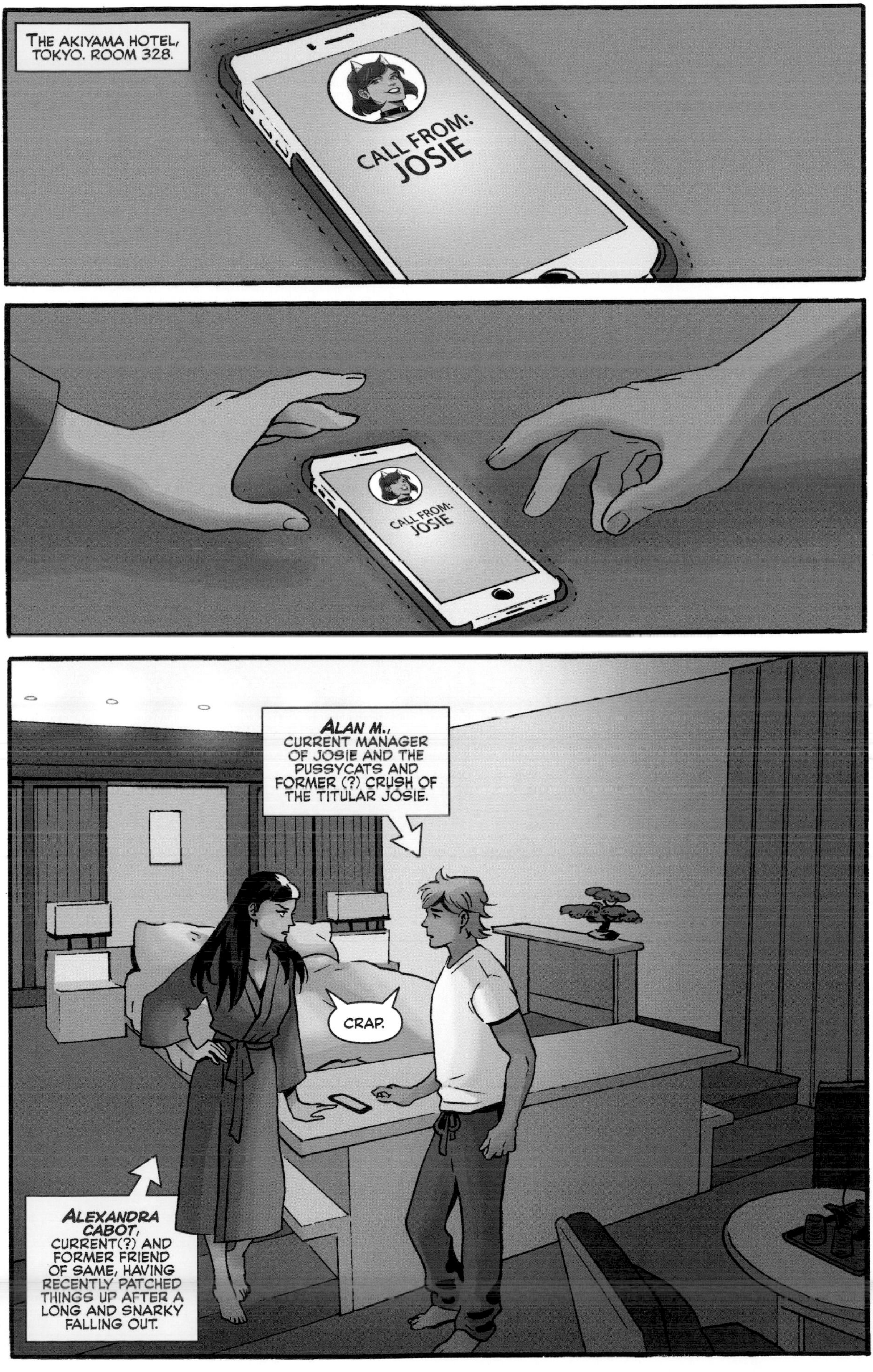
THE AKIYAMA HOTEL, TOKYO. ROOM 328.
CALL FROM: JOSIE
CALL FROM: JOSIE
ALAN M., CURRENT MANAGER OF JOSIE AND THE PUSSYCATS AND FORMER (?) CRUSH OF THE TITULAR JOSIE.
CRAP.
ALEXANDRA CABOT, CURRENT(?) AND FORMER FRIEND OF SAME, HAVING RECENTLY PATCHED THINGS UP AFTER A LONG AND SNARKY FALLING OUT.

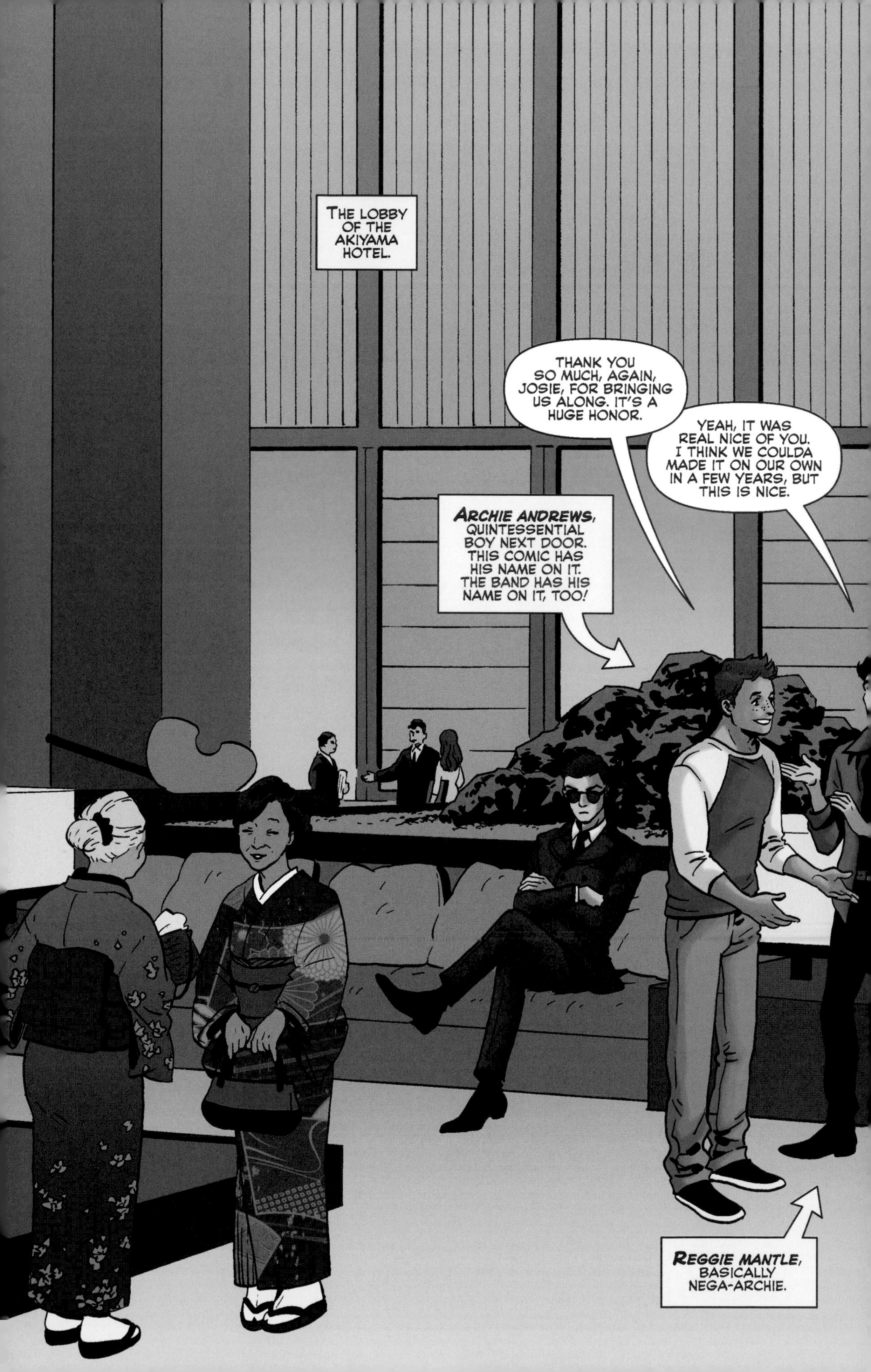

THE LOBBY OF THE AKIYAMA HOTEL.
THANK YOU SO MUCH, AGAIN, JOSIE, FOR BRINGING US ALONG. IT'S A HUGE HONOR.
YEAH, IT WAS REAL NICE OF YOU. I THINK WE COULDA MADE IT ON OUR OWN IN A FEW YEARS, BUT THIS IS NICE.
ARCHIE ANDREWS, QUINTESSENTIAL BOY NEXT DOOR. THIS COMIC HAS HIS NAME ON IT. THE BAND HAS HIS NAME ON IT, TOO!
REGGIE MANTLE, BASICALLY NEGA-ARCHIE.

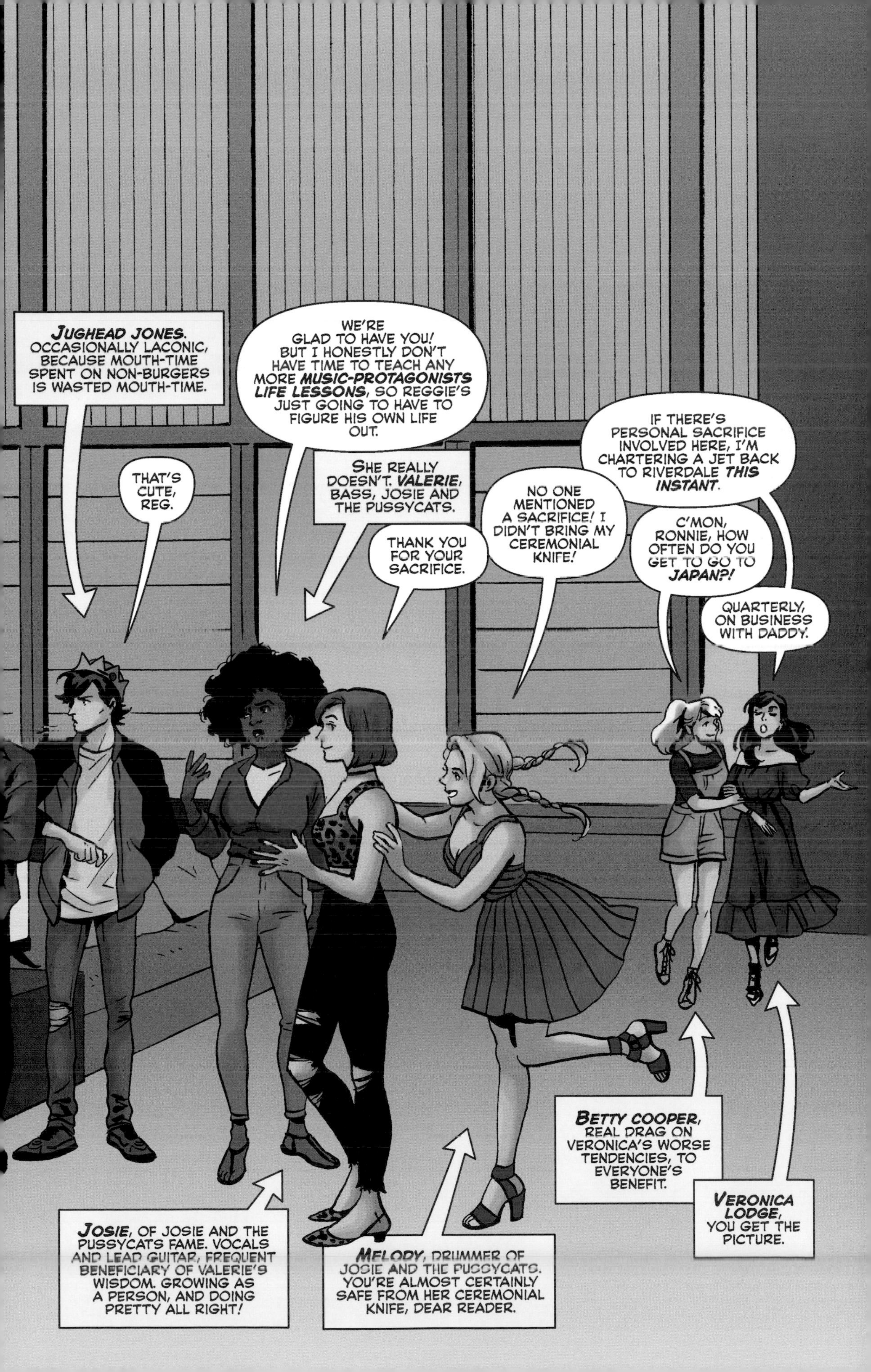
JUGHEAD JONES. OCCASIONALLY LACONIC, BECAUSE MOUTH-TIME SPENT ON NON-BURGERS IS WASTED MOUTH-TIME.
THAT'S CUTE, REG.
WE'RE GLAD TO HAVE YOU! BUT I HONESTLY DON'T HAVE TIME TO TEACH ANY MORE MUSIC-PROTAGONISTS LIFE LESSONS, SO REGGIE'S JUST GOING TO HAVE TO FIGURE HIS OWN LIFE OUT.
SHE REALLY DOESN'T. VALERIE, BASS, JOSIE AND THE PUSSYCATS.
THANK YOU FOR YOUR SACRIFICE.
NO ONE MENTIONED A SACRIFICE! I DIDN'T BRING MY CEREMONIAL KNIFE!
IF THERE'S PERSONAL SACRIFICE INVOLVED HERE, I'M CHARTERING A JET BACK TO RIVERDALE THIS INSTANT.
C'MON, RONNIE, HOW OFTEN DO YOU GET TO GO TO JAPAN?!
QUARTERLY, ON BUSINESS WITH DADDY.
BETTY COOPER, REAL DRAG ON VERONICA'S WORSE TENDENCIES, TO EVERYONE'S BENEFIT.
VERONICA LODGE, YOU GET THE PICTURE.
JOSIE, OF JOSIE AND THE PUSSYCATS FAME. VOCALS AND LEAD GUITAR, FREQUENT BENEFICIARY OF VALERIE'S WISDOM. GROWING AS A PERSON, AND DOING PRETTY ALL RIGHT!
MELODY, DRUMMER OF JOSIE AND THE PUSSYCATS. YOU'RE ALMOST CERTAINLY SAFE FROM HER CEREMONIAL KNIFE, DEAR READER.

LEAVE IT TO RIVERDALE KIDS TO TRAVEL HALFWAY AROUND THE WORLD TO ONE OF THE MOST EXCITING CITIES IN THE WORLD AND SPEND THE ENTIRE TIME *BEING POLITE TO ONE ANOTHER.*

ALEXANDER CABOT III. ALEXANDRA'S BROTHER. NEVER AT RISK OF BEING POLITE TO ANYONE. FORMER ANTARCTIC DESPOT, RECENTLY DEPOSED BY POLAR BEARS AND PUSSYCATS.

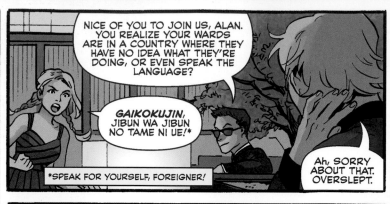

NICE OF YOU TO JOIN US, ALAN. YOU REALIZE YOUR WARDS ARE IN A COUNTRY WHERE THEY HAVE NO IDEA WHAT THEY'RE DOING, OR EVEN SPEAK THE LANGUAGE?

GAIKOKUJIN, JIBUN WA JIBUN NO TAME NI UE!*

*SPEAK FOR YOURSELF, FOREIGNER!

AH, SORRY ABOUT THAT. OVERSLEPT.

WHAT ARE YOU EVEN DOING HERE, ALEXANDER?

AFTER OUR PREVIOUS MISUNDER-STANDING--

YOU MEAN *"FELONY KIDNAP-PING."*

--I'D LIKE TO MAKE THINGS UP TO THE PUSSYCATS. I FIGURED YOU COULD USE A GUIDE DURING YOUR TIME IN TOKYO, AND I HAPPEN TO HAVE EXCELLENT CONTACTS IN THE AREA.

PLEASE DO NOT BE THOSE BORING FOREIGNERS WHO VISIT A NEW COUNTRY AND ONLY GO TO THEIR HOTEL!

WHSSSSH

TRY TO DIG DEEP PAST YOUR MOST GAUCHE IMPULSES TO FIND THE HUMAN CURIOSITY THAT HELPED OUR SPECIES SURVIVE!

HM, THE FORCE IS STRONG IN THIS ONE.

WHA-?!

FINE, ALEXANDRA. LET'S MEET THIS "CONTACT" OF ALEXANDER'S.

WONDERFUL! ALAN, FEEL FREE TO HANG BACK AND GET SOME *MORE REST.*

HEY!

WHAT'S THAT OLD SAYING? NINE'S COMPANY, TEN'S A CROWD?

THERE IS *NO WAY* THAT'S THE SAYING!

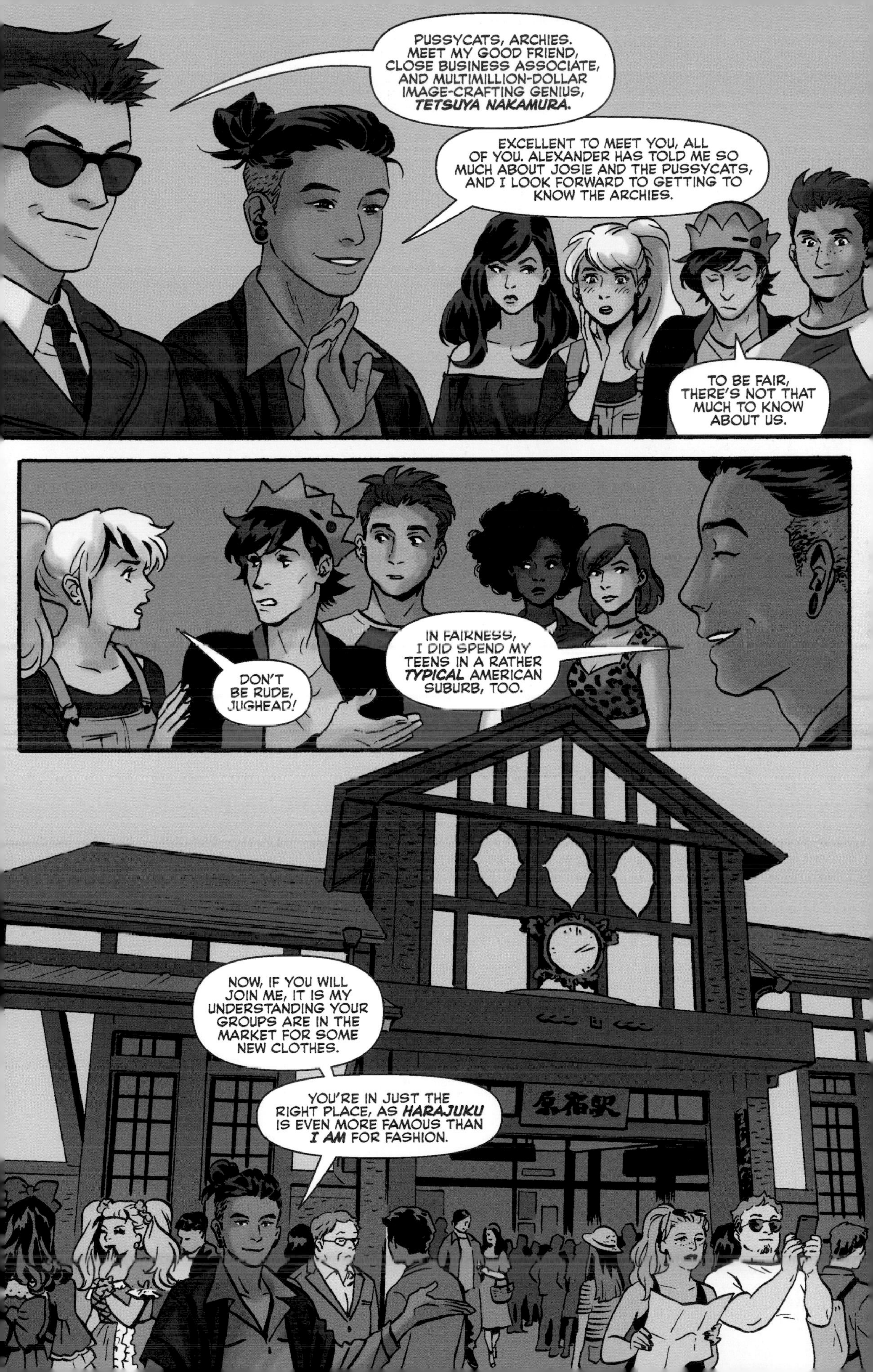
PUSSYCATS, ARCHIES. MEET MY GOOD FRIEND, CLOSE BUSINESS ASSOCIATE, AND MULTIMILLION-DOLLAR IMAGE-CRAFTING GENIUS, ***TETSUYA NAKAMURA.***
EXCELLENT TO MEET YOU, ALL OF YOU. ALEXANDER HAS TOLD ME SO MUCH ABOUT JOSIE AND THE PUSSYCATS, AND I LOOK FORWARD TO GETTING TO KNOW THE ARCHIES.
TO BE FAIR, THERE'S NOT THAT MUCH TO KNOW ABOUT US.
DON'T BE RUDE, JUGHEAD!
IN FAIRNESS, I DID SPEND MY TEENS IN A RATHER ***TYPICAL*** AMERICAN SUBURB, TOO.
NOW, IF YOU WILL JOIN ME, IT IS MY UNDERSTANDING YOUR GROUPS ARE IN THE MARKET FOR SOME NEW CLOTHES.
YOU'RE IN JUST THE RIGHT PLACE, AS ***HARAJUKU*** IS EVEN MORE FAMOUS THAN ***I AM*** FOR FASHION.
原宿駅

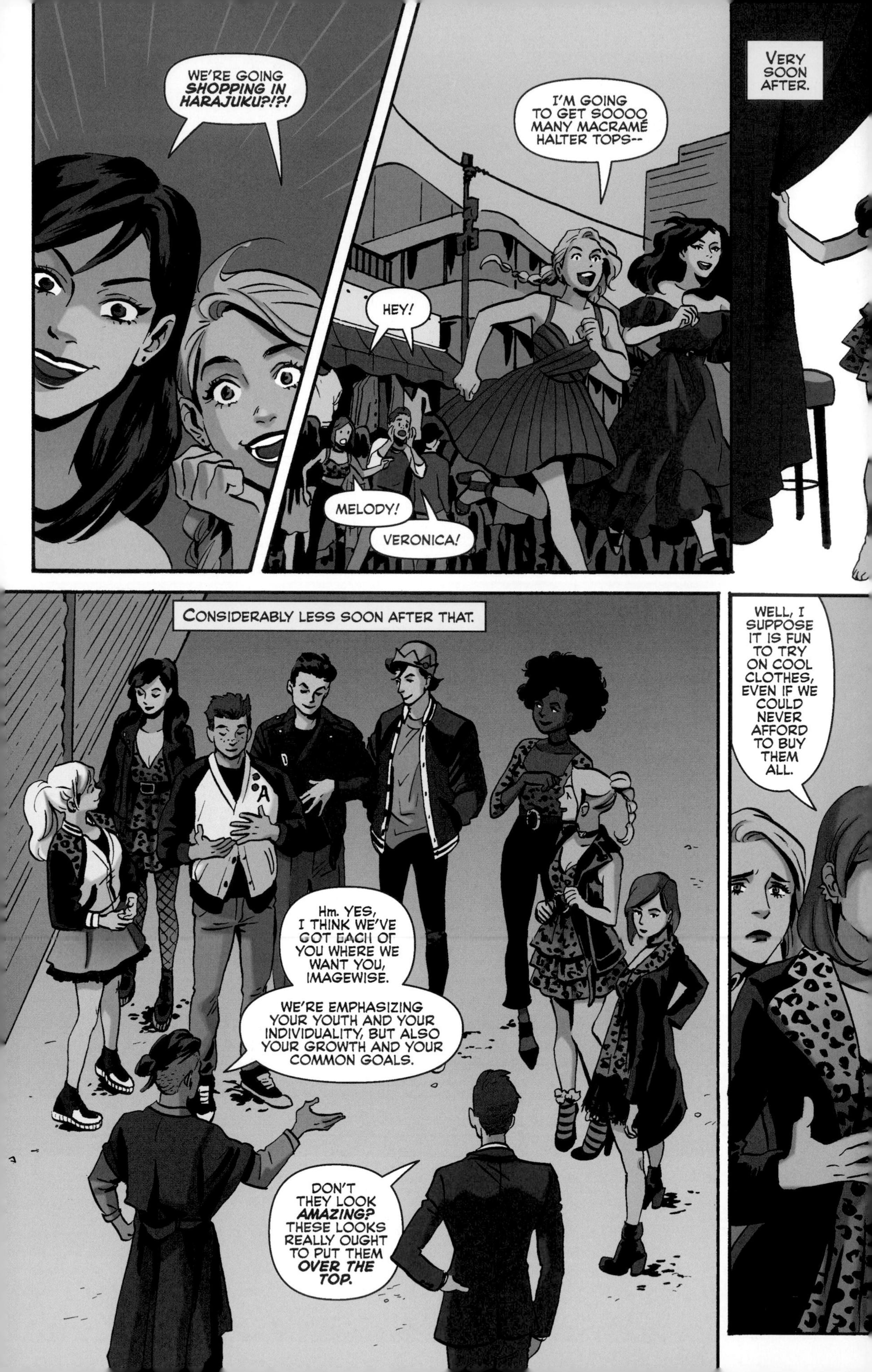
WE'RE GOING SHOPPING IN HARAJUKU?!?!
I'M GOING TO GET SOOOO MANY MACRAMÉ HALTER TOPS--
HEY!
MELODY!
VERONICA!
VERY SOON AFTER.
CONSIDERABLY LESS SOON AFTER THAT.
Hm. YES, I THINK WE'VE GOT EACH OF YOU WHERE WE WANT YOU, IMAGEWISE.
WE'RE EMPHASIZING YOUR YOUTH AND YOUR INDIVIDUALITY, BUT ALSO YOUR GROWTH AND YOUR COMMON GOALS.
DON'T THEY LOOK AMAZING? THESE LOOKS REALLY OUGHT TO PUT THEM OVER THE TOP.
WELL, I SUPPOSE IT IS FUN TO TRY ON COOL CLOTHES, EVEN IF WE COULD NEVER AFFORD TO BUY THEM ALL.

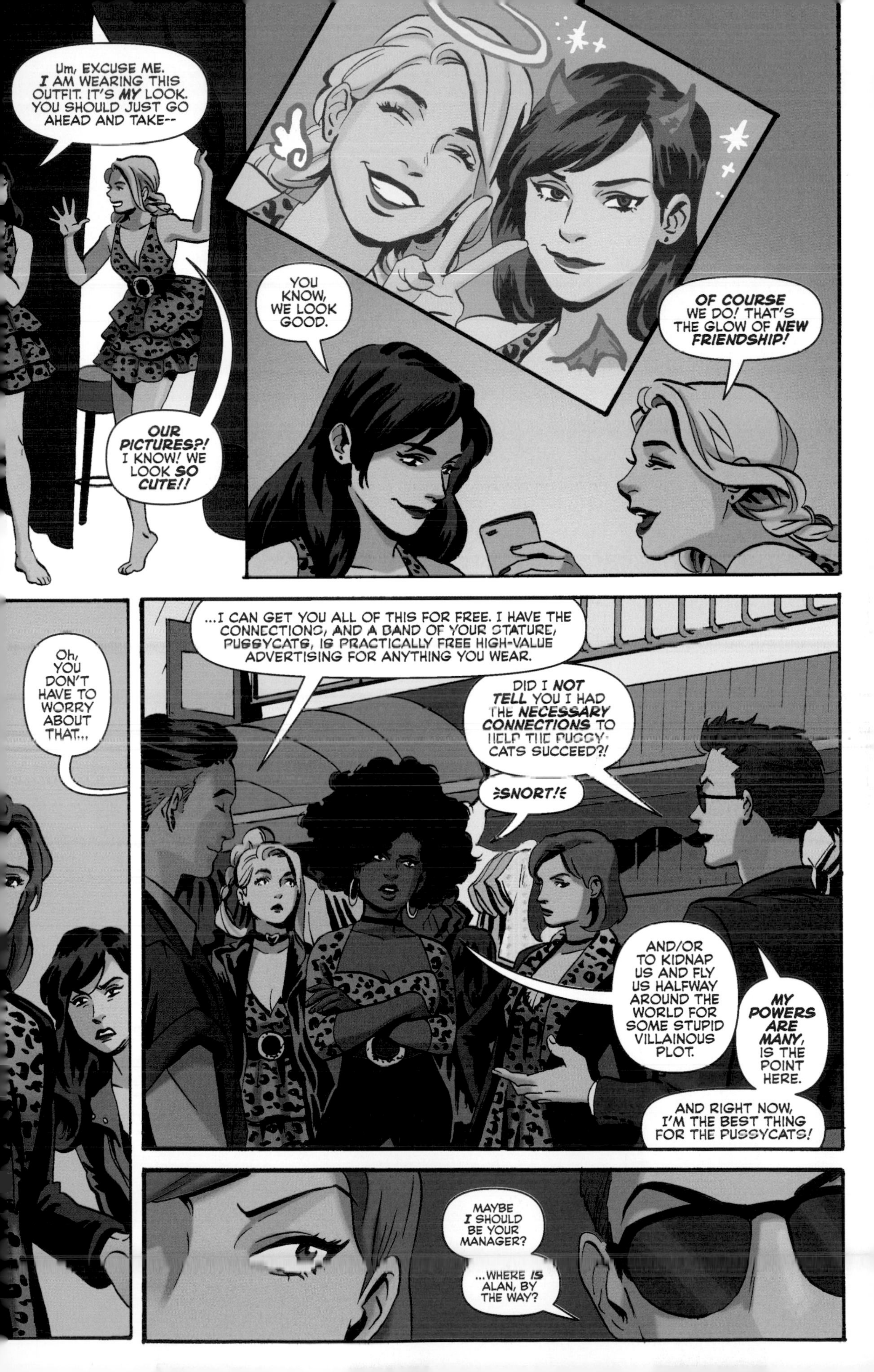
Um, EXCUSE ME. I AM WEARING THIS OUTFIT. IT'S MY LOOK. YOU SHOULD JUST GO AHEAD AND TAKE--
OUR PICTURES?! I KNOW! WE LOOK SO CUTE!!
YOU KNOW, WE LOOK GOOD.
OF COURSE WE DO! THAT'S THE GLOW OF NEW FRIENDSHIP!
Oh, YOU DON'T HAVE TO WORRY ABOUT THAT...
...I CAN GET YOU ALL OF THIS FOR FREE. I HAVE THE CONNECTIONS, AND A BAND OF YOUR STATURE, PUSSYCATS, IS PRACTICALLY FREE HIGH-VALUE ADVERTISING FOR ANYTHING YOU WEAR.
DID I NOT TELL YOU I HAD THE NECESSARY CONNECTIONS TO HELP THE PUSSY-CATS SUCCEED?!
SNORT!
AND/OR TO KIDNAP US AND FLY US HALFWAY AROUND THE WORLD FOR SOME STUPID VILLAINOUS PLOT.
MY POWERS ARE MANY, IS THE POINT HERE.
AND RIGHT NOW, I'M THE BEST THING FOR THE PUSSYCATS!
MAYBE I SHOULD BE YOUR MANAGER?
...WHERE IS ALAN, BY THE WAY?

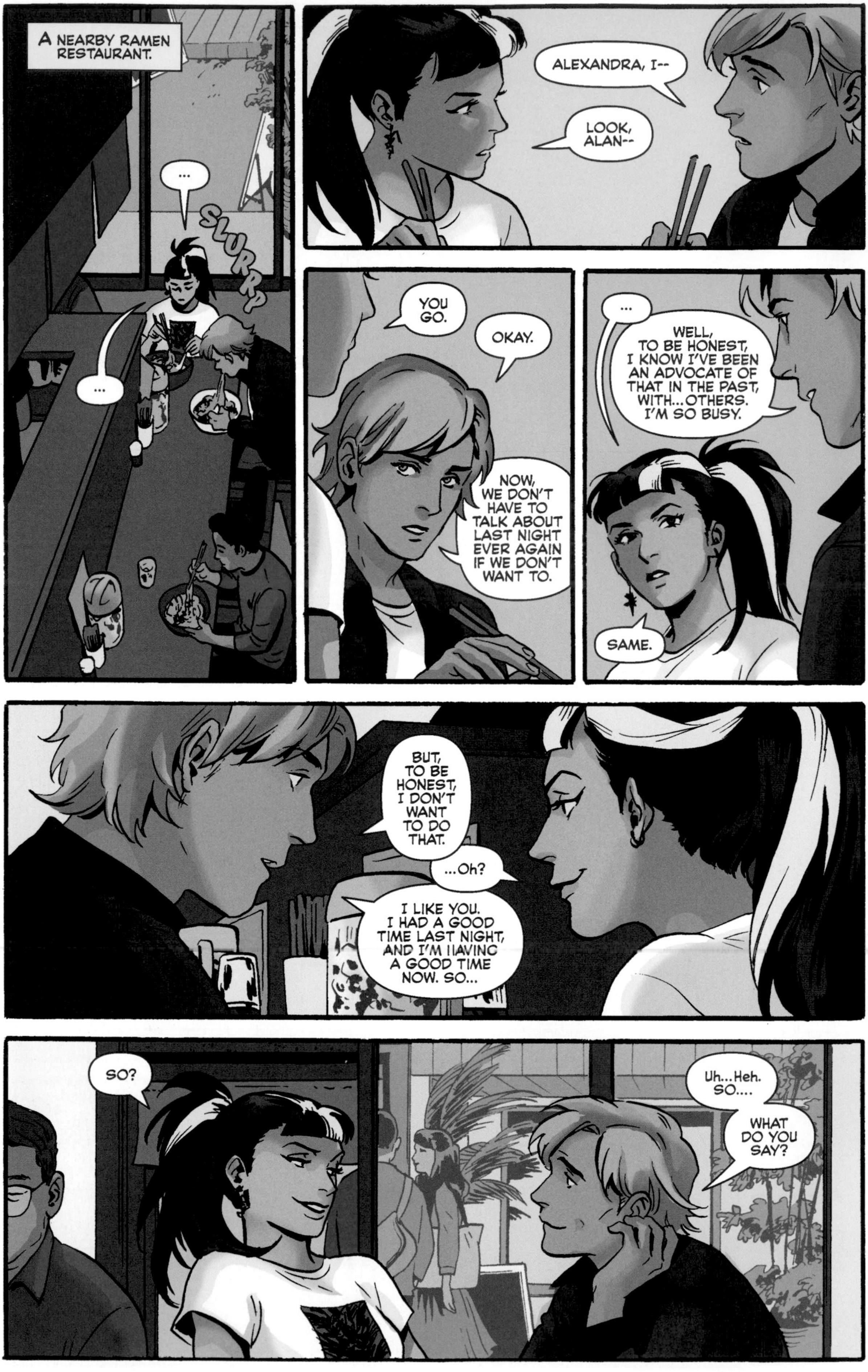
A NEARBY RAMEN RESTAURANT.
...
SLURRP
...
ALEXANDRA, I--
LOOK, ALAN--
YOU GO.
OKAY.
NOW, WE DON'T HAVE TO TALK ABOUT LAST NIGHT EVER AGAIN IF WE DON'T WANT TO.
...
WELL, TO BE HONEST, I KNOW I'VE BEEN AN ADVOCATE OF THAT IN THE PAST, WITH...OTHERS. I'M SO BUSY.
SAME.
BUT, TO BE HONEST, I DON'T WANT TO DO THAT.
...Oh?
I LIKE YOU. I HAD A GOOD TIME LAST NIGHT, AND I'M HAVING A GOOD TIME NOW. SO...
SO?
Uh...Heh. SO....
WHAT DO YOU SAY?

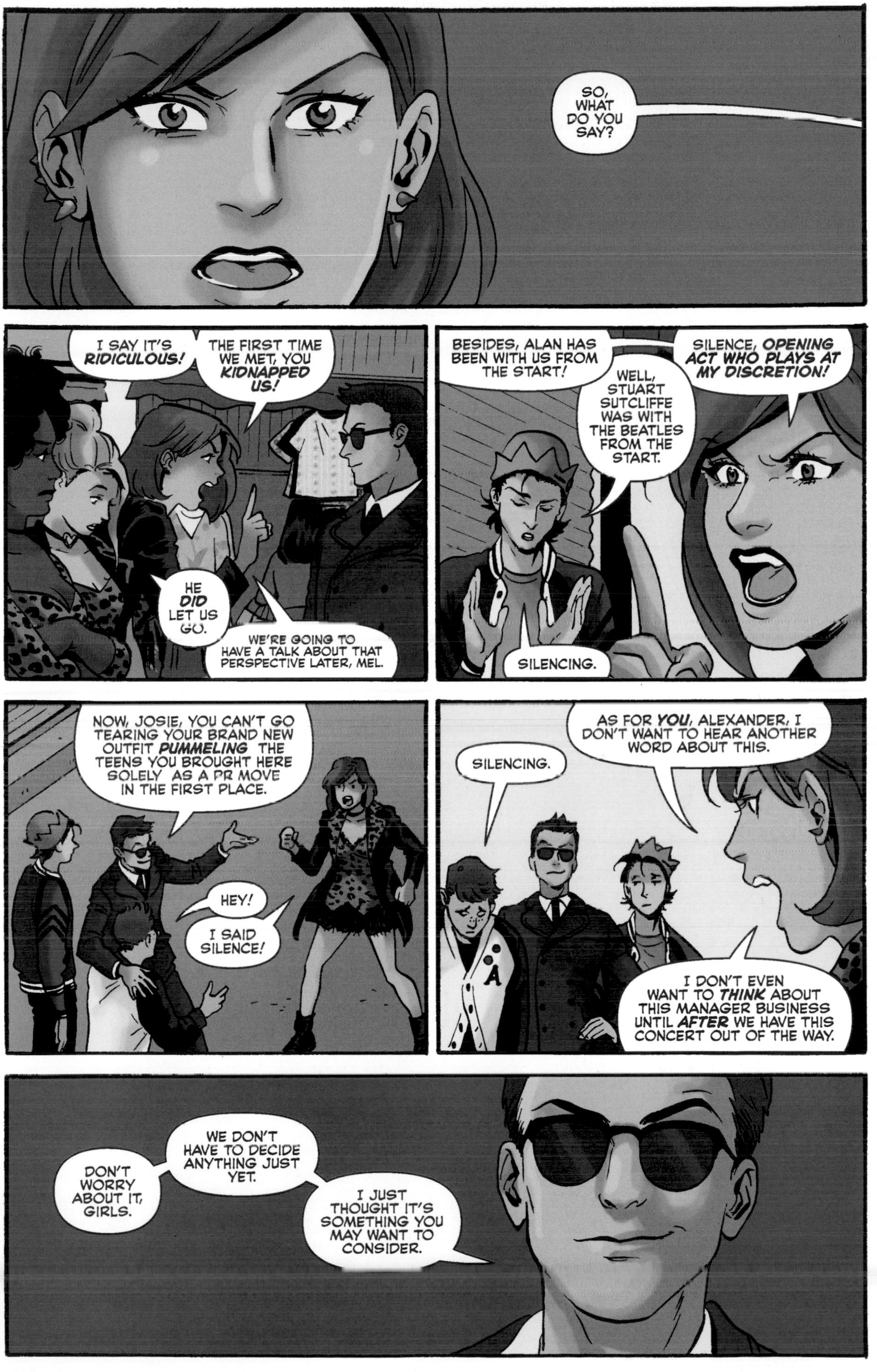
SO, WHAT DO YOU SAY?
I SAY IT'S *RIDICULOUS!*
THE FIRST TIME WE MET, YOU *KIDNAPPED US!*
HE *DID* LET US GO.
WE'RE GOING TO HAVE A TALK ABOUT THAT PERSPECTIVE LATER, MEL.
BESIDES, ALAN HAS BEEN WITH US FROM THE START!
WELL, STUART SUTCLIFFE WAS WITH THE BEATLES FROM THE START.
SILENCE, *OPENING ACT WHO PLAYS AT MY DISCRETION!*
SILENCING.
NOW, JOSIE, YOU CAN'T GO TEARING YOUR BRAND NEW OUTFIT *PUMMELING* THE TEENS YOU BROUGHT HERE SOLELY AS A PR MOVE IN THE FIRST PLACE.
HEY!
I SAID SILENCE!
AS FOR *YOU*, ALEXANDER, I DON'T WANT TO HEAR ANOTHER WORD ABOUT THIS.
SILENCING.
I DON'T EVEN WANT TO *THINK* ABOUT THIS MANAGER BUSINESS UNTIL *AFTER* WE HAVE THIS CONCERT OUT OF THE WAY.
DON'T WORRY ABOUT IT, GIRLS.
WE DON'T HAVE TO DECIDE ANYTHING JUST YET.
I JUST THOUGHT IT'S SOMETHING YOU MAY WANT TO CONSIDER.

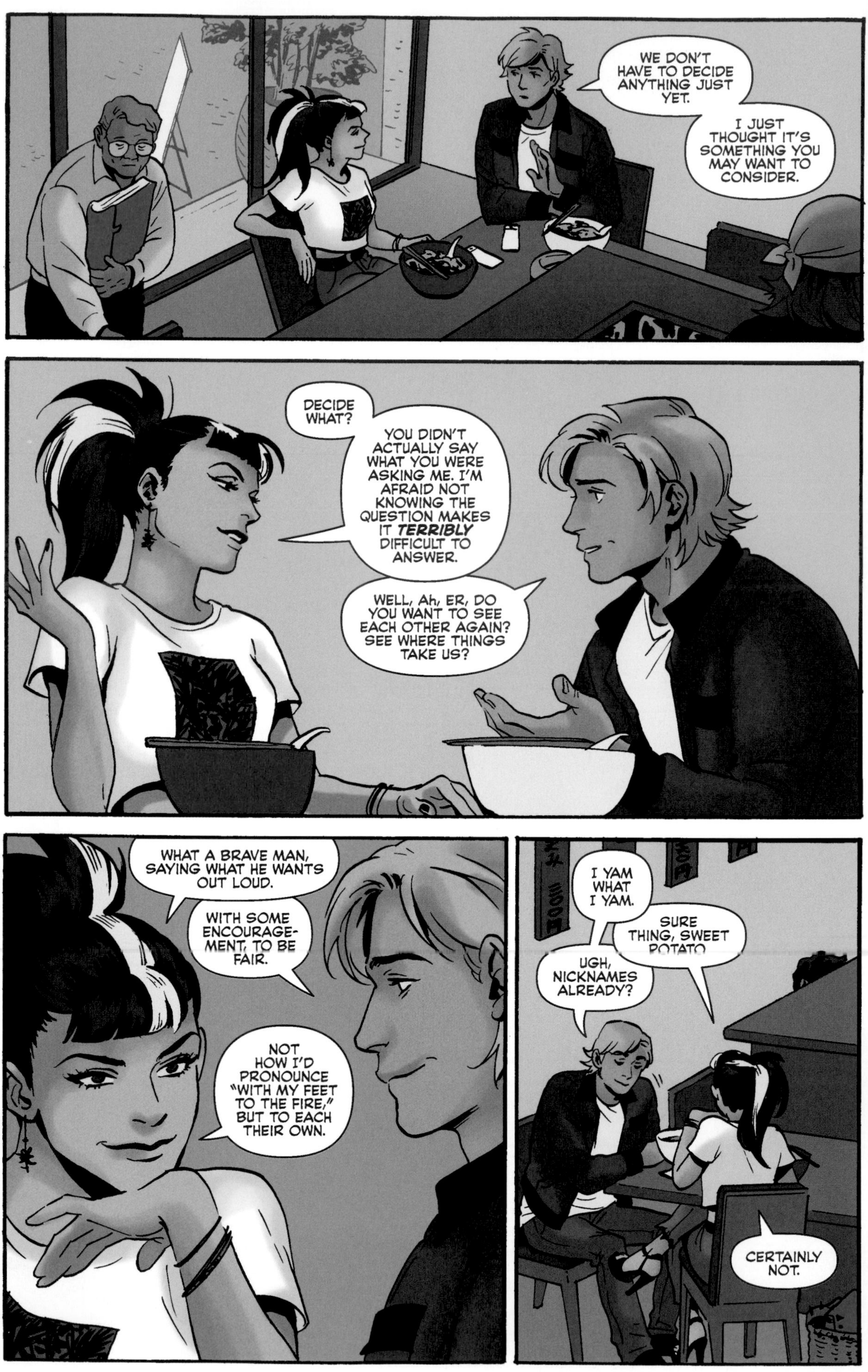
WE DON'T HAVE TO DECIDE ANYTHING JUST YET.
I JUST THOUGHT IT'S SOMETHING YOU MAY WANT TO CONSIDER.
DECIDE WHAT?
YOU DIDN'T ACTUALLY SAY WHAT YOU WERE ASKING ME. I'M AFRAID NOT KNOWING THE QUESTION MAKES IT *TERRIBLY* DIFFICULT TO ANSWER.
WELL, Ah, ER, DO YOU WANT TO SEE EACH OTHER AGAIN? SEE WHERE THINGS TAKE US?
WHAT A BRAVE MAN, SAYING WHAT HE WANTS OUT LOUD.
WITH SOME ENCOURAGE-MENT, TO BE FAIR.
NOT HOW I'D PRONOUNCE "WITH MY FEET TO THE FIRE," BUT TO EACH THEIR OWN.
I YAM WHAT I YAM.
SURE THING, SWEET POTATO.
UGH, NICKNAMES ALREADY?
CERTAINLY NOT.

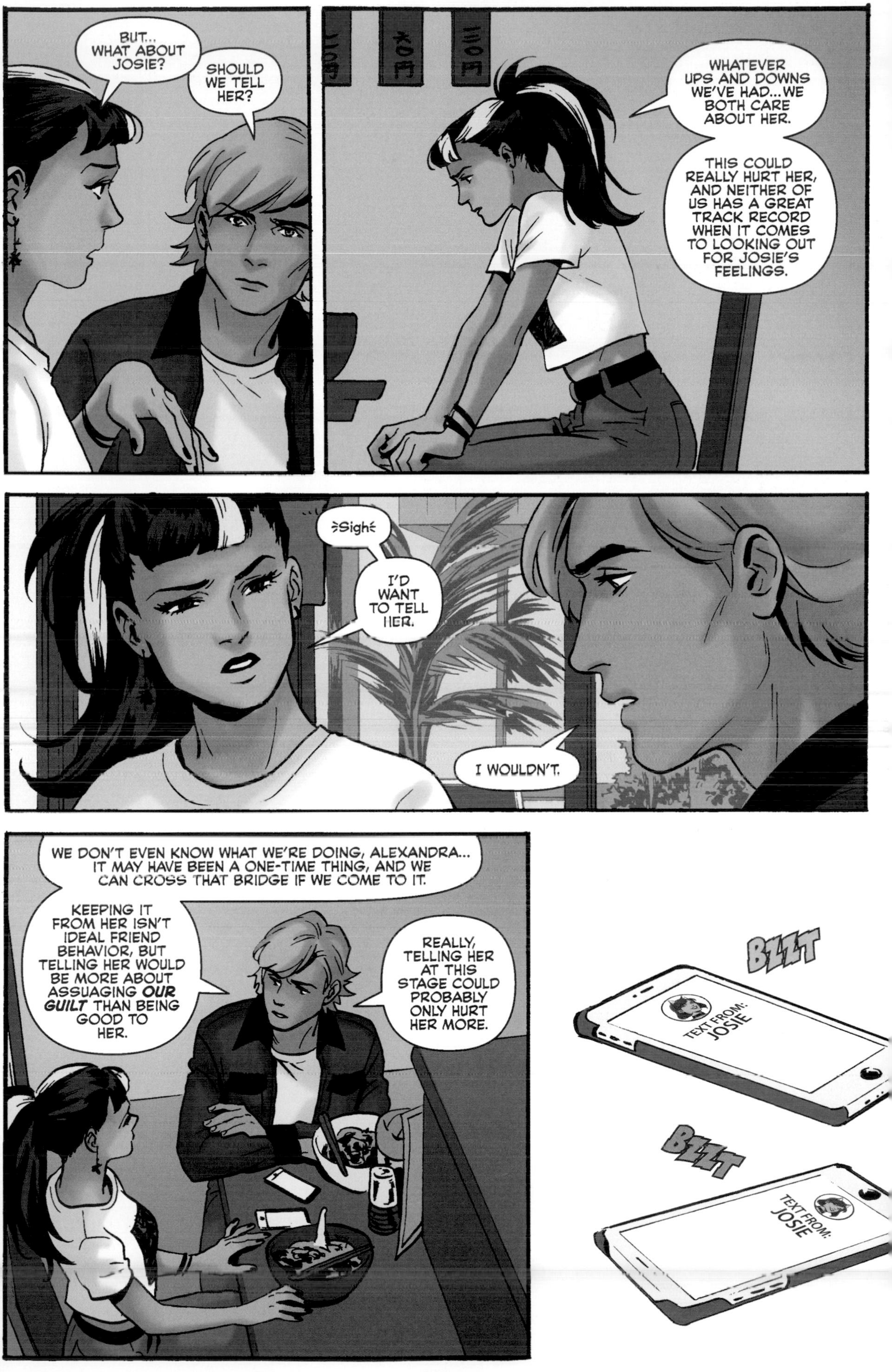
BUT... WHAT ABOUT JOSIE?
SHOULD WE TELL HER?
WHATEVER UPS AND DOWNS WE'VE HAD...WE BOTH CARE ABOUT HER.
THIS COULD REALLY HURT HER, AND NEITHER OF US HAS A GREAT TRACK RECORD WHEN IT COMES TO LOOKING OUT FOR JOSIE'S FEELINGS.
Sigh
I'D WANT TO TELL HER.
I WOULDN'T.
WE DON'T EVEN KNOW WHAT WE'RE DOING, ALEXANDRA... IT MAY HAVE BEEN A ONE-TIME THING, AND WE CAN CROSS THAT BRIDGE IF WE COME TO IT.
KEEPING IT FROM HER ISN'T IDEAL FRIEND BEHAVIOR, BUT TELLING HER WOULD BE MORE ABOUT ASSUAGING OUR GUILT THAN BEING GOOD TO HER.
REALLY, TELLING HER AT THIS STAGE COULD PROBABLY ONLY HURT HER MORE.
BZZT
TEXT FROM: JOSIE
BZZT
TEXT FROM: JOSIE

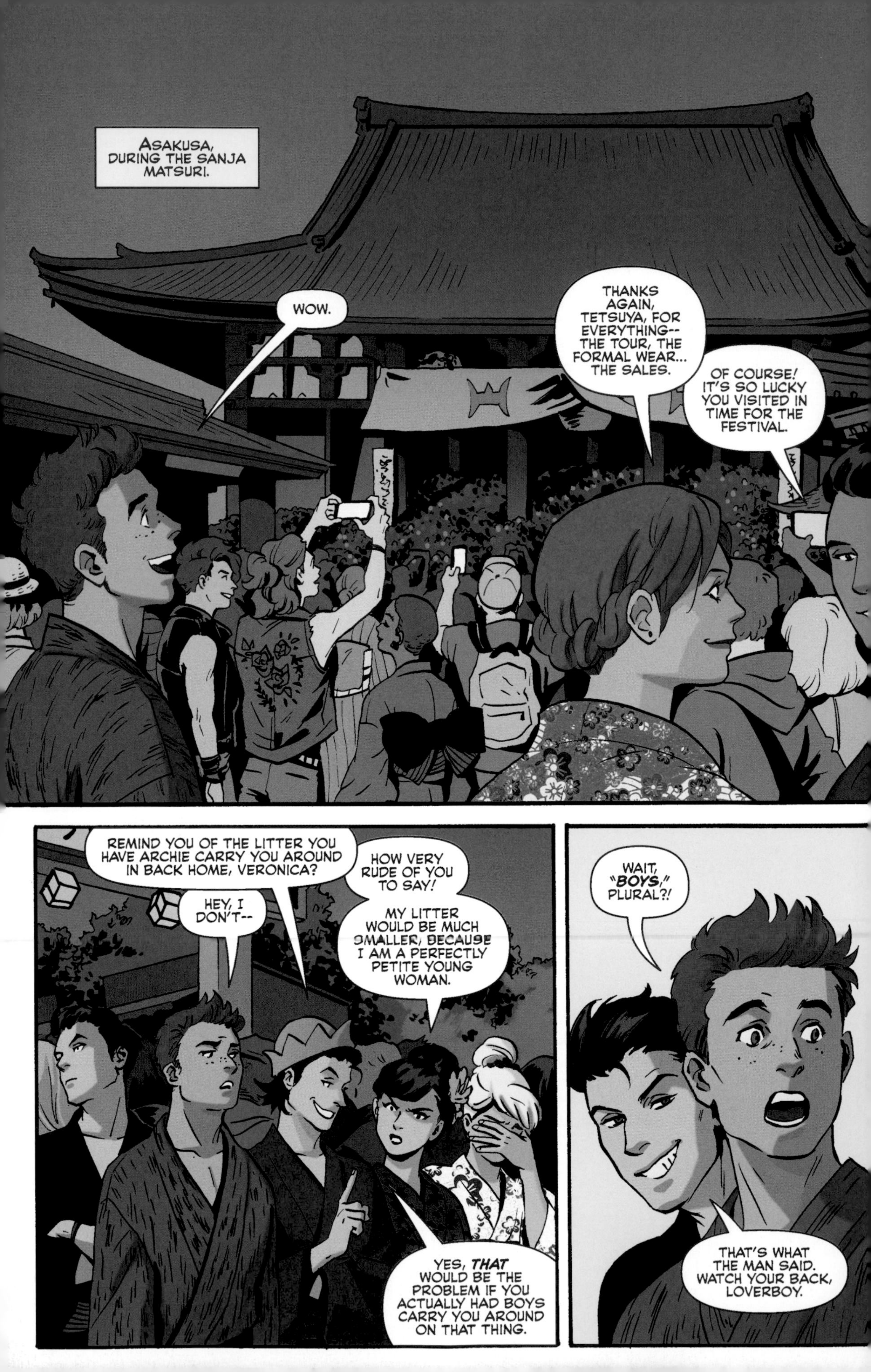

ASAKUSA, DURING THE SANJA MATSURI.
WOW.
THANKS AGAIN, TETSUYA, FOR EVERYTHING-- THE TOUR, THE FORMAL WEAR... THE SALES.
OF COURSE! IT'S SO LUCKY YOU VISITED IN TIME FOR THE FESTIVAL.
REMIND YOU OF THE LITTER YOU HAVE ARCHIE CARRY YOU AROUND IN BACK HOME, VERONICA?
HEY, I DON'T--
HOW VERY RUDE OF YOU TO SAY!
MY LITTER WOULD BE MUCH SMALLER, BECAUSE I AM A PERFECTLY PETITE YOUNG WOMAN.
YES, *THAT* WOULD BE THE PROBLEM IF YOU ACTUALLY HAD BOYS CARRY YOU AROUND ON THAT THING.
WAIT, "*BOYS*," PLURAL?!
THAT'S WHAT THE MAN SAID. WATCH YOUR BACK, LOVERBOY.

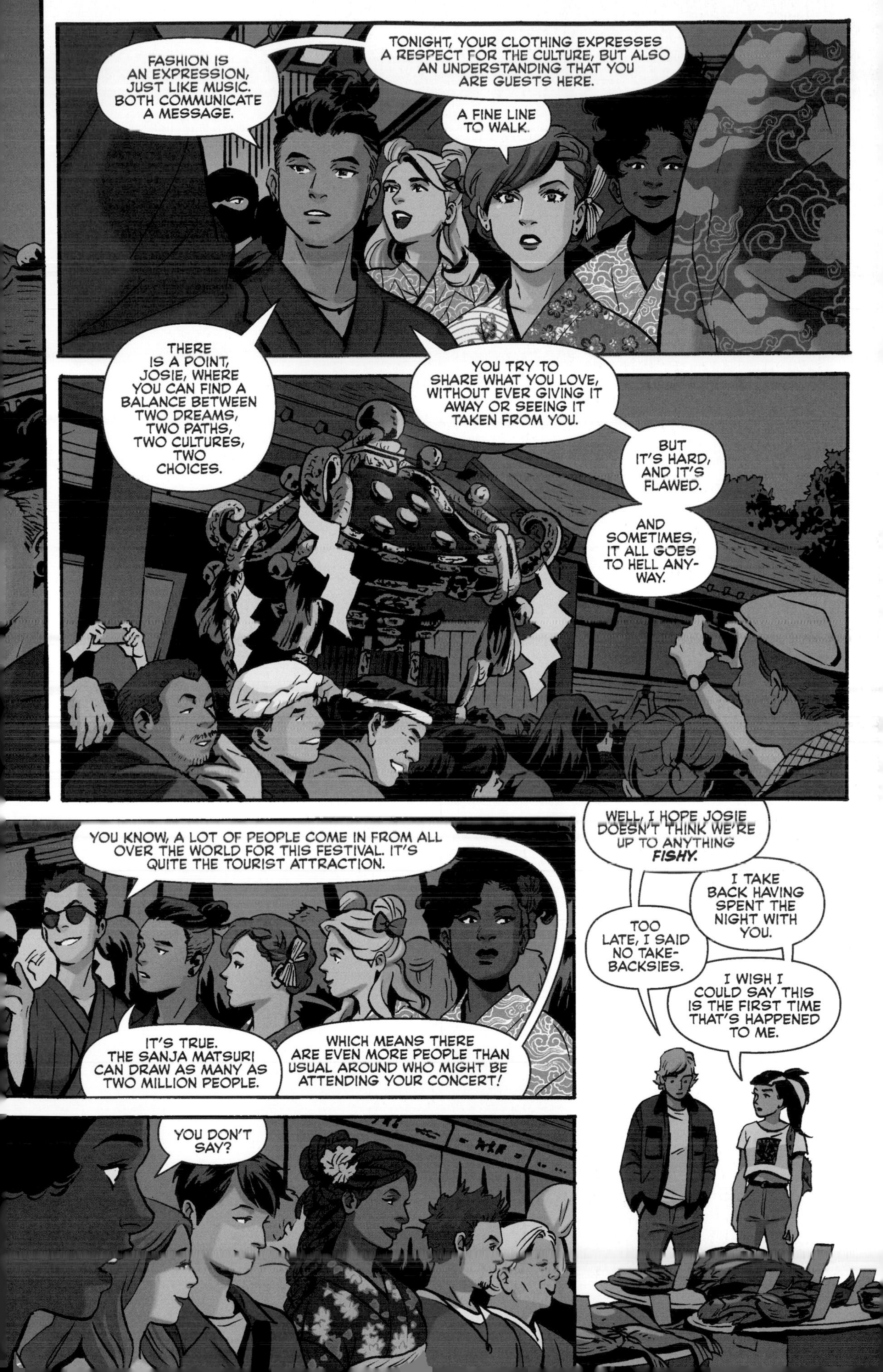
FASHION IS AN EXPRESSION, JUST LIKE MUSIC. BOTH COMMUNICATE A MESSAGE.
TONIGHT, YOUR CLOTHING EXPRESSES A RESPECT FOR THE CULTURE, BUT ALSO AN UNDERSTANDING THAT YOU ARE GUESTS HERE.
A FINE LINE TO WALK.
THERE IS A POINT, JOSIE, WHERE YOU CAN FIND A BALANCE BETWEEN TWO DREAMS, TWO PATHS, TWO CULTURES, TWO CHOICES.
YOU TRY TO SHARE WHAT YOU LOVE, WITHOUT EVER GIVING IT AWAY OR SEEING IT TAKEN FROM YOU.
BUT IT'S HARD, AND IT'S FLAWED.
AND SOMETIMES, IT ALL GOES TO HELL ANY-WAY.
YOU KNOW, A LOT OF PEOPLE COME IN FROM ALL OVER THE WORLD FOR THIS FESTIVAL. IT'S QUITE THE TOURIST ATTRACTION.
IT'S TRUE. THE SANJA MATSURI CAN DRAW AS MANY AS TWO MILLION PEOPLE.
WHICH MEANS THERE ARE EVEN MORE PEOPLE THAN USUAL AROUND WHO MIGHT BE ATTENDING YOUR CONCERT!
YOU DON'T SAY?
WELL, I HOPE JOSIE DOESN'T THINK WE'RE UP TO ANYTHING ***FISHY.***
I TAKE BACK HAVING SPENT THE NIGHT WITH YOU.
TOO LATE, I SAID NO TAKE-BACKSIES.
I WISH I COULD SAY THIS IS THE FIRST TIME THAT'S HAPPENED TO ME.

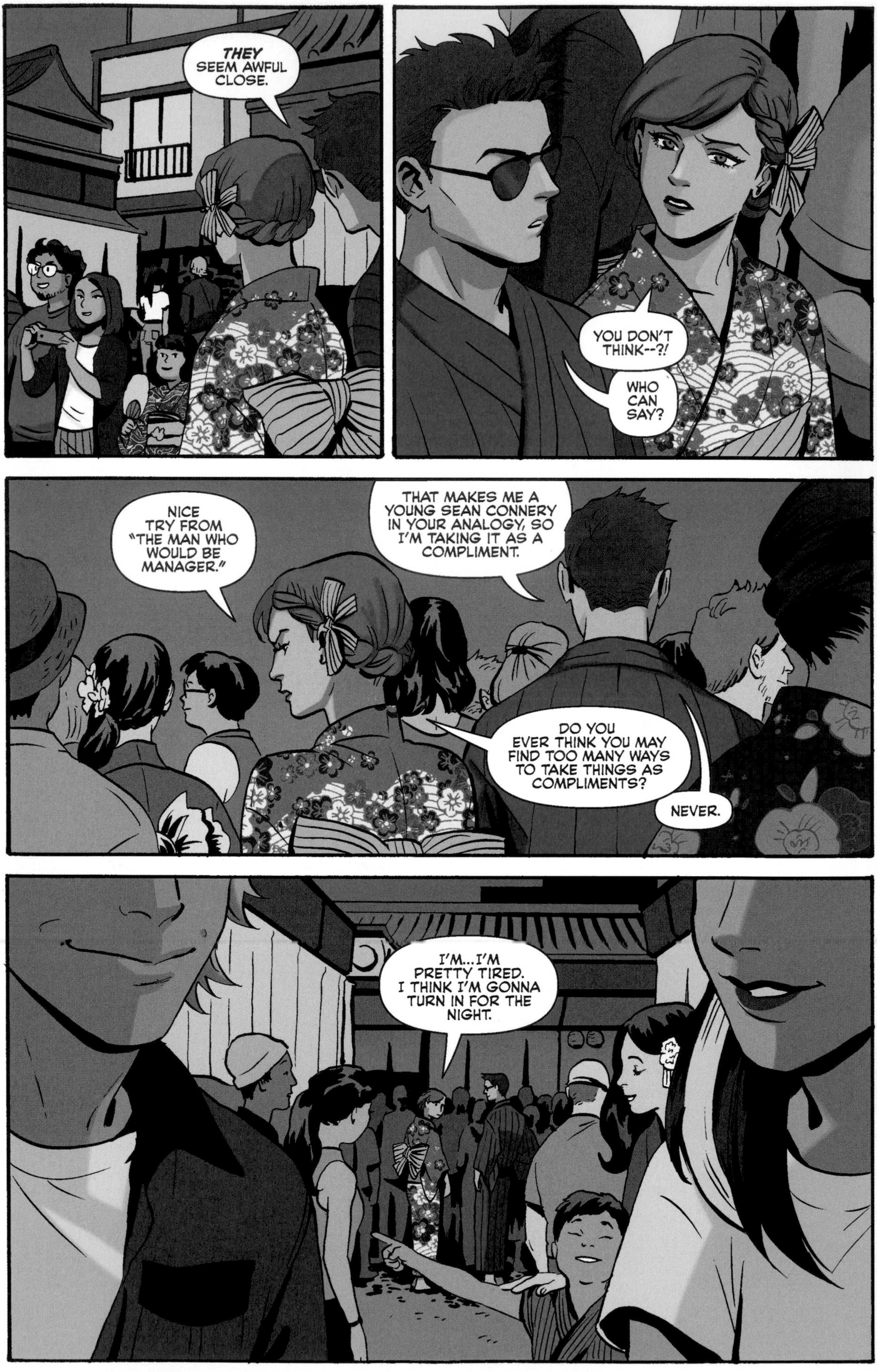
THEY SEEM AWFUL CLOSE.
YOU DON'T THINK--?!
WHO CAN SAY?
NICE TRY FROM "THE MAN WHO WOULD BE MANAGER."
THAT MAKES ME A YOUNG SEAN CONNERY IN YOUR ANALOGY, SO I'M TAKING IT AS A COMPLIMENT.
DO YOU EVER THINK YOU MAY FIND TOO MANY WAYS TO TAKE THINGS AS COMPLIMENTS?
NEVER.
I'M...I'M PRETTY TIRED. I THINK I'M GONNA TURN IN FOR THE NIGHT.

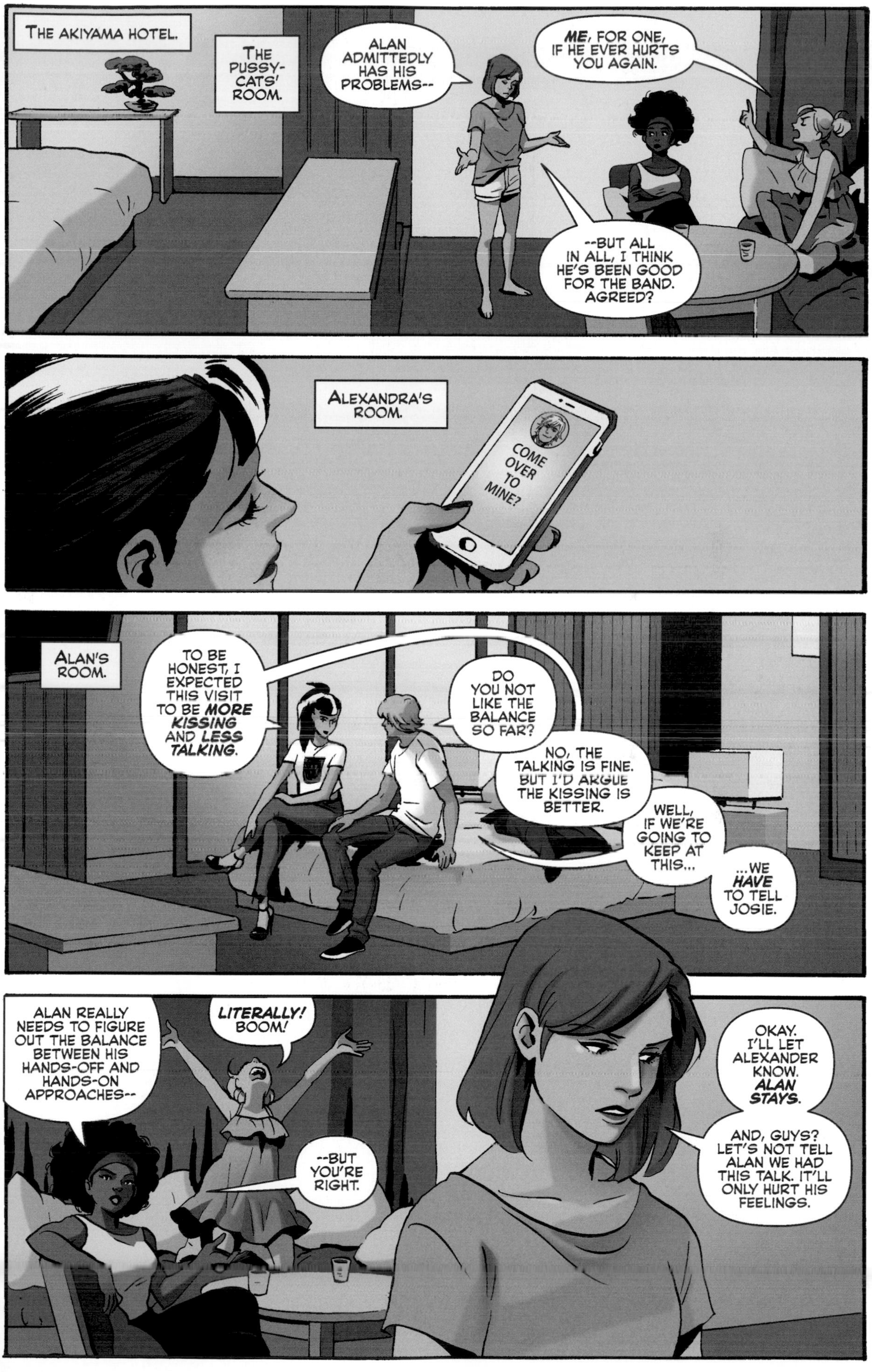
THE AKIYAMA HOTEL.
THE PUSSY-CATS' ROOM.
ALAN ADMITTEDLY HAS HIS PROBLEMS--
--BUT ALL IN ALL, I THINK HE'S BEEN GOOD FOR THE BAND. AGREED?
ME, FOR ONE, IF HE EVER HURTS YOU AGAIN.
ALEXANDRA'S ROOM.
COME OVER TO MINE?
ALAN'S ROOM.
TO BE HONEST, I EXPECTED THIS VISIT TO BE MORE KISSING AND LESS TALKING.
DO YOU NOT LIKE THE BALANCE SO FAR?
NO, THE TALKING IS FINE. BUT I'D ARGUE THE KISSING IS BETTER.
WELL, IF WE'RE GOING TO KEEP AT THIS...
...WE HAVE TO TELL JOSIE.
ALAN REALLY NEEDS TO FIGURE OUT THE BALANCE BETWEEN HIS HANDS-OFF AND HANDS-ON APPROACHES--
LITERALLY! BOOM!
--BUT YOU'RE RIGHT.
OKAY. I'LL LET ALEXANDER KNOW. ALAN STAYS.
AND, GUYS? LET'S NOT TELL ALAN WE HAD THIS TALK. IT'LL ONLY HURT HIS FEELINGS.

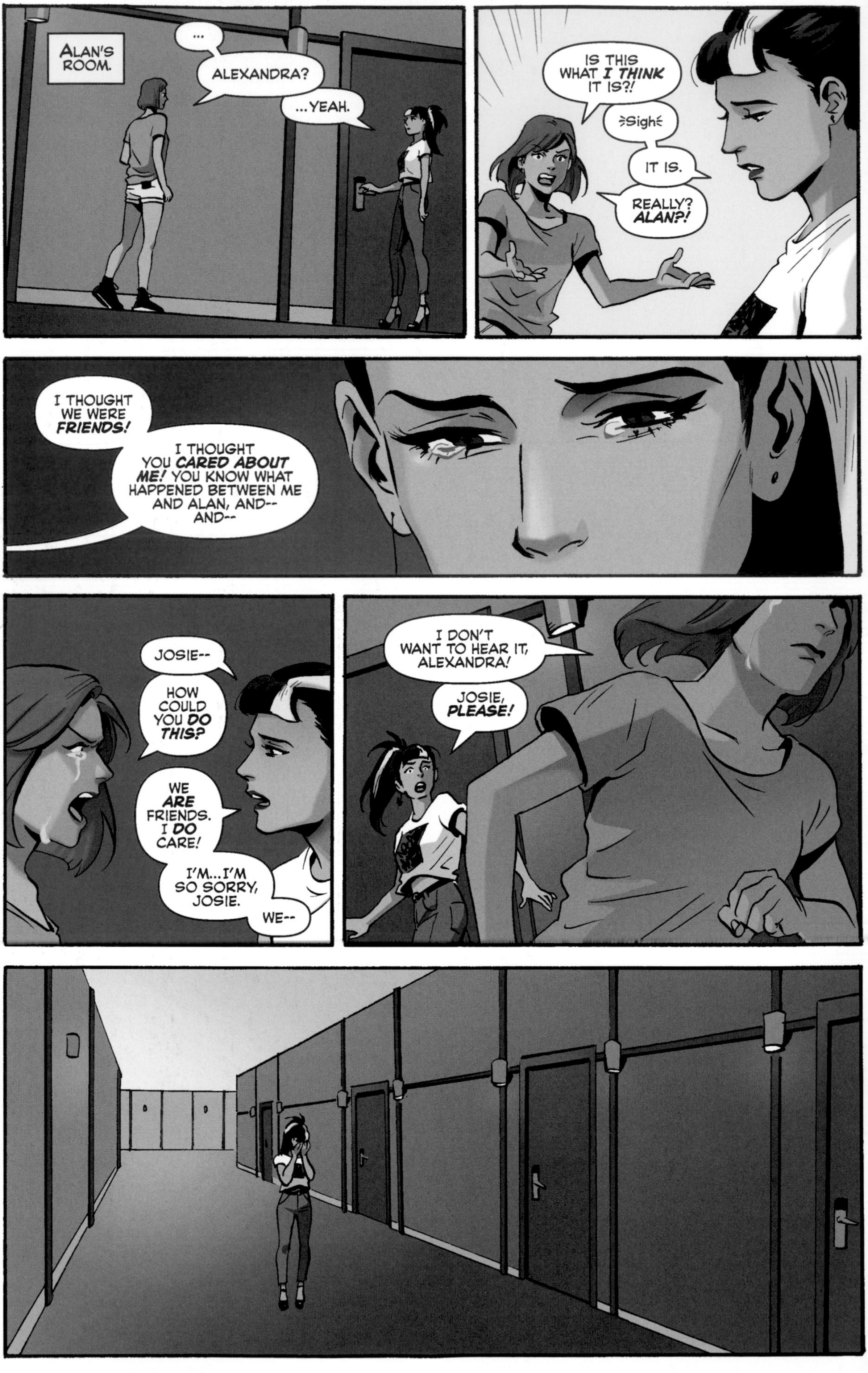
ALAN'S ROOM.
...
ALEXANDRA?
...YEAH.
IS THIS WHAT I THINK IT IS?!
Sigh
IT IS.
REALLY? ALAN?!
I THOUGHT WE WERE FRIENDS!
I THOUGHT YOU CARED ABOUT ME! YOU KNOW WHAT HAPPENED BETWEEN ME AND ALAN, AND-- AND--
JOSIE--
HOW COULD YOU DO THIS?
WE ARE FRIENDS. I DO CARE!
I'M...I'M SO SORRY, JOSIE.
WE--
I DON'T WANT TO HEAR IT, ALEXANDRA!
JOSIE, PLEASE!

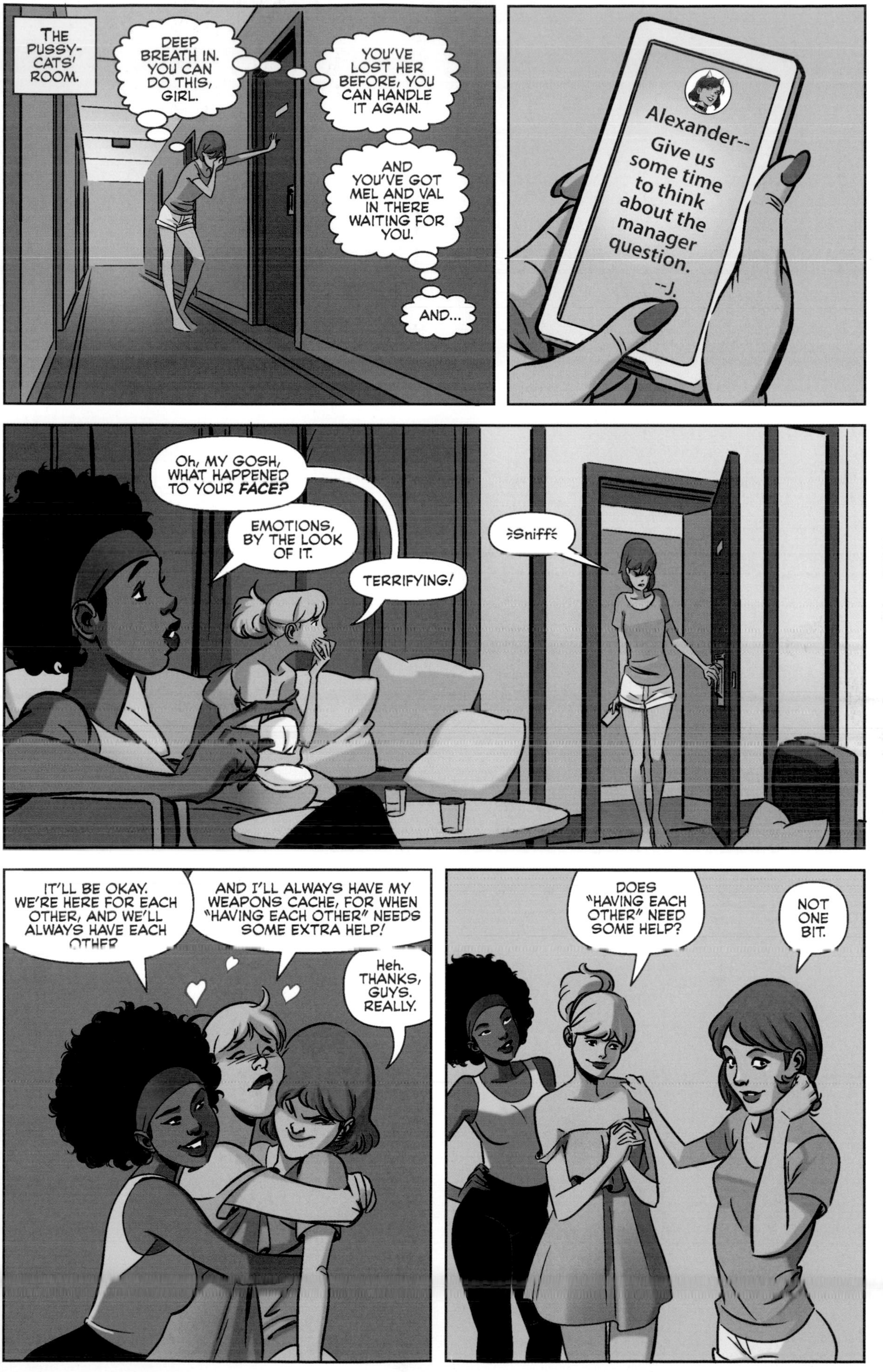
THE PUSSY-CATS' ROOM.
DEEP BREATH IN. YOU CAN DO THIS, GIRL.
YOU'VE LOST HER BEFORE, YOU CAN HANDLE IT AGAIN.
AND YOU'VE GOT MEL AND VAL IN THERE WAITING FOR YOU.
AND...
Alexander-- Give us some time to think about the manager question. --J.
Oh, MY GOSH, WHAT HAPPENED TO YOUR FACE?
EMOTIONS, BY THE LOOK OF IT.
TERRIFYING!
Sniff
IT'LL BE OKAY. WE'RE HERE FOR EACH OTHER, AND WE'LL ALWAYS HAVE EACH OTHER.
AND I'LL ALWAYS HAVE MY WEAPONS CACHE, FOR WHEN "HAVING EACH OTHER" NEEDS SOME EXTRA HELP!
Heh. THANKS, GUYS. REALLY.
DOES "HAVING EACH OTHER" NEED SOME HELP?
NOT ONE BIT.

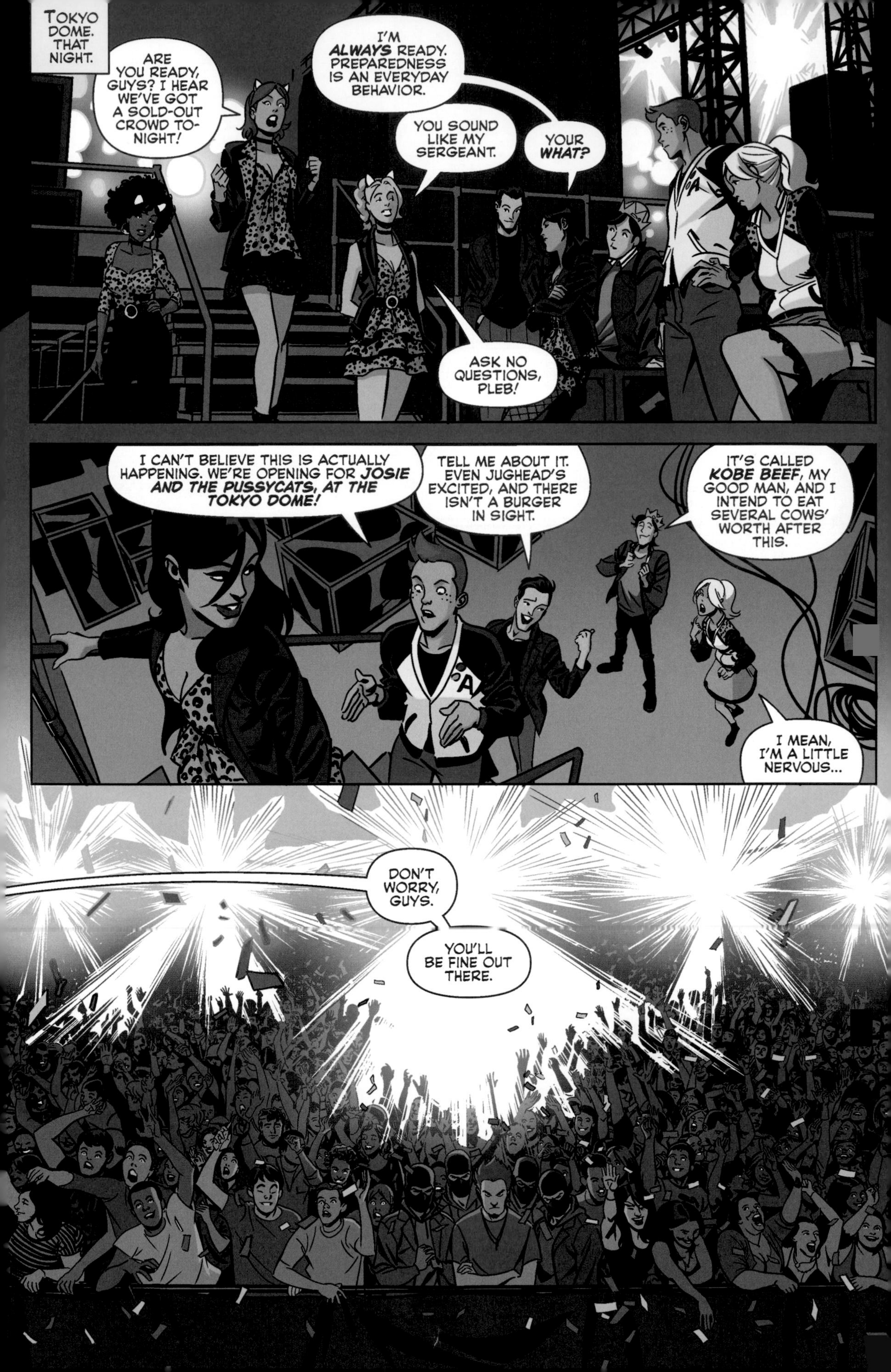
TOKYO DOME. THAT NIGHT.
ARE YOU READY, GUYS? I HEAR WE'VE GOT A SOLD-OUT CROWD TO-NIGHT!
I'M *ALWAYS* READY. PREPAREDNESS IS AN EVERYDAY BEHAVIOR.
YOU SOUND LIKE MY SERGEANT.
YOUR *WHAT?*
ASK NO QUESTIONS, PLEB!
I CAN'T BELIEVE THIS IS ACTUALLY HAPPENING. WE'RE OPENING FOR *JOSIE AND THE PUSSYCATS, AT THE TOKYO DOME!*
TELL ME ABOUT IT. EVEN JUGHEAD'S EXCITED, AND THERE ISN'T A BURGER IN SIGHT.
IT'S CALLED *KOBE BEEF*, MY GOOD MAN, AND I INTEND TO EAT SEVERAL COWS' WORTH AFTER THIS.
I MEAN, I'M A LITTLE NERVOUS...
DON'T WORRY, GUYS.
YOU'LL BE FINE OUT THERE.

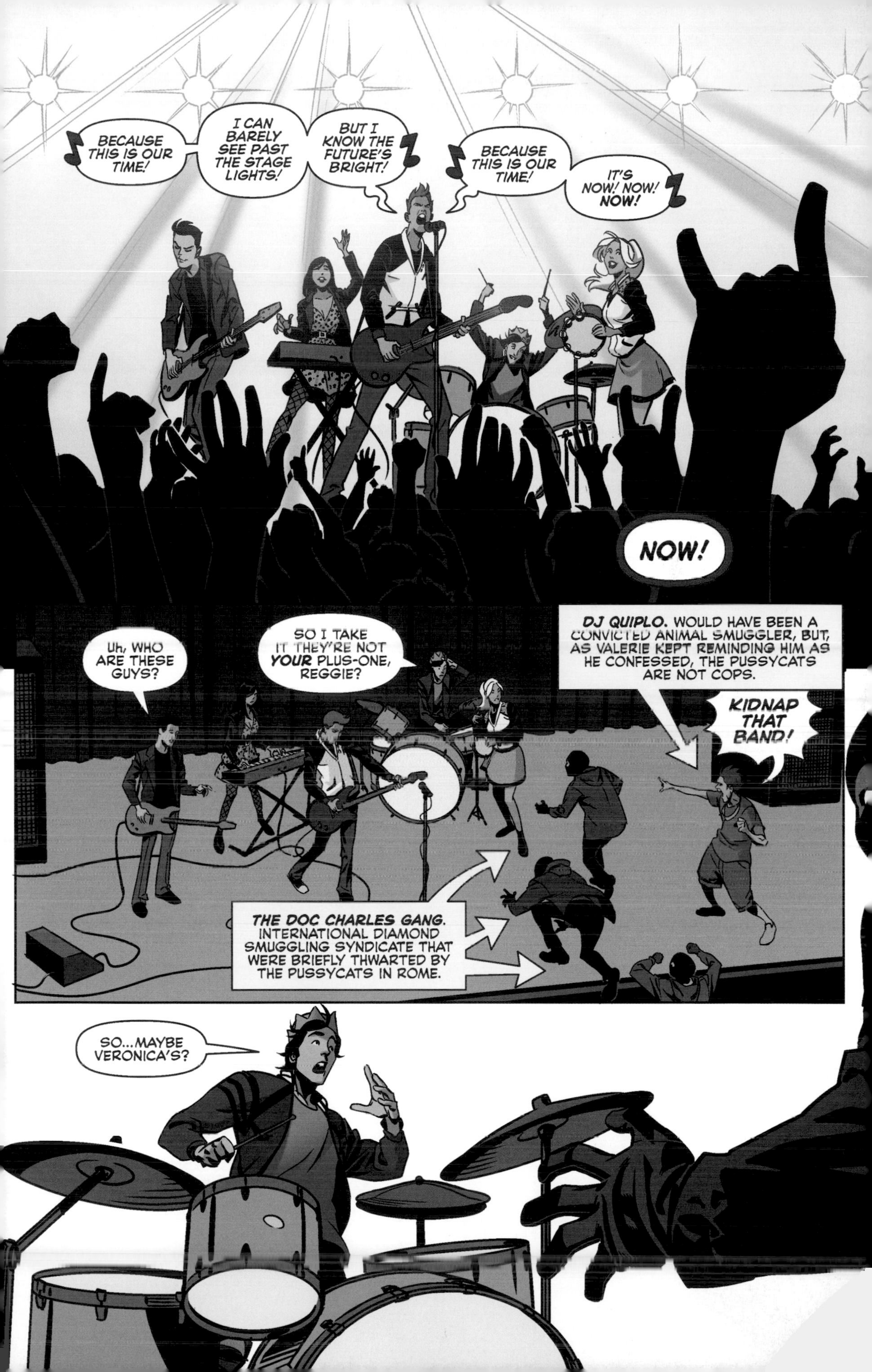

BECAUSE THIS IS OUR TIME!
I CAN BARELY SEE PAST THE STAGE LIGHTS!
BUT I KNOW THE FUTURE'S BRIGHT!
BECAUSE THIS IS OUR TIME!
IT'S NOW! NOW! NOW!
NOW!
UH, WHO ARE THESE GUYS?
SO I TAKE IT THEY'RE NOT YOUR PLUS-ONE, REGGIE?
DJ QUIPLO. WOULD HAVE BEEN A CONVICTED ANIMAL SMUGGLER, BUT, AS VALERIE KEPT REMINDING HIM AS HE CONFESSED, THE PUSSYCATS ARE NOT COPS.
KIDNAP THAT BAND!
THE DOC CHARLES GANG. INTERNATIONAL DIAMOND SMUGGLING SYNDICATE THAT WERE BRIEFLY THWARTED BY THE PUSSYCATS IN ROME.
SO...MAYBE VERONICA'S?

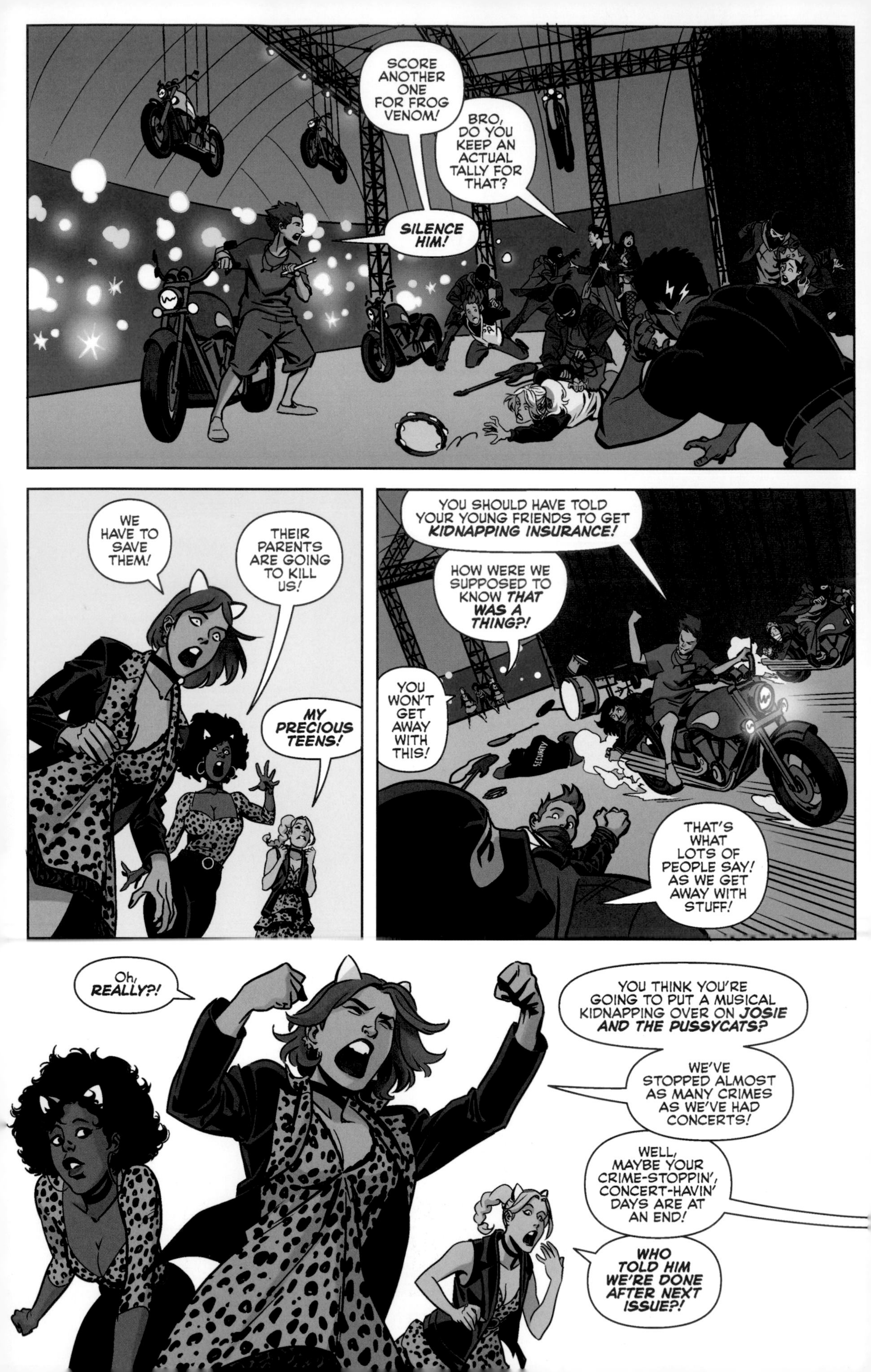

SCORE ANOTHER ONE FOR FROG VENOM!
BRO, DO YOU KEEP AN ACTUAL TALLY FOR THAT?
SILENCE HIM!
WE HAVE TO SAVE THEM!
THEIR PARENTS ARE GOING TO KILL US!
MY PRECIOUS TEENS!
YOU SHOULD HAVE TOLD YOUR YOUNG FRIENDS TO GET KIDNAPPING INSURANCE!
HOW WERE WE SUPPOSED TO KNOW THAT WAS A THING?!
YOU WON'T GET AWAY WITH THIS!
THAT'S WHAT LOTS OF PEOPLE SAY! AS WE GET AWAY WITH STUFF!
SECURITY
Oh, REALLY?!
YOU THINK YOU'RE GOING TO PUT A MUSICAL KIDNAPPING OVER ON JOSIE AND THE PUSSYCATS?
WE'VE STOPPED ALMOST AS MANY CRIMES AS WE'VE HAD CONCERTS!
WELL, MAYBE YOUR CRIME-STOPPIN', CONCERT-HAVIN' DAYS ARE AT AN END!
WHO TOLD HIM WE'RE DONE AFTER NEXT ISSUE?!

TO BE CONTINUED...

ISSUE NINE

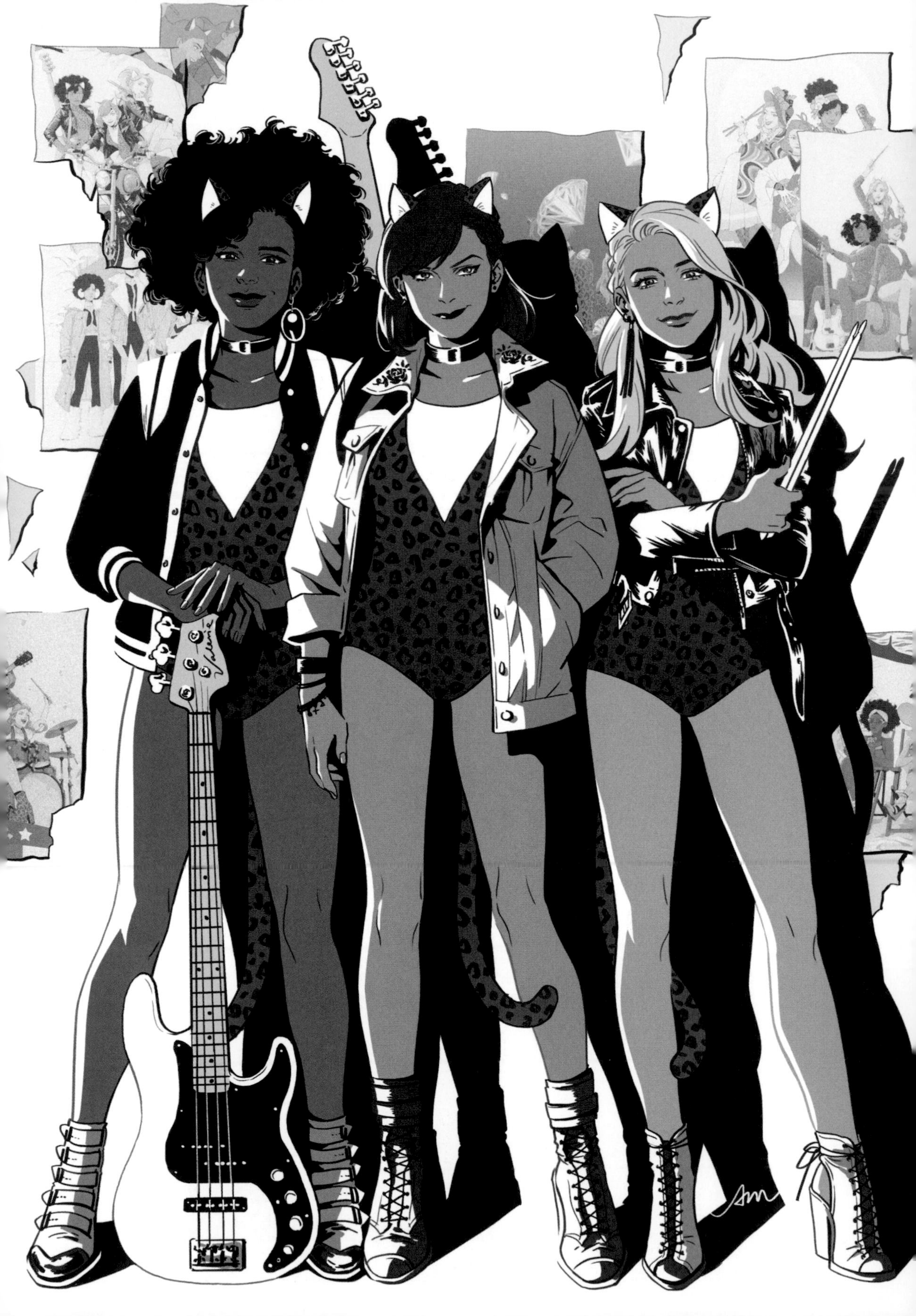

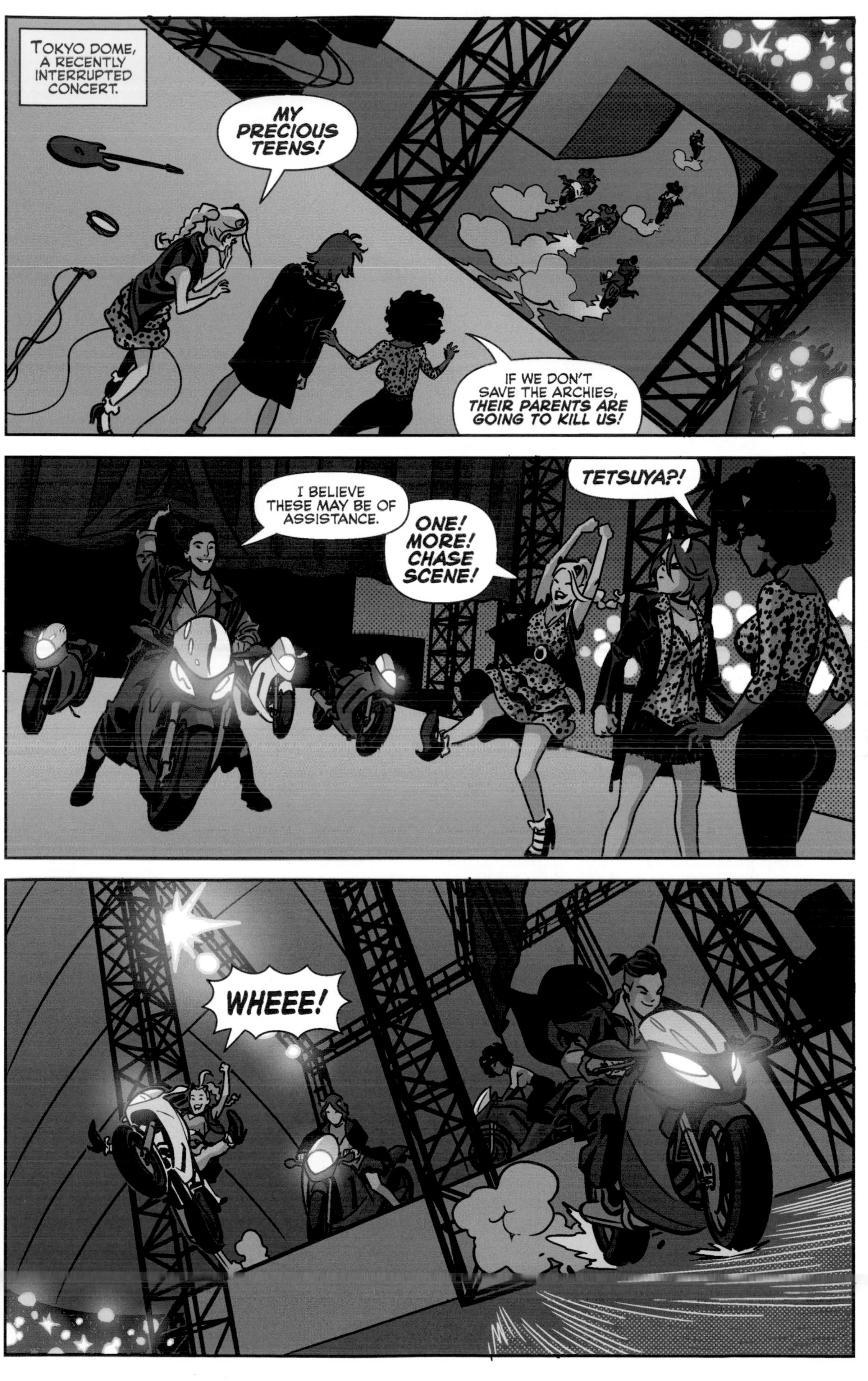
TOKYO DOME, A RECENTLY INTERRUPTED CONCERT.
MY PRECIOUS TEENS!
IF WE DON'T SAVE THE ARCHIES, THEIR PARENTS ARE GOING TO KILL US!
I BELIEVE THESE MAY BE OF ASSISTANCE.
TETSUYA?!
ONE! MORE! CHASE SCENE!
WHEEE!

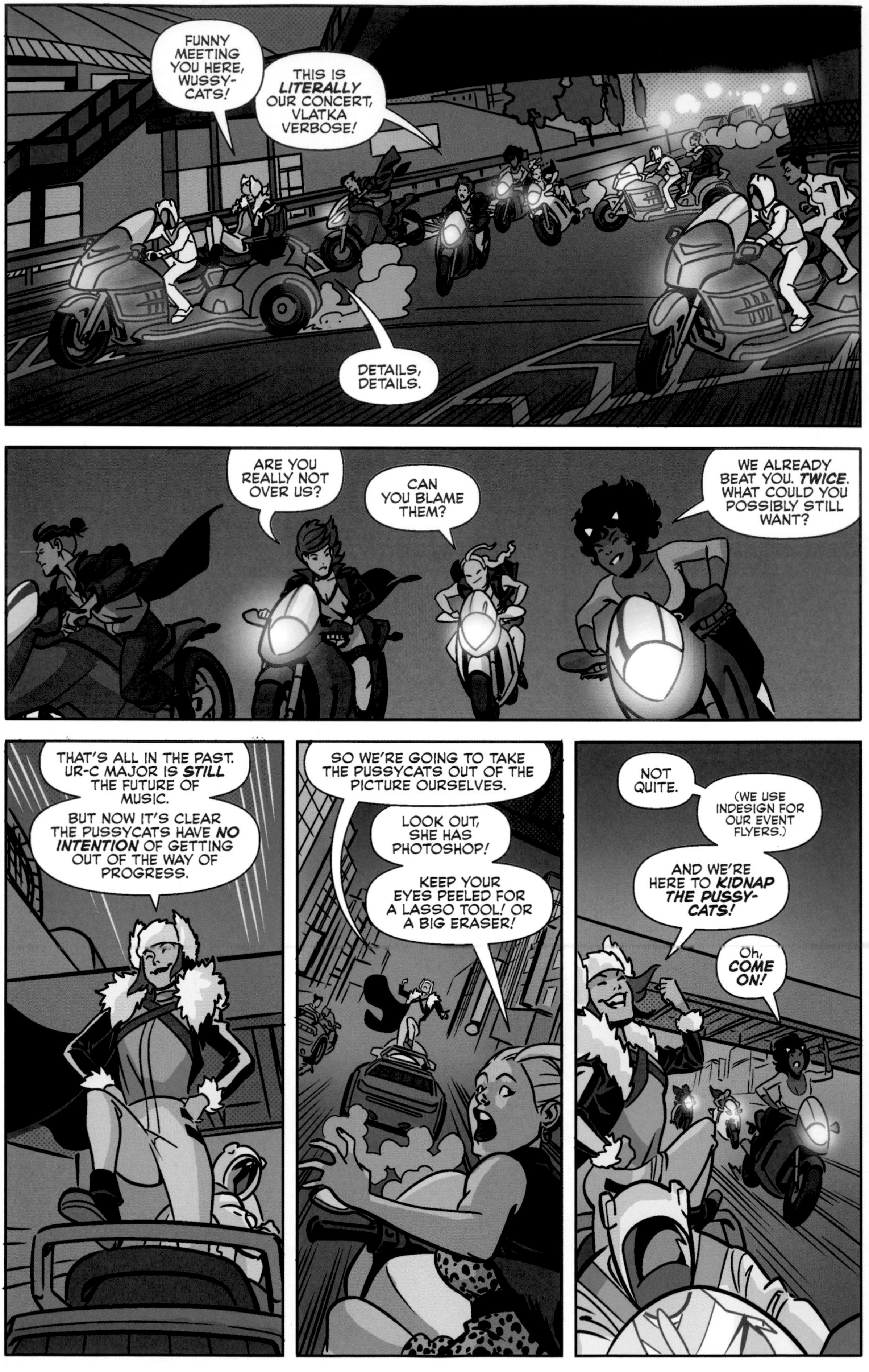

FUNNY MEETING YOU HERE, WUSSY-CATS!
THIS IS LITERALLY OUR CONCERT, VLATKA VERBOSE!
DETAILS, DETAILS.
ARE YOU REALLY NOT OVER US?
CAN YOU BLAME THEM?
WE ALREADY BEAT YOU. TWICE. WHAT COULD YOU POSSIBLY STILL WANT?
THAT'S ALL IN THE PAST. UR-C MAJOR IS STILL THE FUTURE OF MUSIC.
BUT NOW IT'S CLEAR THE PUSSYCATS HAVE NO INTENTION OF GETTING OUT OF THE WAY OF PROGRESS.
SO WE'RE GOING TO TAKE THE PUSSYCATS OUT OF THE PICTURE OURSELVES.
LOOK OUT, SHE HAS PHOTOSHOP!
KEEP YOUR EYES PEELED FOR A LASSO TOOL! OR A BIG ERASER!
NOT QUITE.
(WE USE INDESIGN FOR OUR EVENT FLYERS.)
AND WE'RE HERE TO KIDNAP THE PUSSY-CATS!
Oh, COME ON!

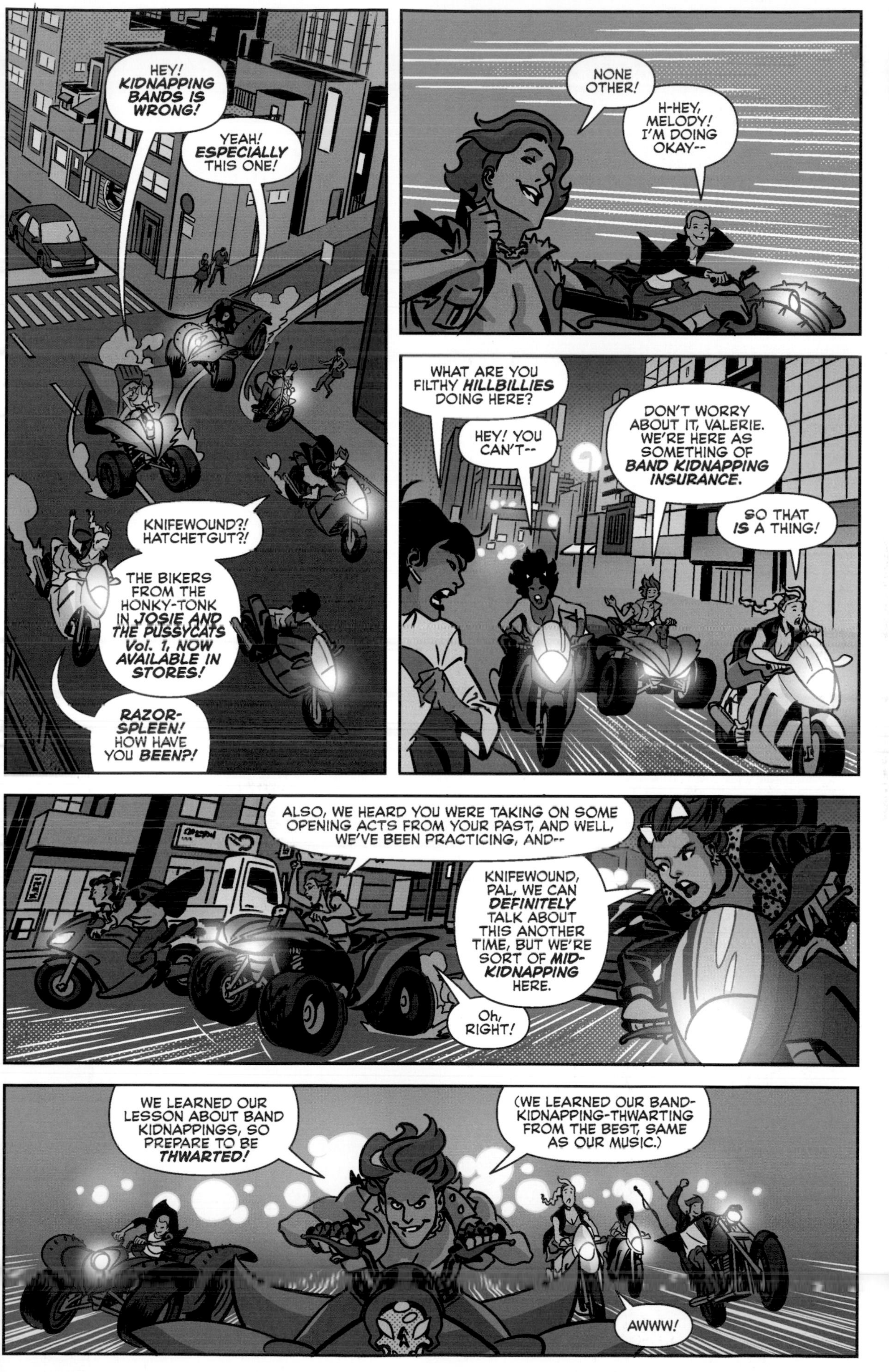
HEY! KIDNAPPING BANDS IS WRONG!
YEAH! ESPECIALLY THIS ONE!
KNIFEWOUND?! HATCHETGUT?!
THE BIKERS FROM THE HONKY-TONK IN JOSIE AND THE PUSSYCATS Vol. 1, NOW AVAILABLE IN STORES!
RAZOR-SPLEEN! HOW HAVE YOU BEEN?!
NONE OTHER!
H-HEY, MELODY! I'M DOING OKAY--
WHAT ARE YOU FILTHY HILLBILLIES DOING HERE?
HEY! YOU CAN'T--
DON'T WORRY ABOUT IT, VALERIE. WE'RE HERE AS SOMETHING OF BAND KIDNAPPING INSURANCE.
SO THAT IS A THING!
ALSO, WE HEARD YOU WERE TAKING ON SOME OPENING ACTS FROM YOUR PAST, AND WELL, WE'VE BEEN PRACTICING, AND--
KNIFEWOUND, PAL, WE CAN DEFINITELY TALK ABOUT THIS ANOTHER TIME, BUT WE'RE SORT OF MID-KIDNAPPING HERE.
Oh, RIGHT!
WE LEARNED OUR LESSON ABOUT BAND KIDNAPPINGS, SO PREPARE TO BE THWARTED!
(WE LEARNED OUR BAND-KIDNAPPING-THWARTING FROM THE BEST, SAME AS OUR MUSIC.)
AWWW!

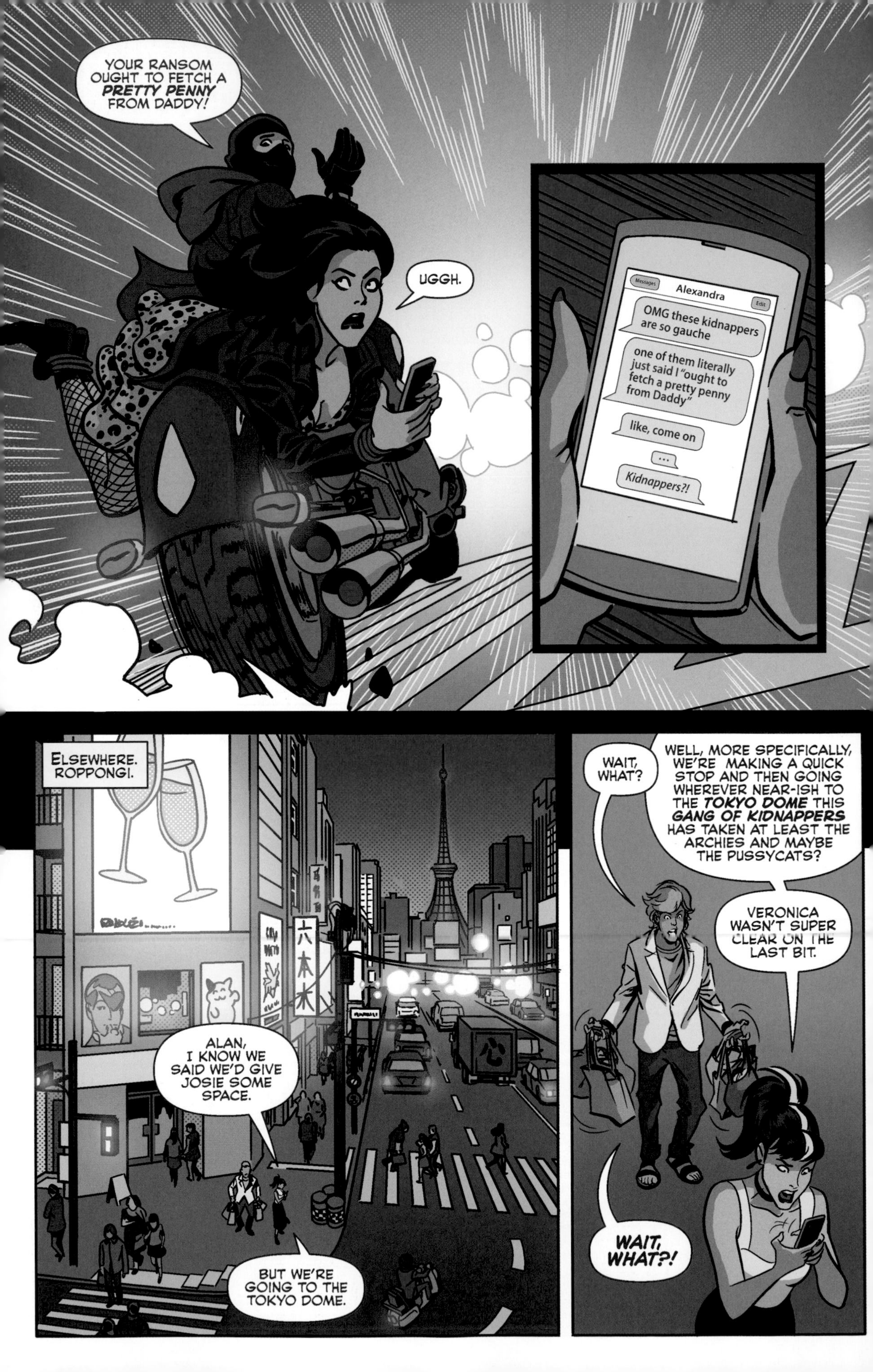
YOUR RANSOM OUGHT TO FETCH A PRETTY PENNY FROM DADDY!
UGGH.
Messages
Alexandra
Edit
OMG these kidnappers are so gauche
one of them literally just said I "ought to fetch a pretty penny from Daddy"
like, come on
...
Kidnappers?!
ELSEWHERE. ROPPONGI.
六本木
ALAN, I KNOW WE SAID WE'D GIVE JOSIE SOME SPACE.
BUT WE'RE GOING TO THE TOKYO DOME.
WAIT, WHAT?
WELL, MORE SPECIFICALLY, WE'RE MAKING A QUICK STOP AND THEN GOING WHEREVER NEAR-ISH TO THE TOKYO DOME THIS GANG OF KIDNAPPERS HAS TAKEN AT LEAST THE ARCHIES AND MAYBE THE PUSSYCATS?
VERONICA WASN'T SUPER CLEAR ON THE LAST BIT.
WAIT, WHAT?!

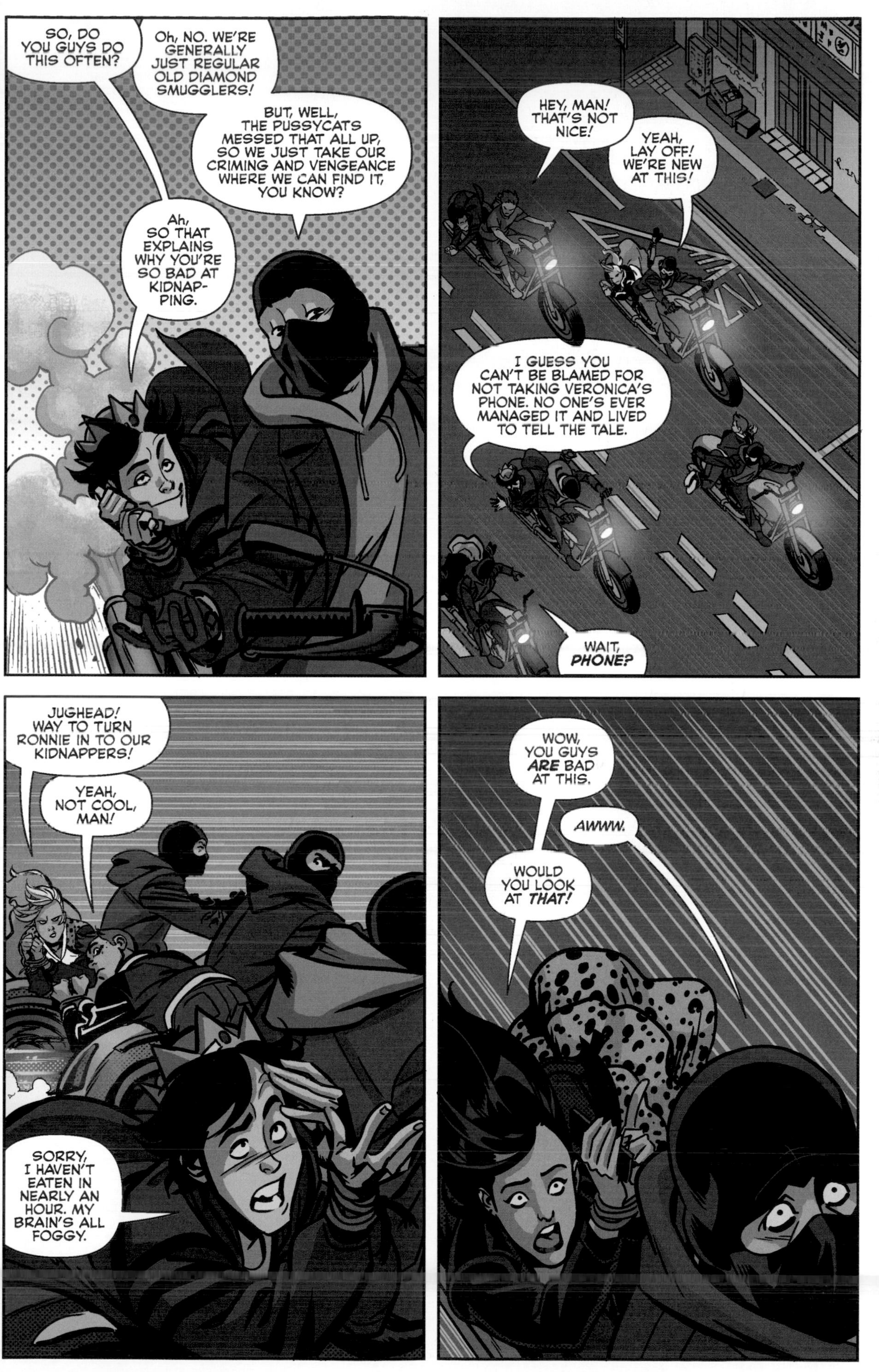
SO, DO YOU GUYS DO THIS OFTEN?
Oh, NO. WE'RE GENERALLY JUST REGULAR OLD DIAMOND SMUGGLERS!
BUT, WELL, THE PUSSYCATS MESSED THAT ALL UP, SO WE JUST TAKE OUR CRIMING AND VENGEANCE WHERE WE CAN FIND IT, YOU KNOW?
Ah, SO THAT EXPLAINS WHY YOU'RE SO BAD AT KIDNAP-PING.
HEY, MAN! THAT'S NOT NICE!
YEAH, LAY OFF! WE'RE NEW AT THIS!
I GUESS YOU CAN'T BE BLAMED FOR NOT TAKING VERONICA'S PHONE. NO ONE'S EVER MANAGED IT AND LIVED TO TELL THE TALE.
WAIT, PHONE?
JUGHEAD! WAY TO TURN RONNIE IN TO OUR KIDNAPPERS!
YEAH, NOT COOL, MAN!
SORRY, I HAVEN'T EATEN IN NEARLY AN HOUR. MY BRAIN'S ALL FOGGY.
WOW, YOU GUYS ARE BAD AT THIS.
AWWW.
WOULD YOU LOOK AT THAT!

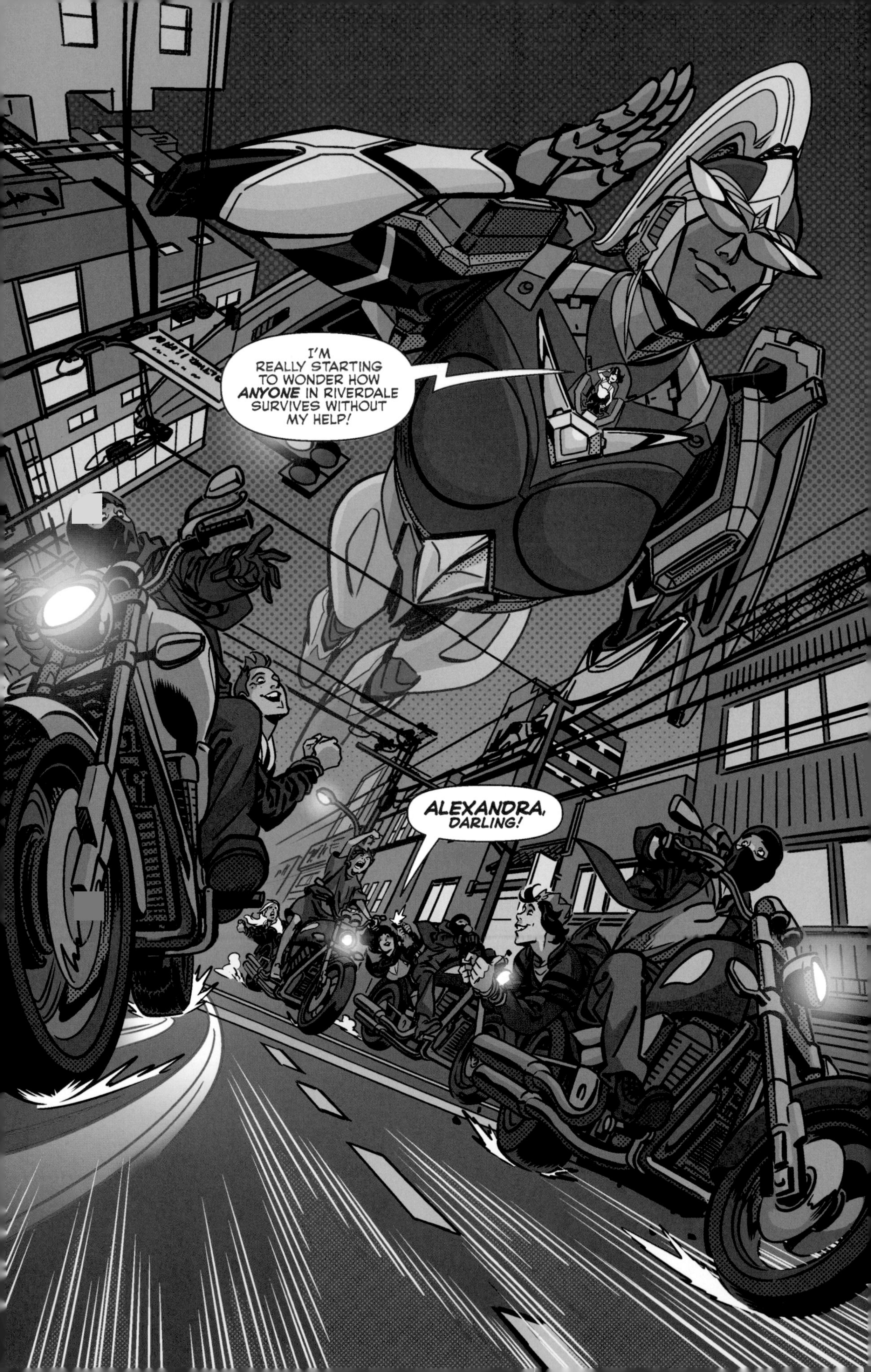
I'M REALLY STARTING TO WONDER HOW ANYONE IN RIVERDALE SURVIVES WITHOUT MY HELP!
ALEXANDRA, DARLING!

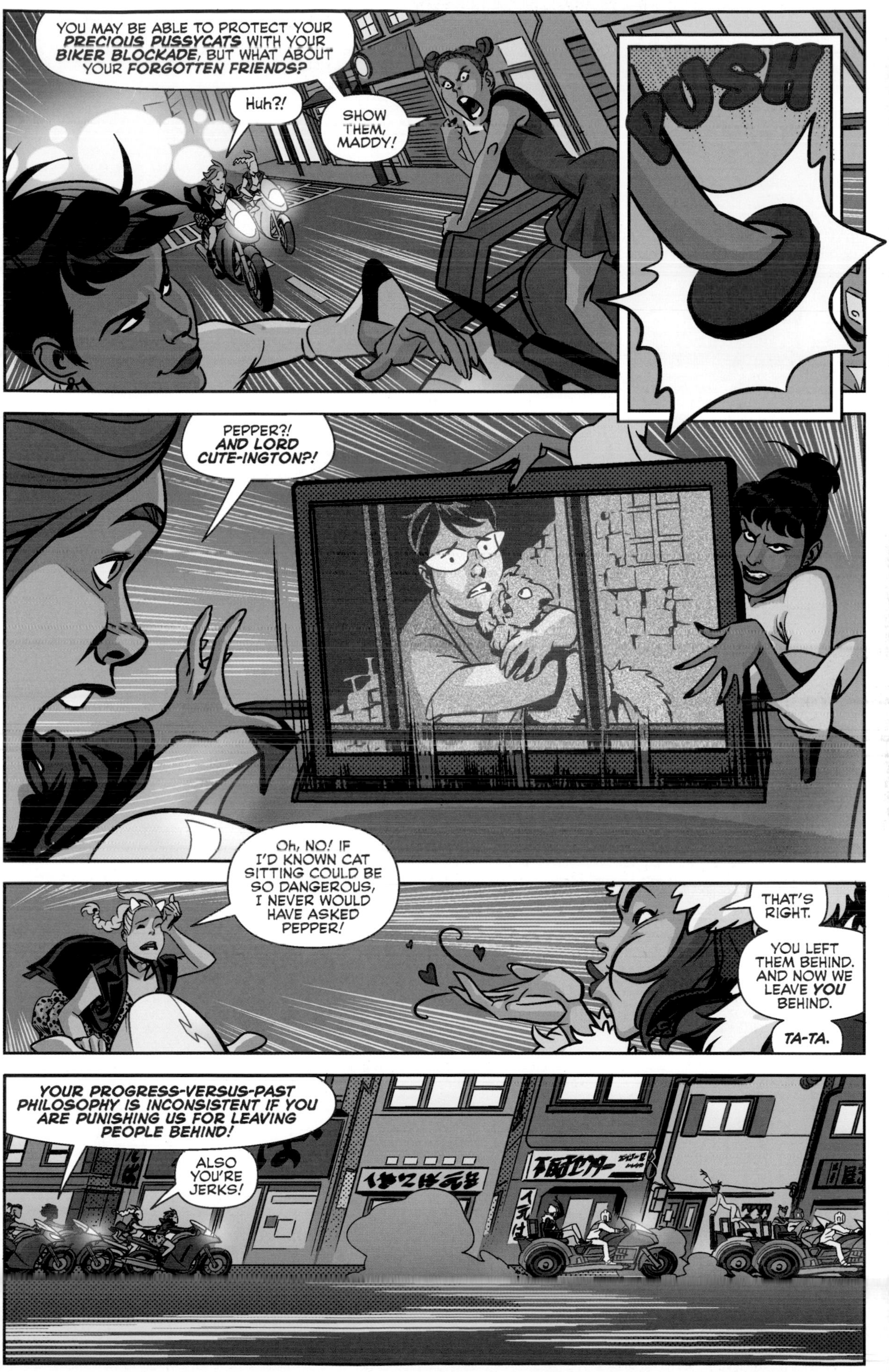

YOU MAY BE ABLE TO PROTECT YOUR PRECIOUS PUSSYCATS WITH YOUR BIKER BLOCKADE, BUT WHAT ABOUT YOUR FORGOTTEN FRIENDS?
Huh?!
SHOW THEM, MADDY!
PUSH
PEPPER?! AND LORD CUTE-INGTON?!
Oh, NO! IF I'D KNOWN CAT SITTING COULD BE SO DANGEROUS, I NEVER WOULD HAVE ASKED PEPPER!
THAT'S RIGHT.
YOU LEFT THEM BEHIND. AND NOW WE LEAVE YOU BEHIND.
TA-TA.
YOUR PROGRESS-VERSUS-PAST PHILOSOPHY IS INCONSISTENT IF YOU ARE PUNISHING US FOR LEAVING PEOPLE BEHIND!
ALSO YOU'RE JERKS!

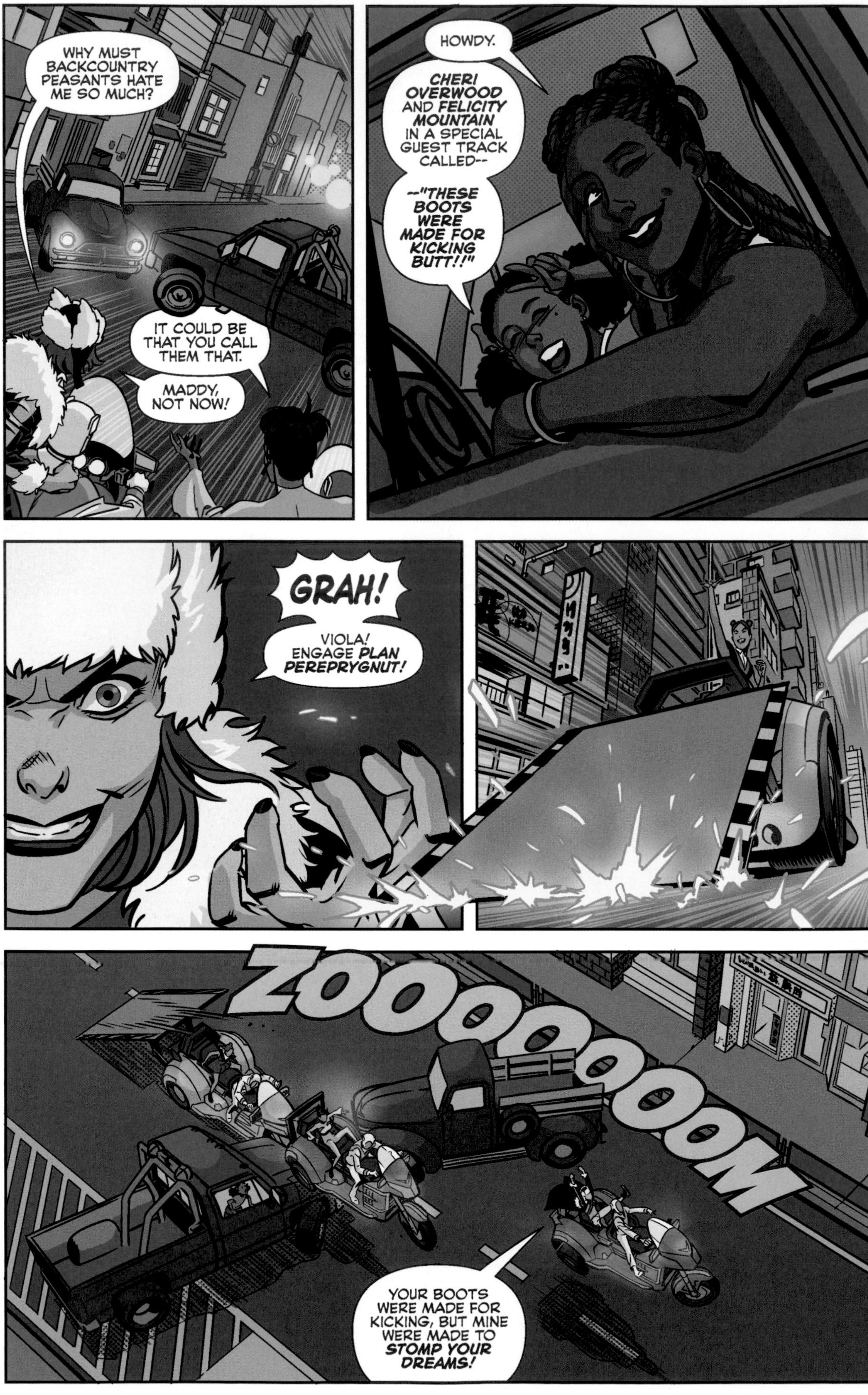
WHY MUST BACKCOUNTRY PEASANTS HATE ME SO MUCH?
IT COULD BE THAT YOU CALL THEM THAT.
MADDY, NOT NOW!
HOWDY.
CHERI OVERWOOD AND FELICITY MOUNTAIN IN A SPECIAL GUEST TRACK CALLED--
--"THESE BOOTS WERE MADE FOR KICKING BUTT!!"
GRAH!
VIOLA! ENGAGE PLAN PEREPRYGNUT!
ZOOOOOOOOM
YOUR BOOTS WERE MADE FOR KICKING, BUT MINE WERE MADE TO STOMP YOUR DREAMS!

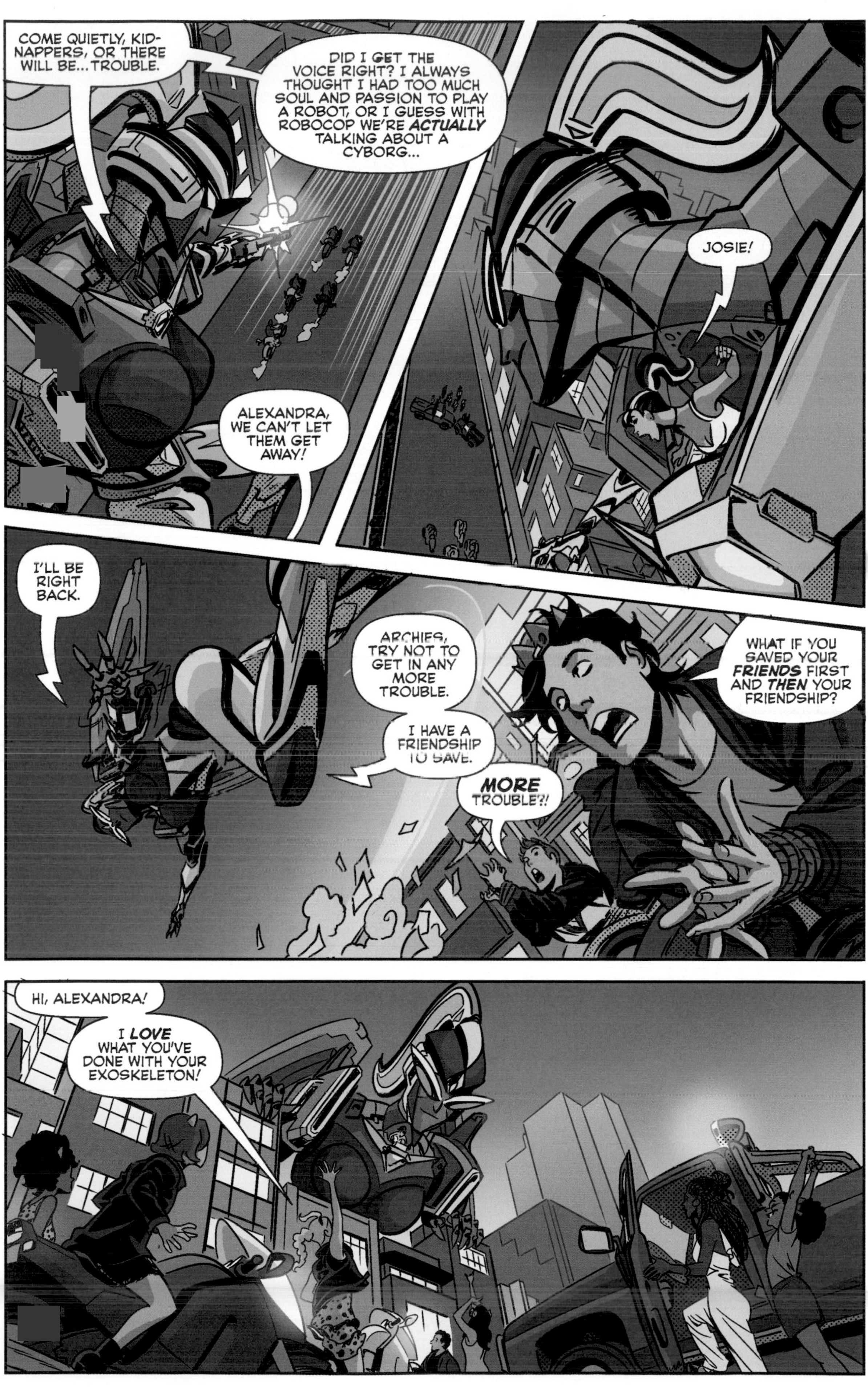
COME QUIETLY, KID-NAPPERS, OR THERE WILL BE... TROUBLE.
DID I GET THE VOICE RIGHT? I ALWAYS THOUGHT I HAD TOO MUCH SOUL AND PASSION TO PLAY A ROBOT, OR I GUESS WITH ROBOCOP WE'RE ***ACTUALLY*** TALKING ABOUT A CYBORG...
ALEXANDRA, WE CAN'T LET THEM GET AWAY!
JOSIE!
I'LL BE RIGHT BACK.
ARCHIES, TRY NOT TO GET IN ANY MORE TROUBLE.
I HAVE A FRIENDSHIP TO SAVE.
MORE TROUBLE?!
WHAT IF YOU SAVED YOUR ***FRIENDS*** FIRST AND ***THEN*** YOUR FRIENDSHIP?
HI, ALEXANDRA!
I ***LOVE*** WHAT YOU'VE DONE WITH YOUR EXOSKELETON!

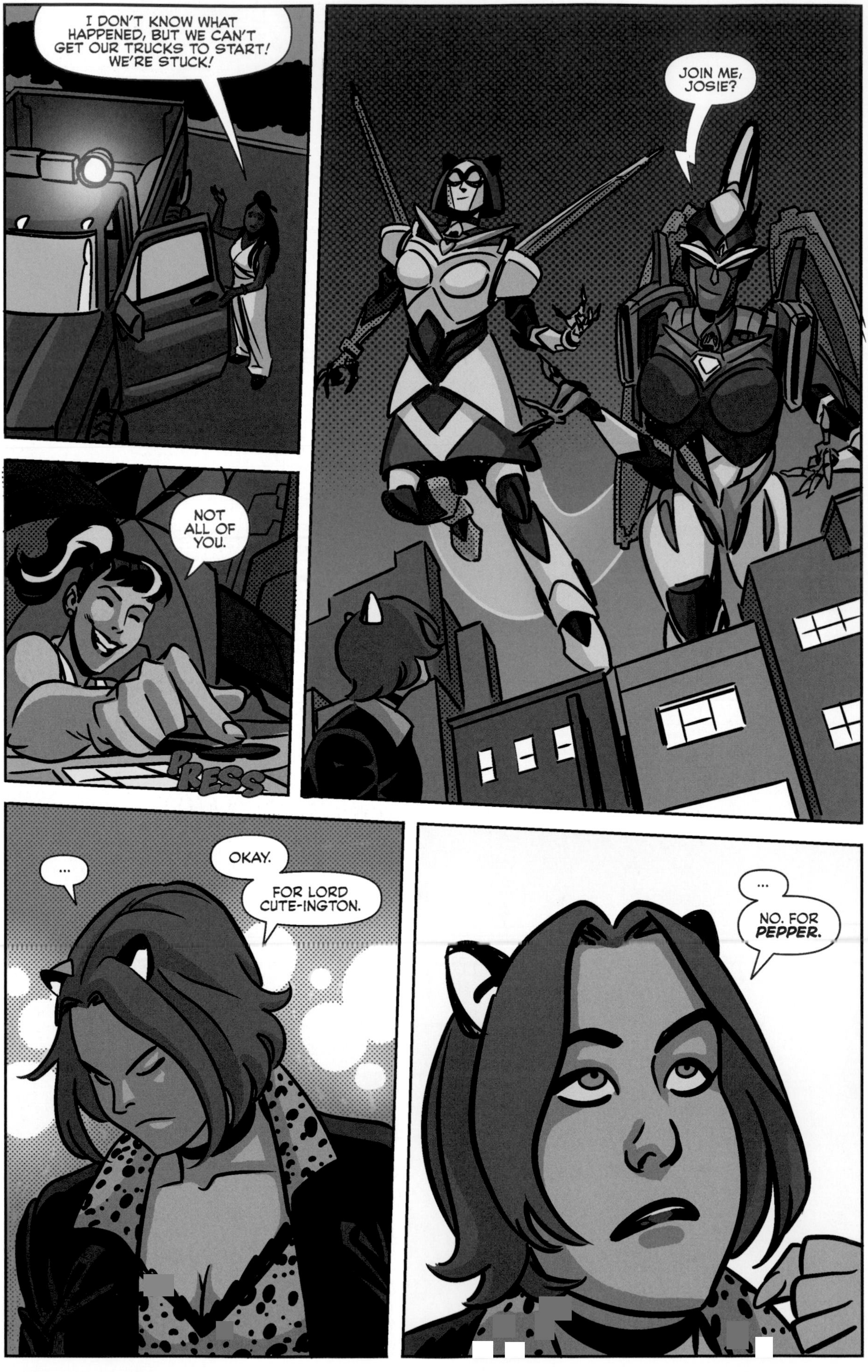
I DON'T KNOW WHAT HAPPENED, BUT WE CAN'T GET OUR TRUCKS TO START! WE'RE STUCK!
NOT ALL OF YOU.
PRESS
JOIN ME, JOSIE?
...
OKAY.
FOR LORD CUTE-INGTON.
...
NO. FOR *PEPPER*.

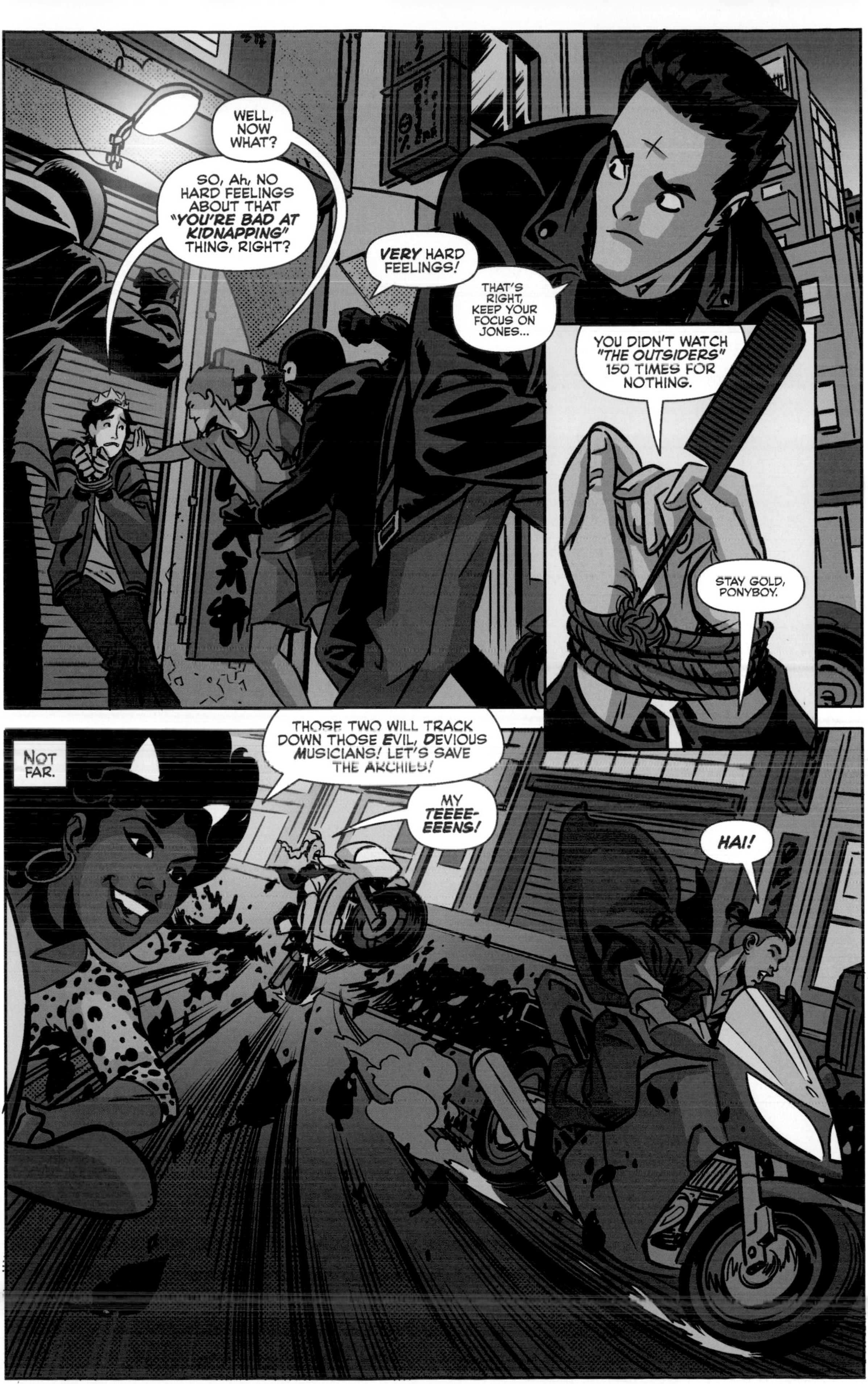

WELL, NOW WHAT?
SO, Ah, NO HARD FEELINGS ABOUT THAT "YOU'RE BAD AT KIDNAPPING" THING, RIGHT?
VERY HARD FEELINGS!
THAT'S RIGHT, KEEP YOUR FOCUS ON JONES...
YOU DIDN'T WATCH "THE OUTSIDERS" 150 TIMES FOR NOTHING.
STAY GOLD, PONYBOY.
NOT FAR.
THOSE TWO WILL TRACK DOWN THOSE EVIL, DEVIOUS MUSICIANS! LET'S SAVE THE ARCHIES!
MY TEEEE-EEENS!
HAI!

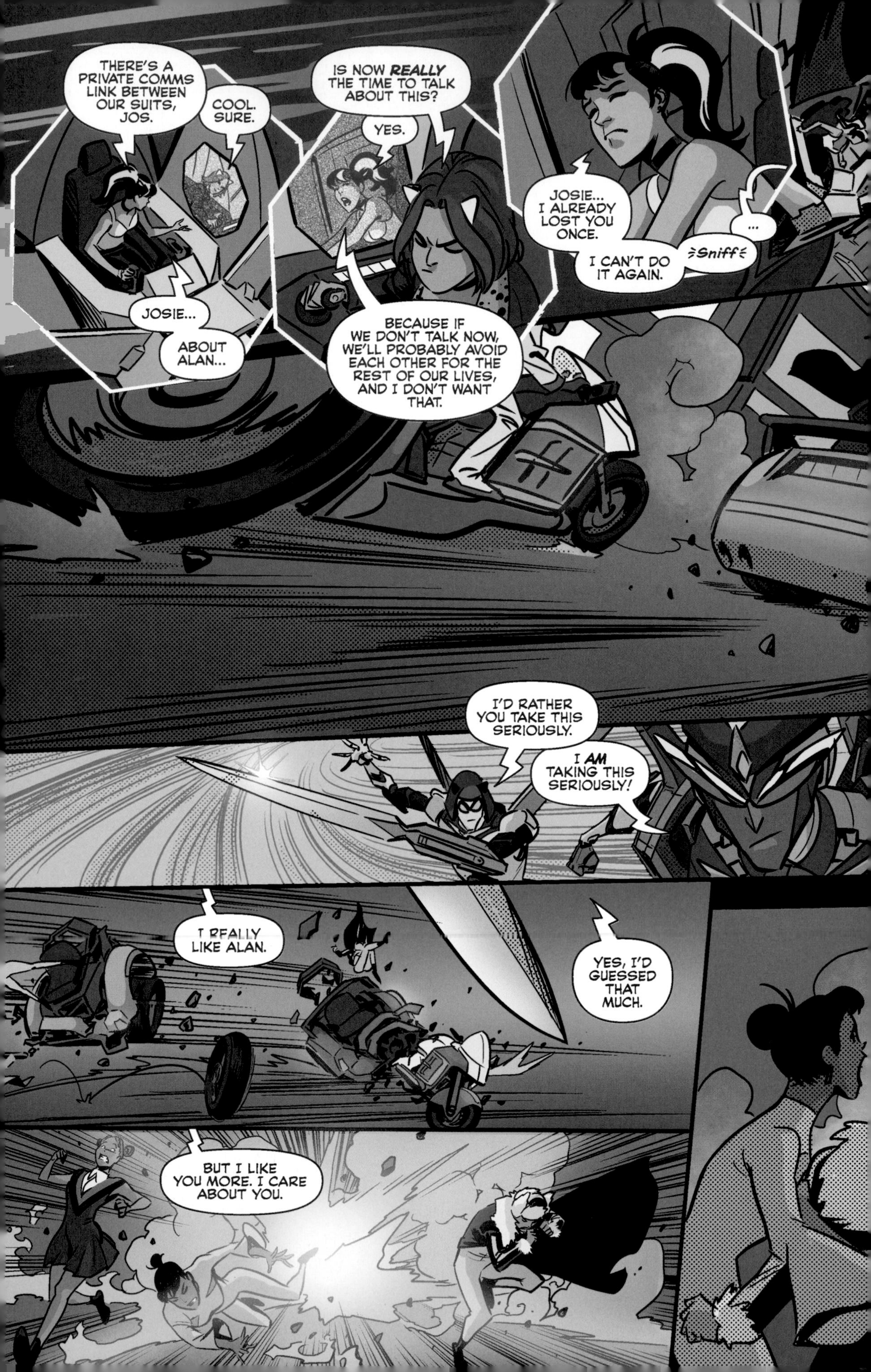
THERE'S A PRIVATE COMMS LINK BETWEEN OUR SUITS, JOS.
COOL. SURE.
JOSIE...
ABOUT ALAN...
IS NOW REALLY THE TIME TO TALK ABOUT THIS?
YES.
BECAUSE IF WE DON'T TALK NOW, WE'LL PROBABLY AVOID EACH OTHER FOR THE REST OF OUR LIVES, AND I DON'T WANT THAT.
JOSIE... I ALREADY LOST YOU ONCE.
I CAN'T DO IT AGAIN.
Sniff
...
I'D RATHER YOU TAKE THIS SERIOUSLY.
I AM TAKING THIS SERIOUSLY!
I REALLY LIKE ALAN.
YES, I'D GUESSED THAT MUCH.
BUT I LIKE YOU MORE. I CARE ABOUT YOU.

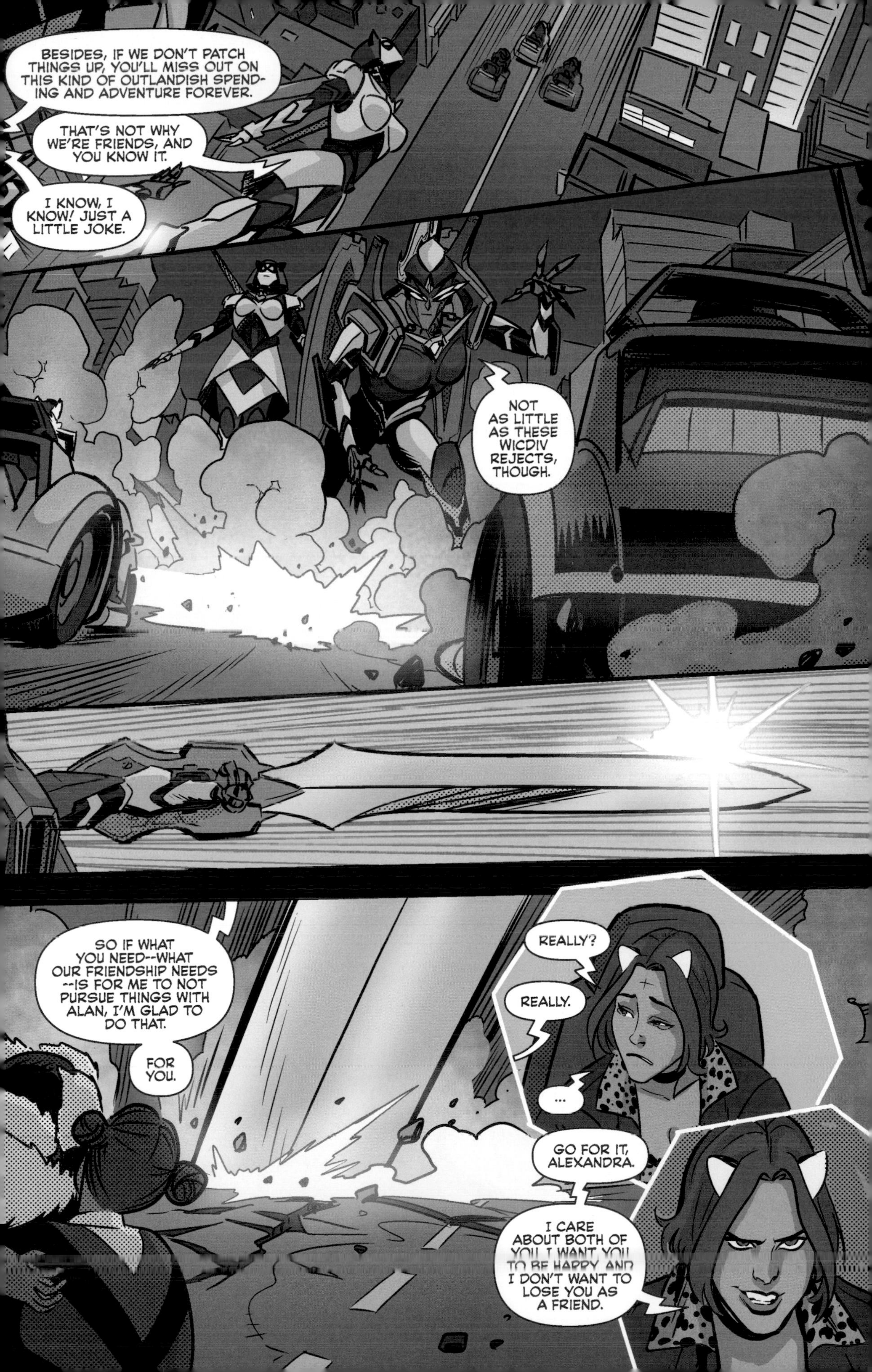
BESIDES, IF WE DON'T PATCH THINGS UP, YOU'LL MISS OUT ON THIS KIND OF OUTLANDISH SPENDING AND ADVENTURE FOREVER.
THAT'S NOT WHY WE'RE FRIENDS, AND YOU KNOW IT.
I KNOW, I KNOW! JUST A LITTLE JOKE.
NOT AS LITTLE AS THESE WICDIV REJECTS, THOUGH.
SO IF WHAT YOU NEED--WHAT OUR FRIENDSHIP NEEDS --IS FOR ME TO NOT PURSUE THINGS WITH ALAN, I'M GLAD TO DO THAT.
FOR YOU.
REALLY?
REALLY.
...
GO FOR IT, ALEXANDRA.
I CARE ABOUT BOTH OF YOU. I WANT YOU TO BE HAPPY AND I DON'T WANT TO LOSE YOU AS A FRIEND.

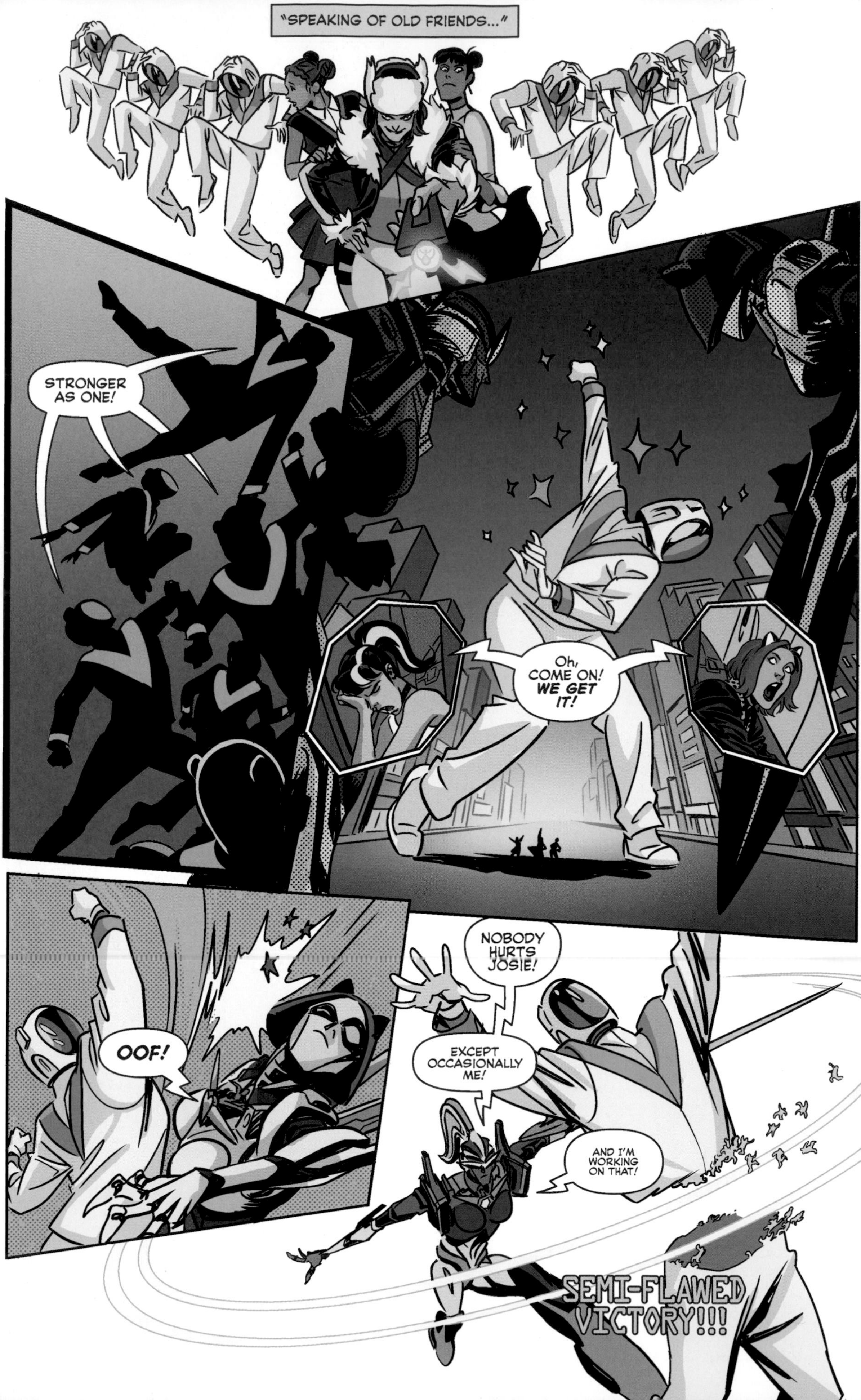
"SPEAKING OF OLD FRIENDS..."
STRONGER AS ONE!
Oh, COME ON! WE GET IT!
OOF!
NOBODY HURTS JOSIE!
EXCEPT OCCASIONALLY ME!
AND I'M WORKING ON THAT!
SEMI-FLAWED VICTORY!!!

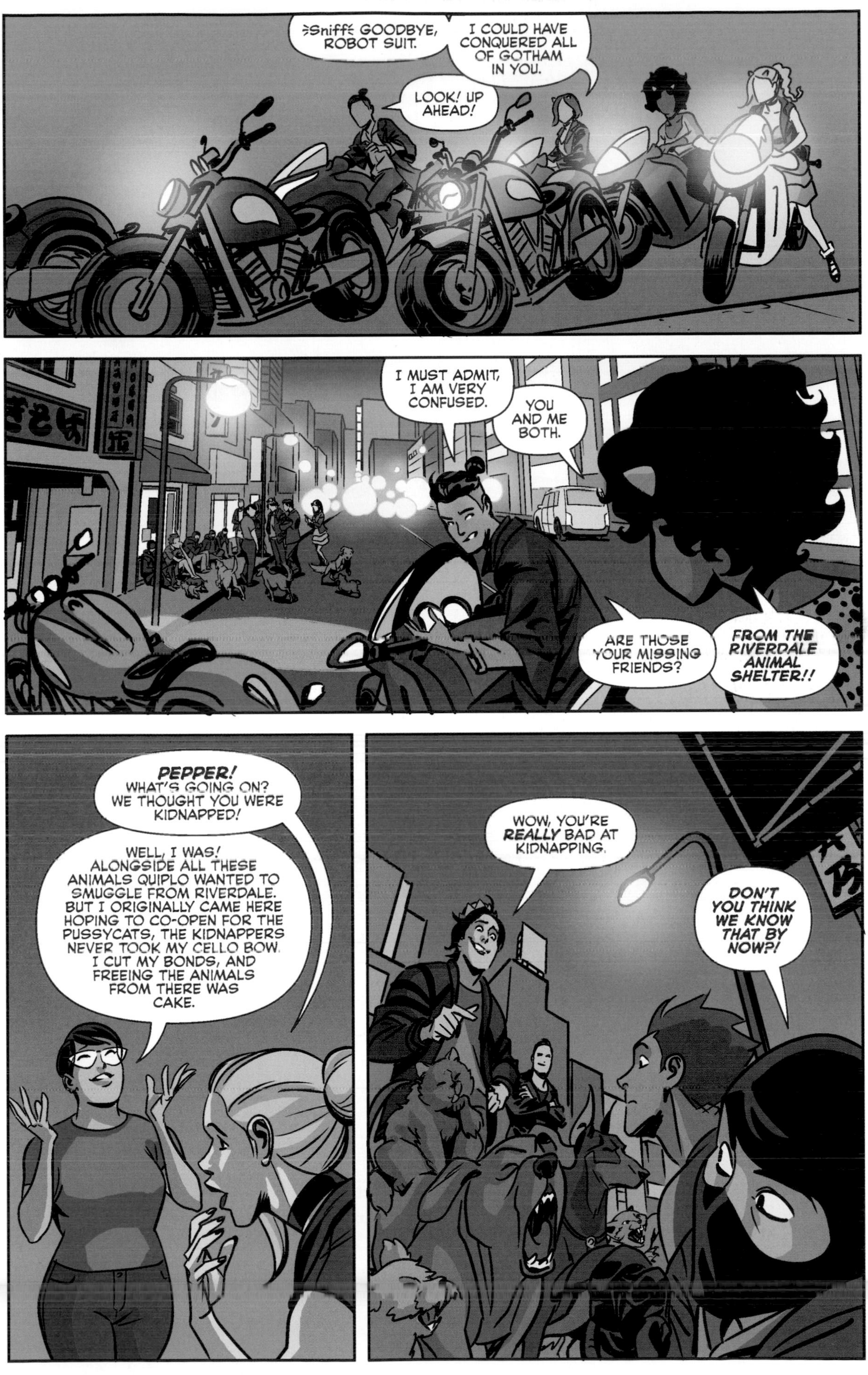
Sniff GOODBYE, ROBOT SUIT.
I COULD HAVE CONQUERED ALL OF GOTHAM IN YOU.
LOOK! UP AHEAD!
I MUST ADMIT, I AM VERY CONFUSED.
YOU AND ME BOTH.
ARE THOSE YOUR MISSING FRIENDS?
FROM THE RIVERDALE ANIMAL SHELTER!!
PEPPER! WHAT'S GOING ON? WE THOUGHT YOU WERE KIDNAPPED!
WELL, I WAS! ALONGSIDE ALL THESE ANIMALS QUIPLO WANTED TO SMUGGLE FROM RIVERDALE. BUT I ORIGINALLY CAME HERE HOPING TO CO-OPEN FOR THE PUSSYCATS, THE KIDNAPPERS NEVER TOOK MY CELLO BOW. I CUT MY BONDS, AND FREEING THE ANIMALS FROM THERE WAS CAKE.
WOW, YOU'RE REALLY BAD AT KIDNAPPING.
DON'T YOU THINK WE KNOW THAT BY NOW?!

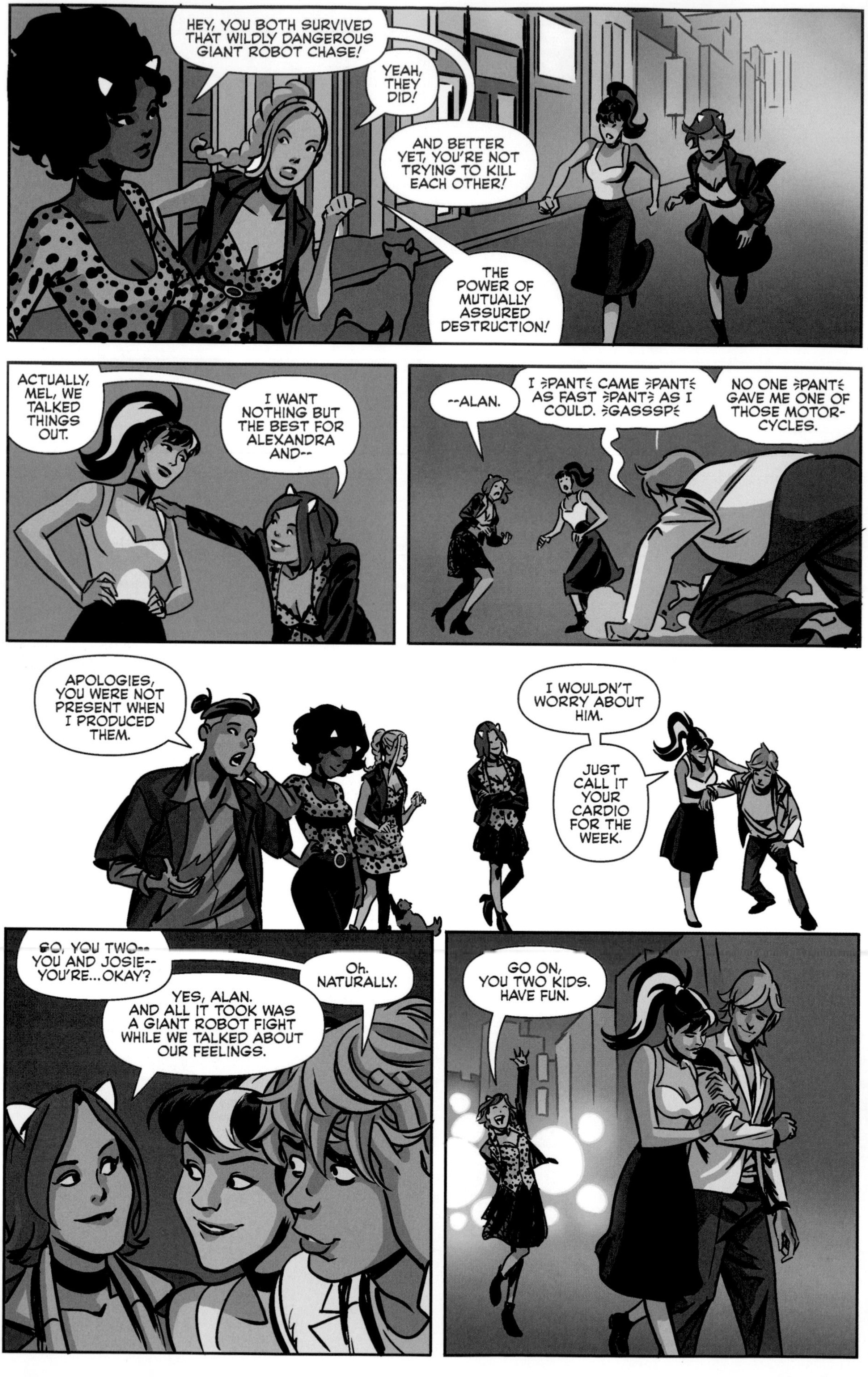
HEY, YOU BOTH SURVIVED THAT WILDLY DANGEROUS GIANT ROBOT CHASE!
YEAH, THEY DID!
AND BETTER YET, YOU'RE NOT TRYING TO KILL EACH OTHER!
THE POWER OF MUTUALLY ASSURED DESTRUCTION!
ACTUALLY, MEL, WE TALKED THINGS OUT.
I WANT NOTHING BUT THE BEST FOR ALEXANDRA AND--
--ALAN.
I ≶PANT≷ CAME ≶PANT≷ AS FAST ≶PANT≷ AS I COULD. ≶GASSSP≷
NO ONE ≶PANT≷ GAVE ME ONE OF THOSE MOTOR-CYCLES.
APOLOGIES, YOU WERE NOT PRESENT WHEN I PRODUCED THEM.
I WOULDN'T WORRY ABOUT HIM.
JUST CALL IT YOUR CARDIO FOR THE WEEK.
SO, YOU TWO-- YOU AND JOSIE-- YOU'RE...OKAY?
Oh. NATURALLY.
YES, ALAN. AND ALL IT TOOK WAS A GIANT ROBOT FIGHT WHILE WE TALKED ABOUT OUR FEELINGS.
GO ON, YOU TWO KIDS. HAVE FUN.

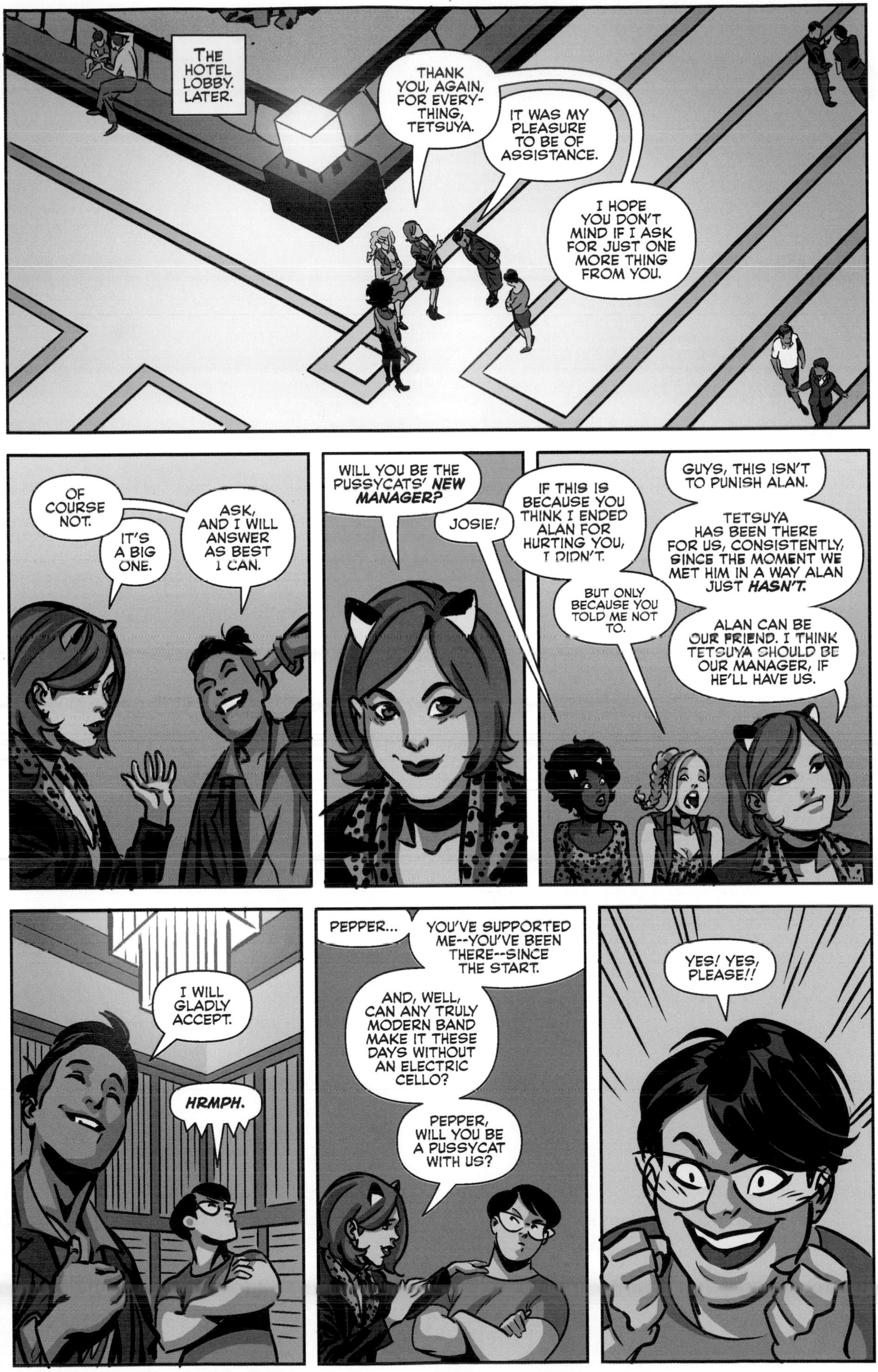
THE HOTEL LOBBY. LATER.
THANK YOU, AGAIN, FOR EVERYTHING, TETSUYA.
IT WAS MY PLEASURE TO BE OF ASSISTANCE.
I HOPE YOU DON'T MIND IF I ASK FOR JUST ONE MORE THING FROM YOU.
OF COURSE NOT.
IT'S A BIG ONE.
ASK, AND I WILL ANSWER AS BEST I CAN.
WILL YOU BE THE PUSSYCATS' NEW MANAGER?
JOSIE!
IF THIS IS BECAUSE YOU THINK I ENDED ALAN FOR HURTING YOU, I DIDN'T.
BUT ONLY BECAUSE YOU TOLD ME NOT TO.
GUYS, THIS ISN'T TO PUNISH ALAN.
TETSUYA HAS BEEN THERE FOR US, CONSISTENTLY, SINCE THE MOMENT WE MET HIM IN A WAY ALAN JUST HASN'T.
ALAN CAN BE OUR FRIEND. I THINK TETSUYA SHOULD BE OUR MANAGER, IF HE'LL HAVE US.
I WILL GLADLY ACCEPT.
HRMPH.
PEPPER...
YOU'VE SUPPORTED ME--YOU'VE BEEN THERE--SINCE THE START.
AND, WELL, CAN ANY TRULY MODERN BAND MAKE IT THESE DAYS WITHOUT AN ELECTRIC CELLO?
PEPPER, WILL YOU BE A PUSSYCAT WITH US?
YES! YES, PLEASE!!

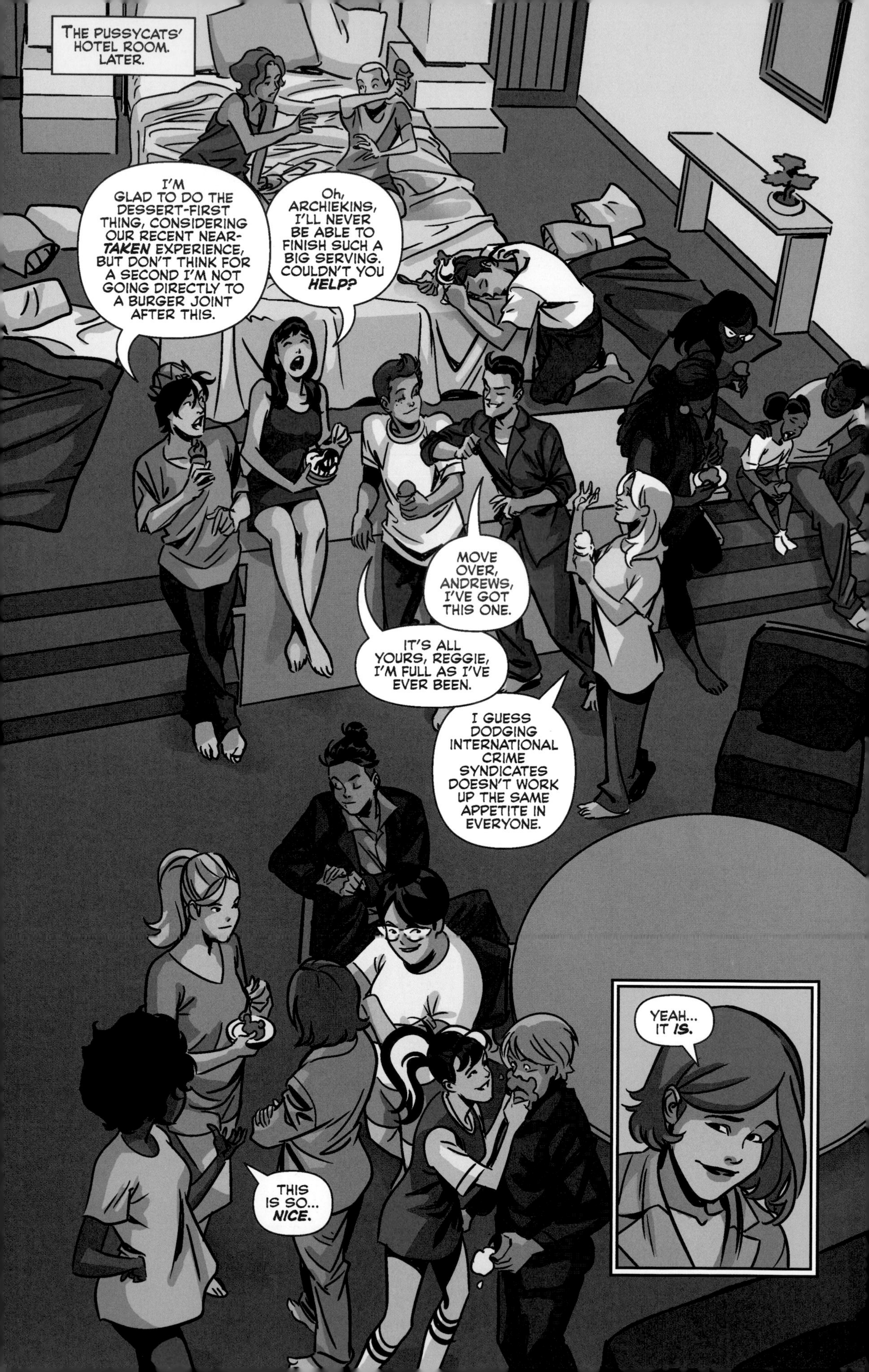

THE PUSSYCATS' HOTEL ROOM. LATER.
I'M GLAD TO DO THE DESSERT-FIRST THING, CONSIDERING OUR RECENT NEAR-*TAKEN* EXPERIENCE, BUT DON'T THINK FOR A SECOND I'M NOT GOING DIRECTLY TO A BURGER JOINT AFTER THIS.
Oh, ARCHIEKINS, I'LL NEVER BE ABLE TO FINISH SUCH A BIG SERVING. COULDN'T YOU *HELP?*
MOVE OVER, ANDREWS, I'VE GOT THIS ONE.
IT'S ALL YOURS, REGGIE, I'M FULL AS I'VE EVER BEEN.
I GUESS DODGING INTERNATIONAL CRIME SYNDICATES DOESN'T WORK UP THE SAME APPETITE IN EVERYONE.
THIS IS SO... ***NICE.***
YEAH... IT ***IS.***

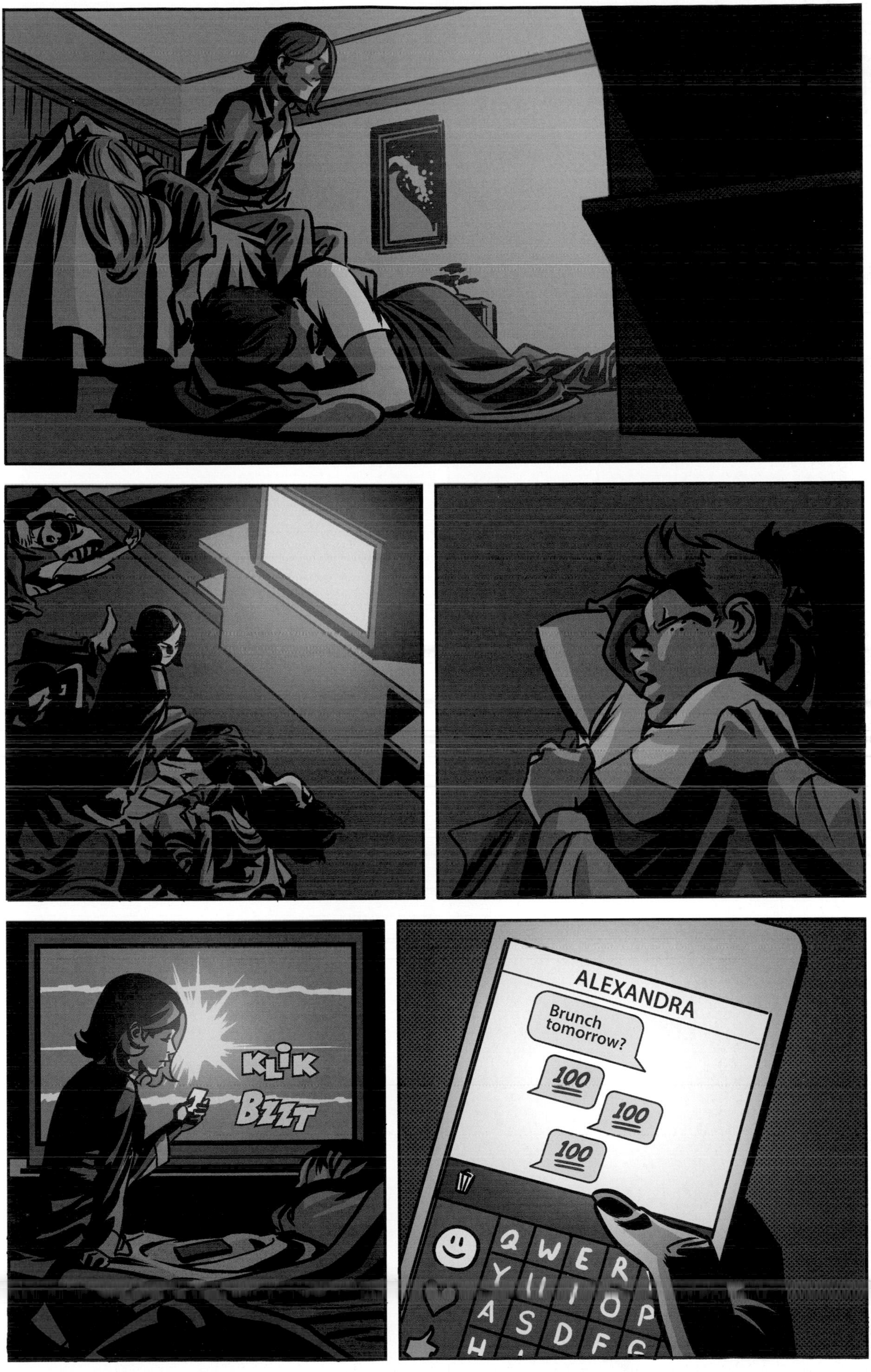

KLIK
BZZT
ALEXANDRA
Brunch tomorrow?
100
100
100

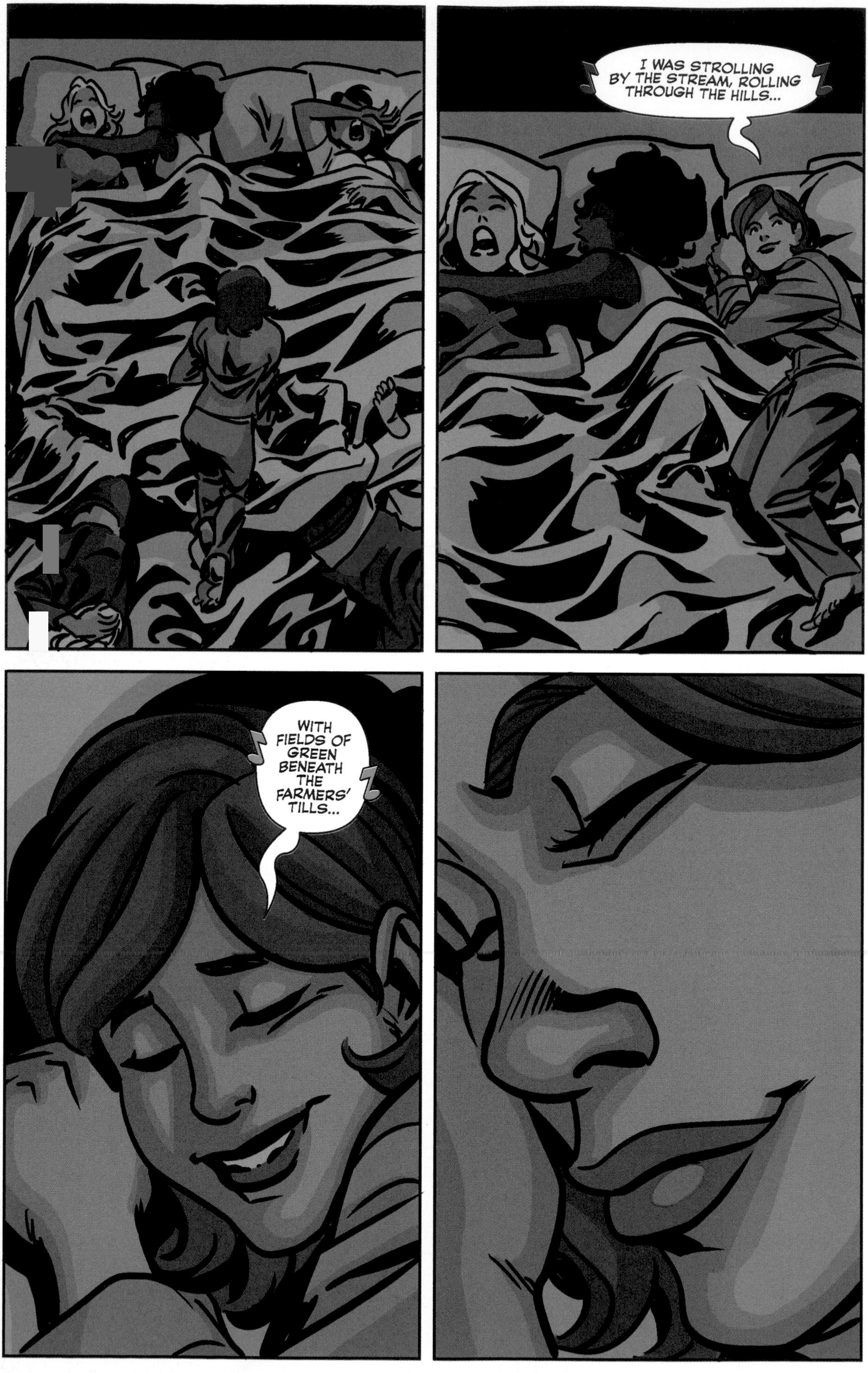
I WAS STROLLING BY THE STREAM, ROLLING THROUGH THE HILLS...
WITH FIELDS OF GREEN BENEATH THE FARMERS' TILLS...

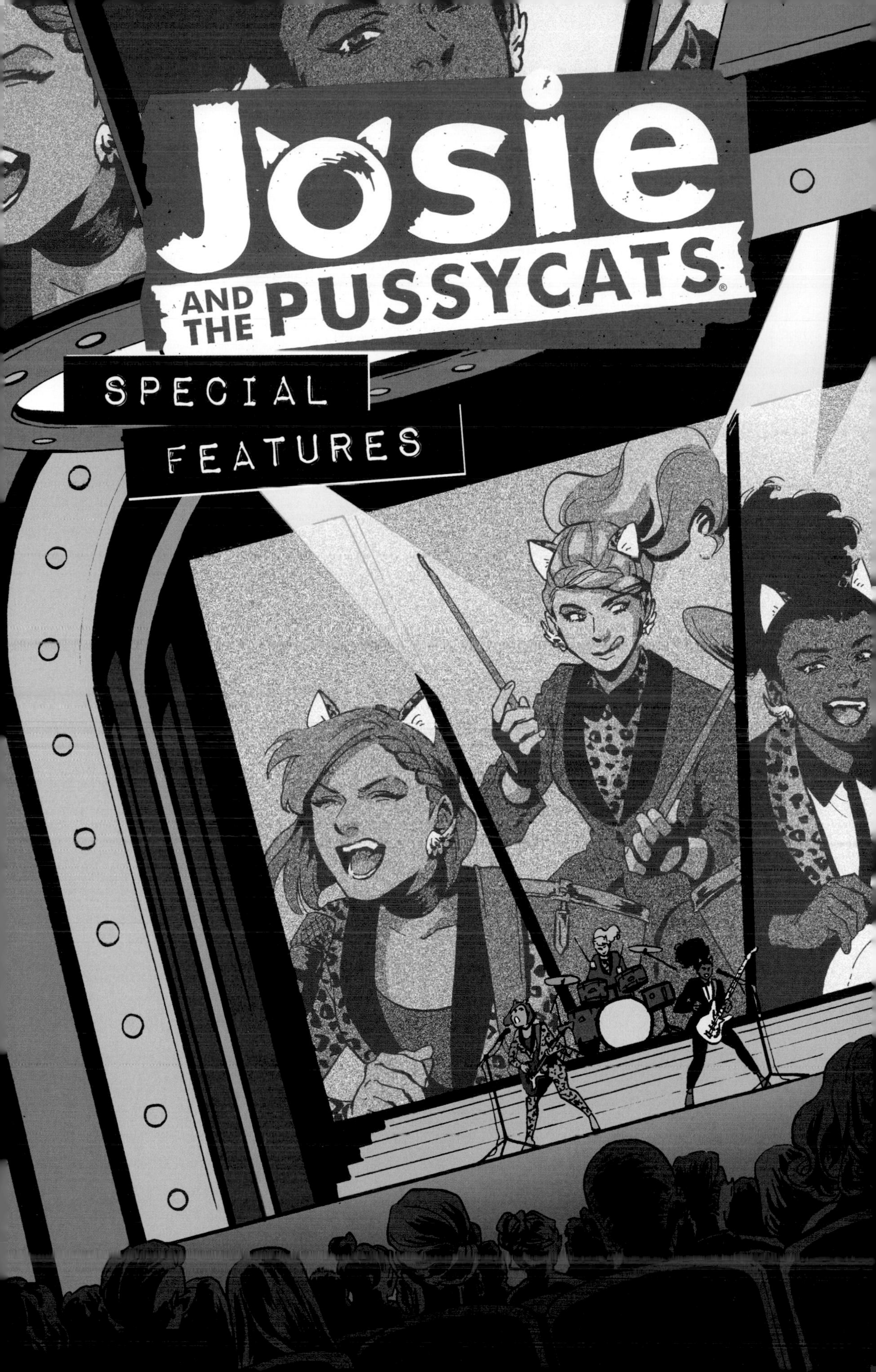
Josie AND THE PUSSYCATS
SPECIAL FEATURES

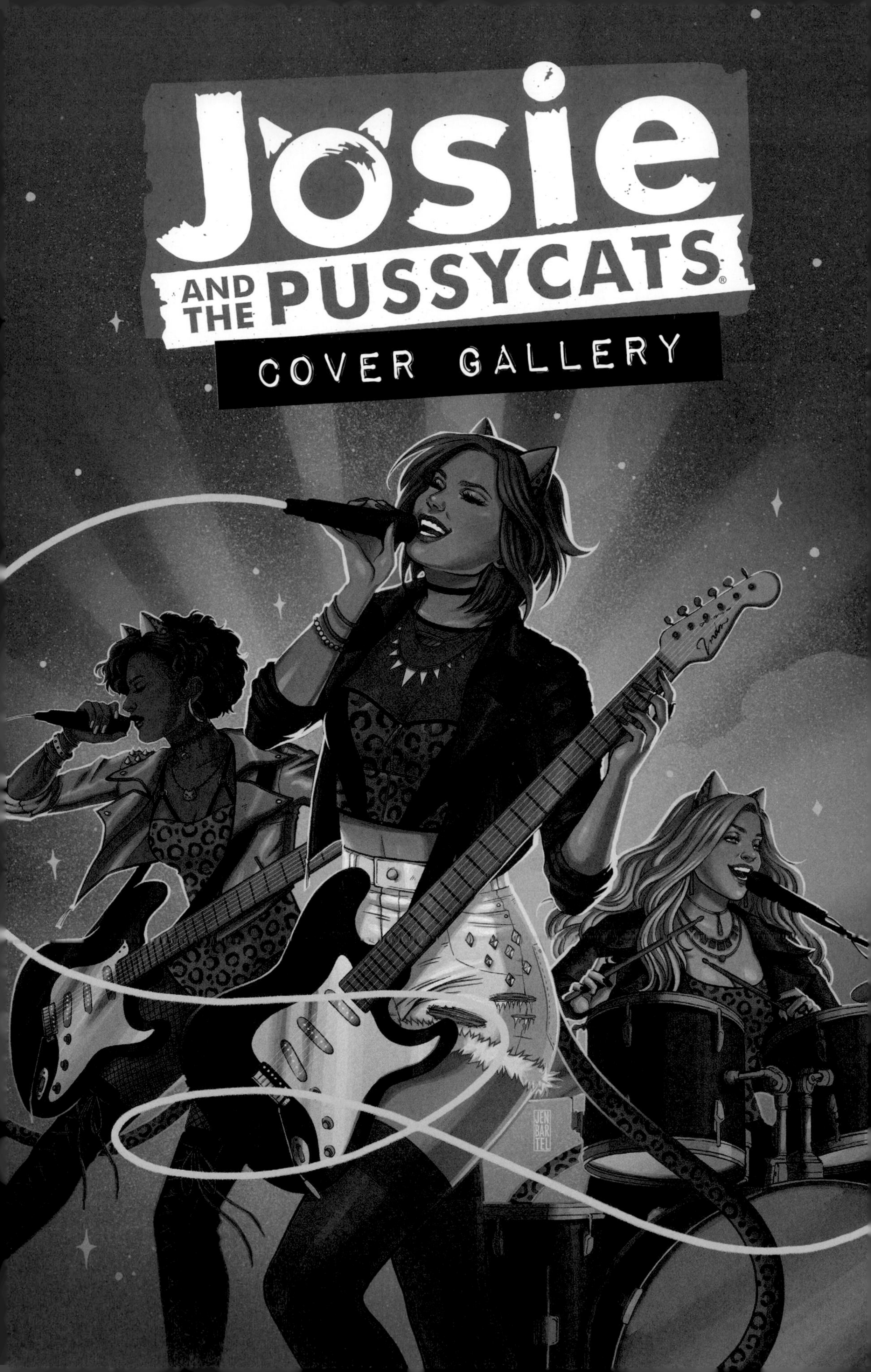
Josie
AND THE PUSSYCATS®
COVER GALLERY
JEN BARTEL

ISSUE SIX

AUDREY MOK

Josie

MICHAEL ALLRED

Josie
AND THE
PUSSYCATS

BEN CALDWELL

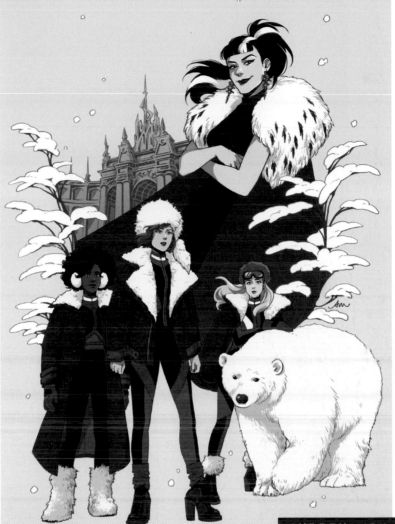

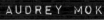

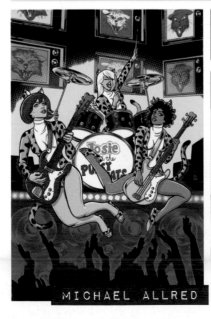

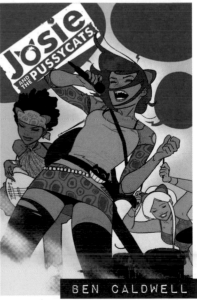

ISSUE SEVEN

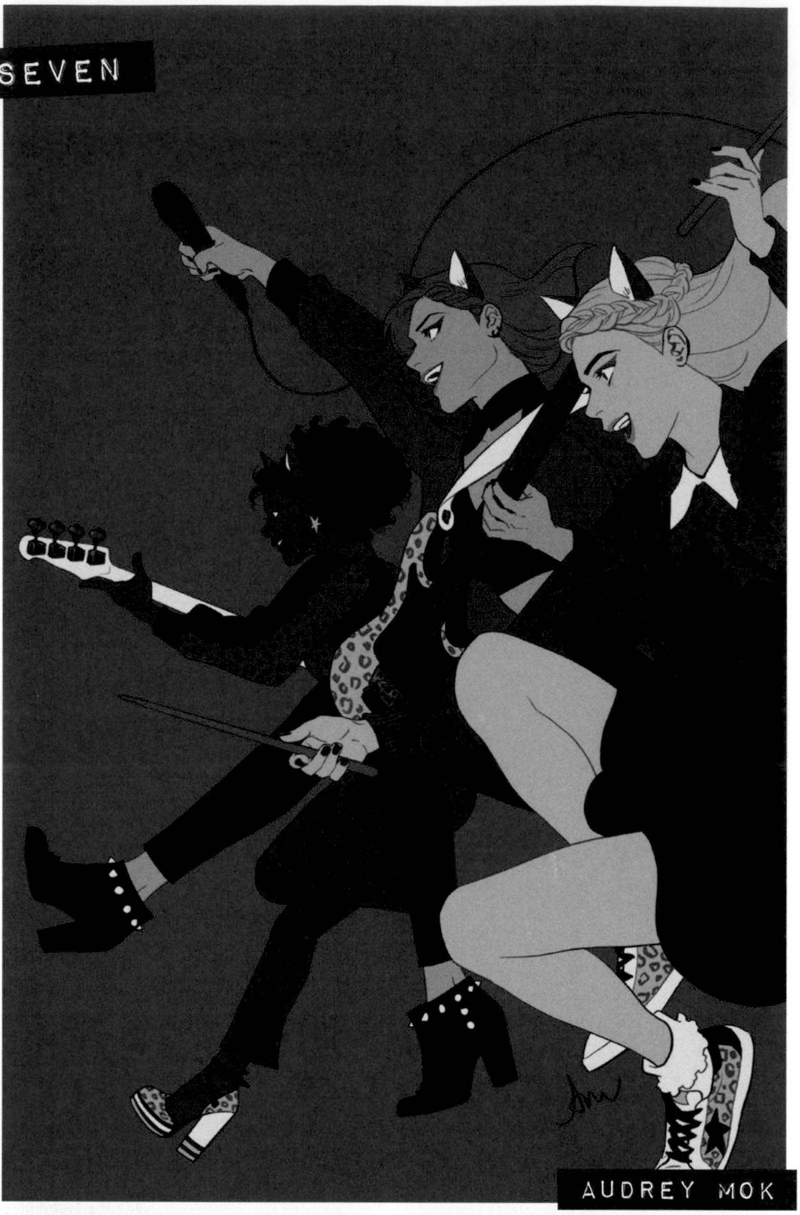

AUDREY MOK

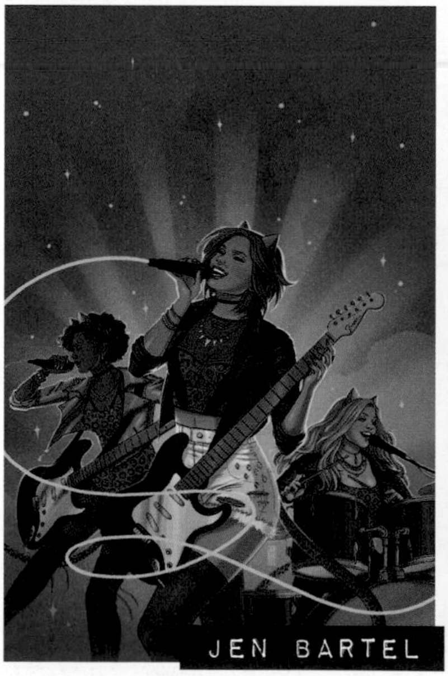

JEN BARTEL

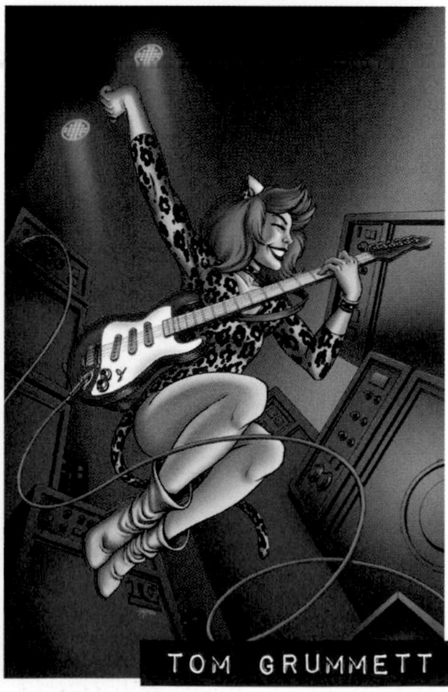

TOM GRUMMETT

ISSUE EIGHT

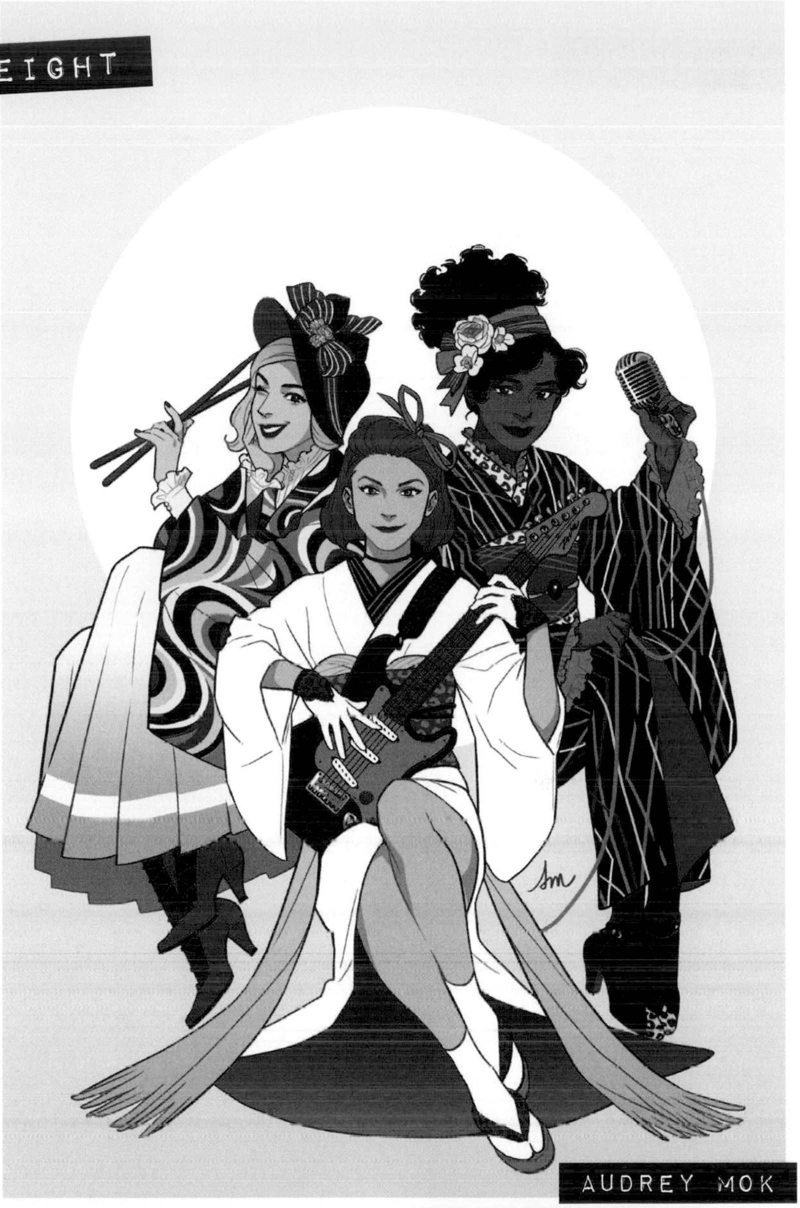

AUDREY MOK

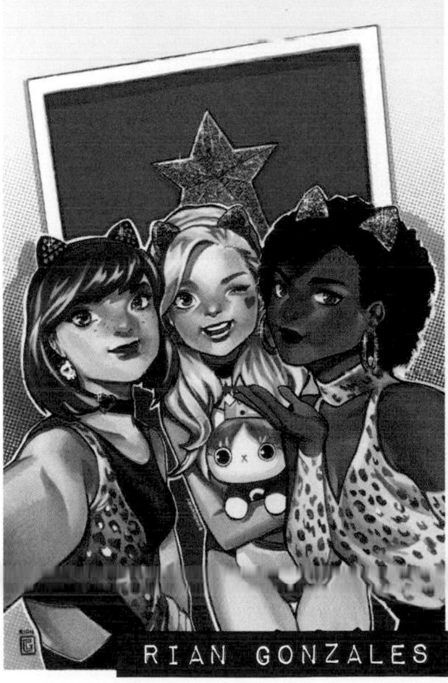

RIAN GONZALES

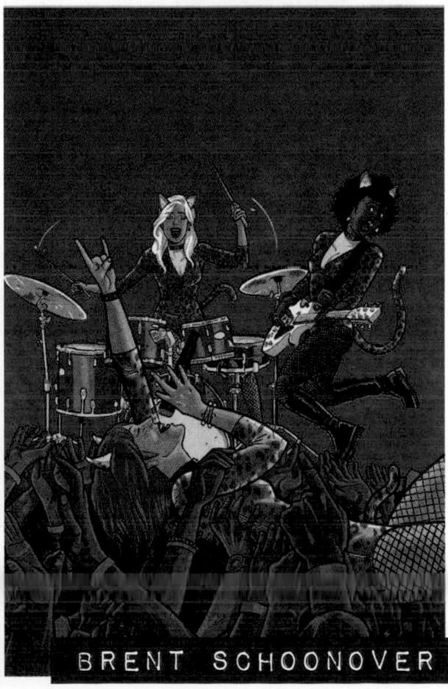

BRENT SCHOONOVER

ISSUE NINE

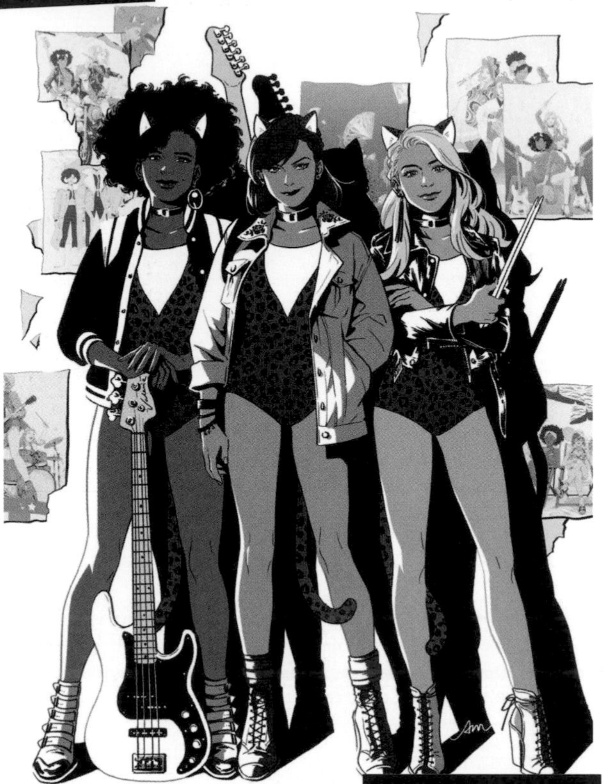

AUDREY MOK

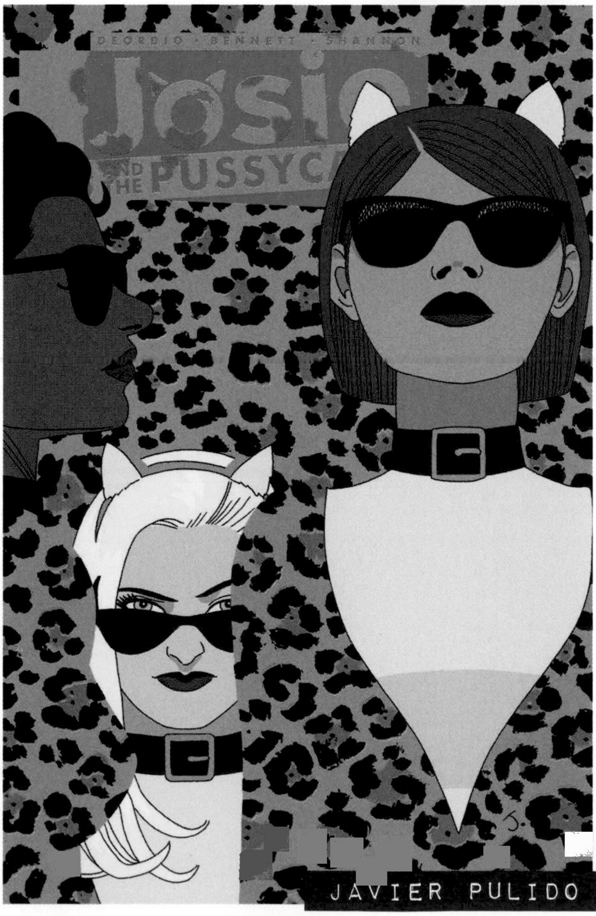
DEORDIO · BENNETT · SHANNON
Josie
AND THE PUSSYCA

JAVIER PULIDO

SPECIAL PREVIEW

Betty & Veronica® Vixens

STORY BY:
Jamie Lee Rotante

ART BY:
Eva Cabrera

COLORS BY:
Elaina Unger

LETTERS BY:
Rachel Deering

Here's a very special preview of the brand new ongoing series **BETTY & VERONICA: VIXENS.** The toughest gang in Riverdale is one you'd least expect: the Vixens, led by Riverdale High's own Betty and Veronica! This action-packed thrilling series not only puts the ladies of Riverdale at the forefront, it's also created by an all-female team. You can find individual issues in comic shops everywhere now!

ISSUE ONE

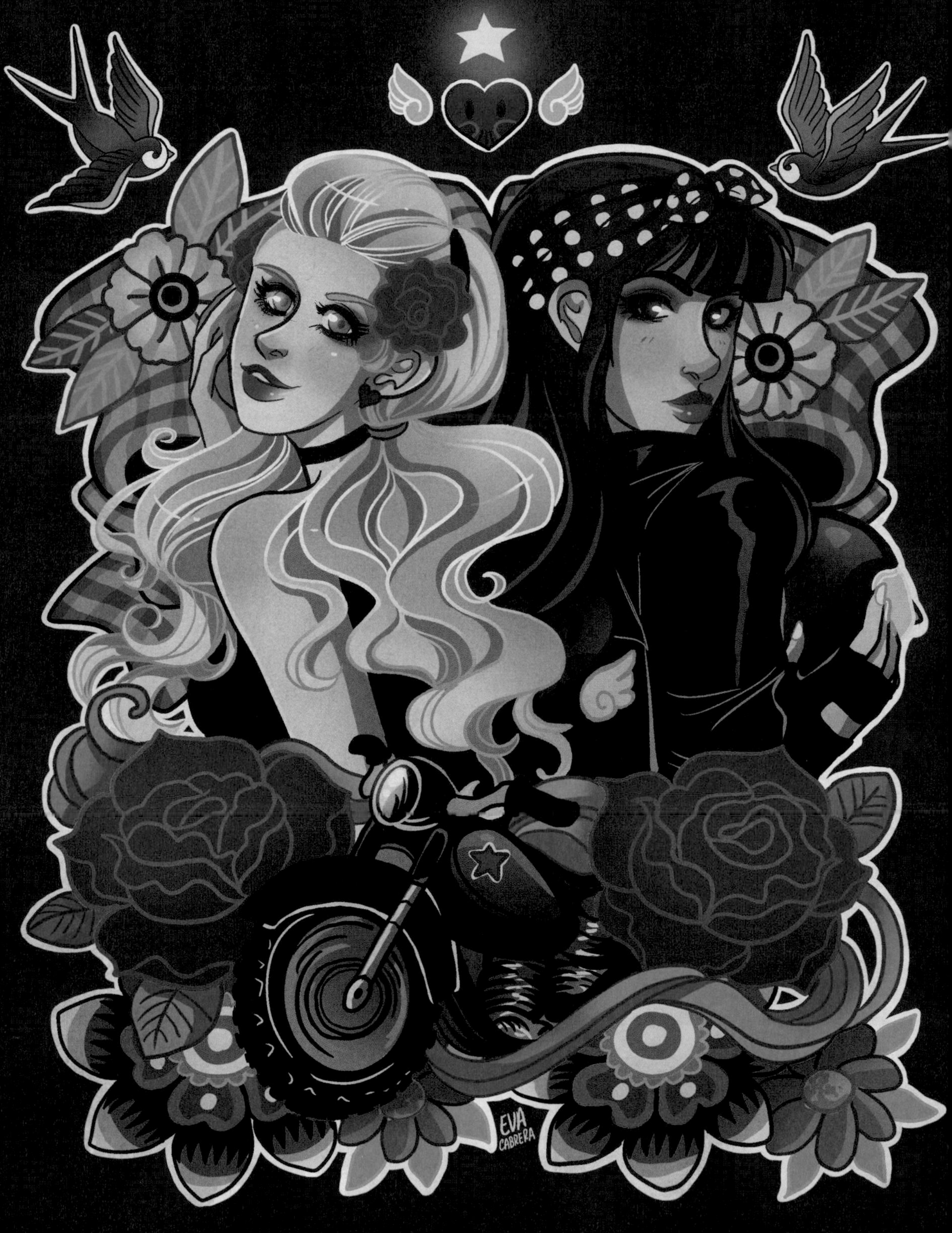
EVA CABRERA

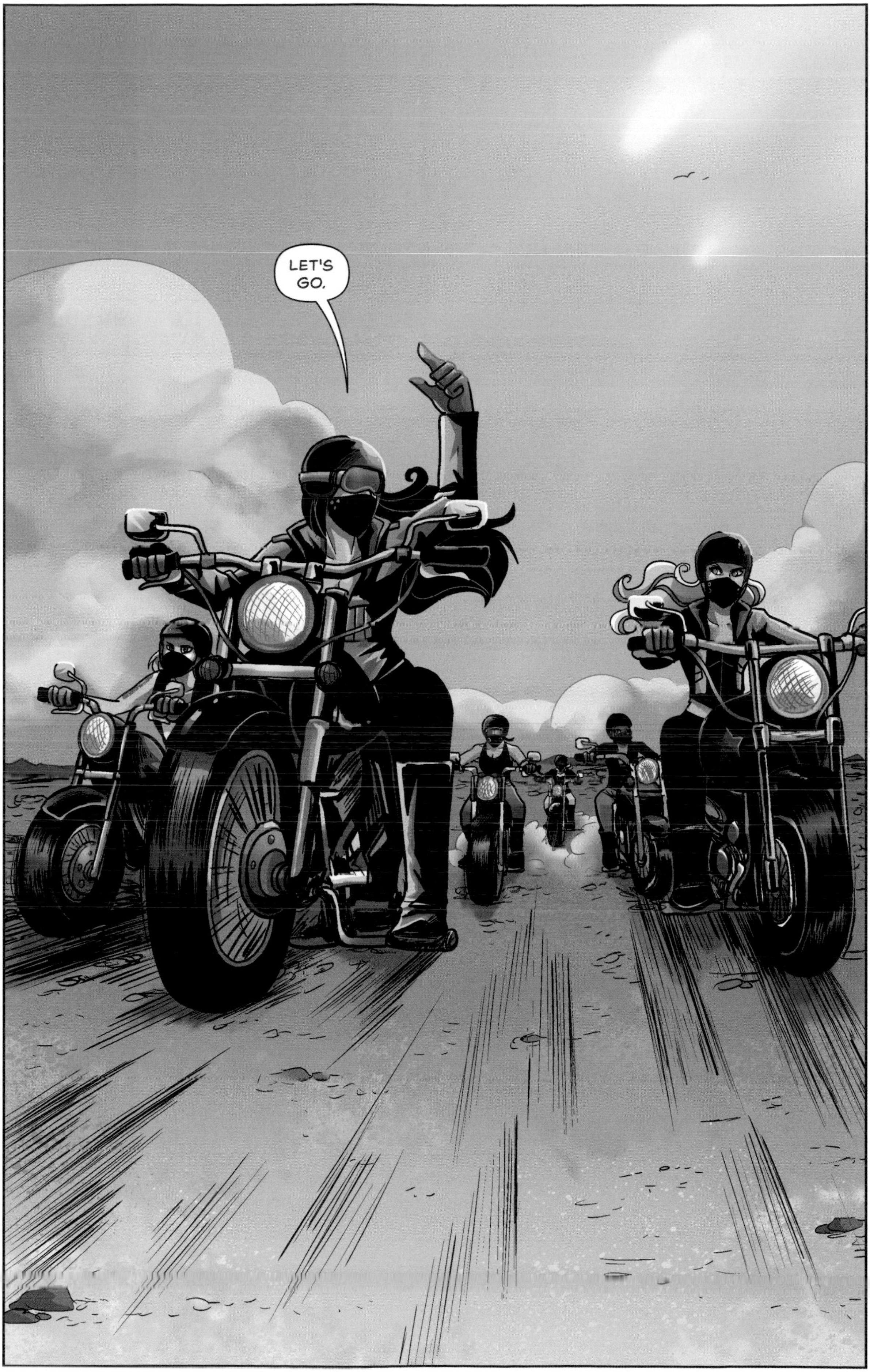
LET'S GO.

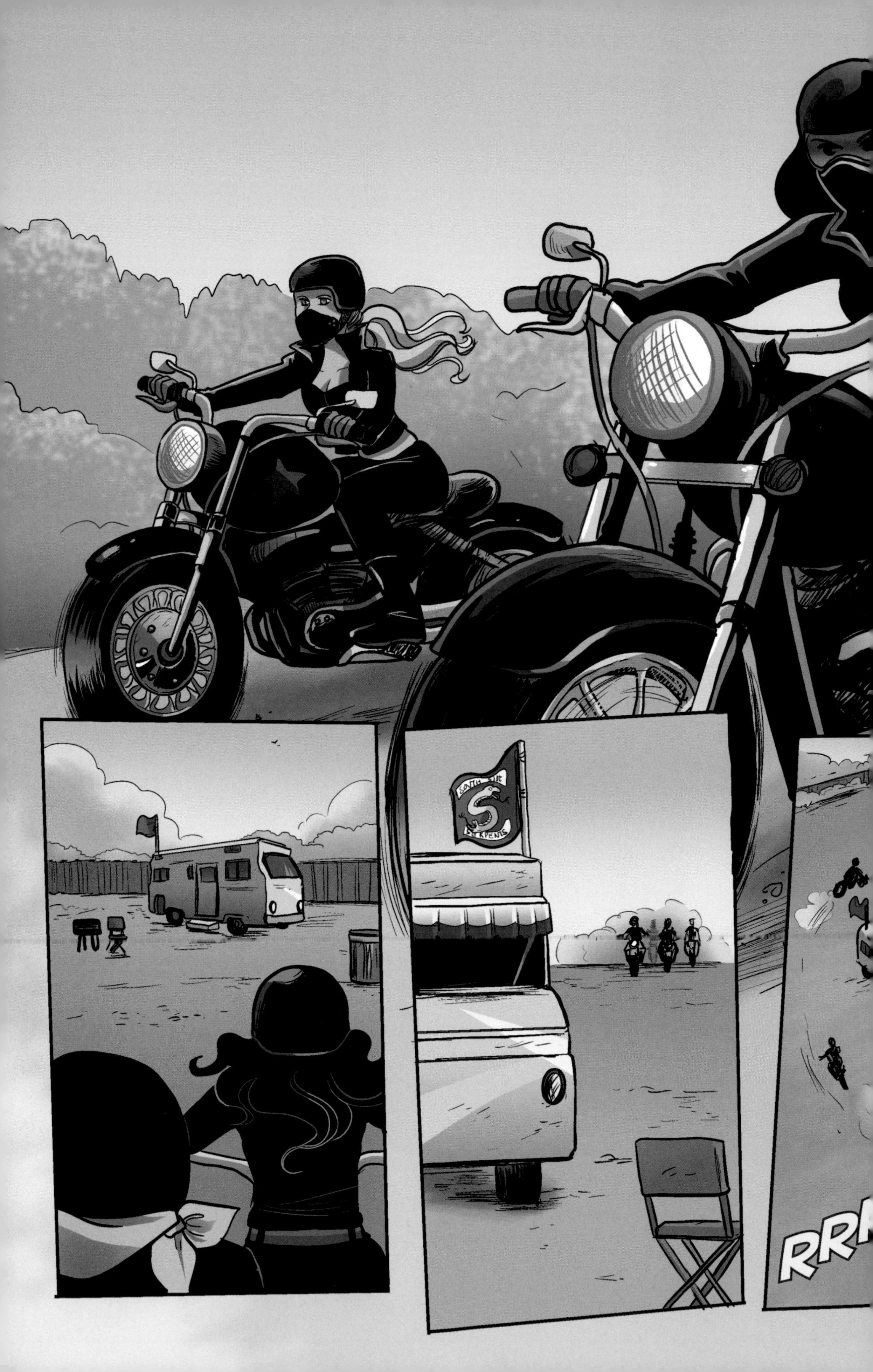
RR

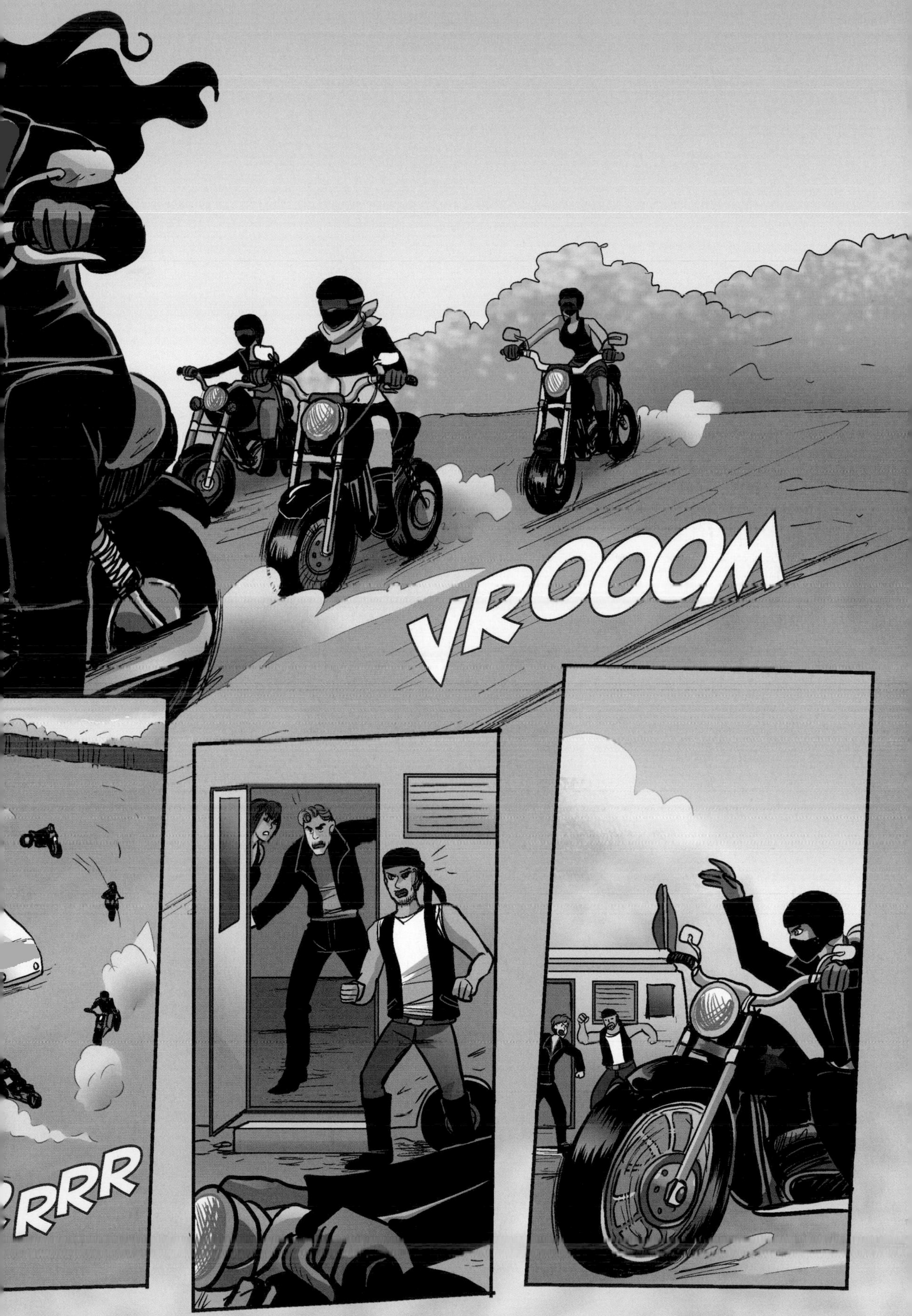
VROOOM
RRR

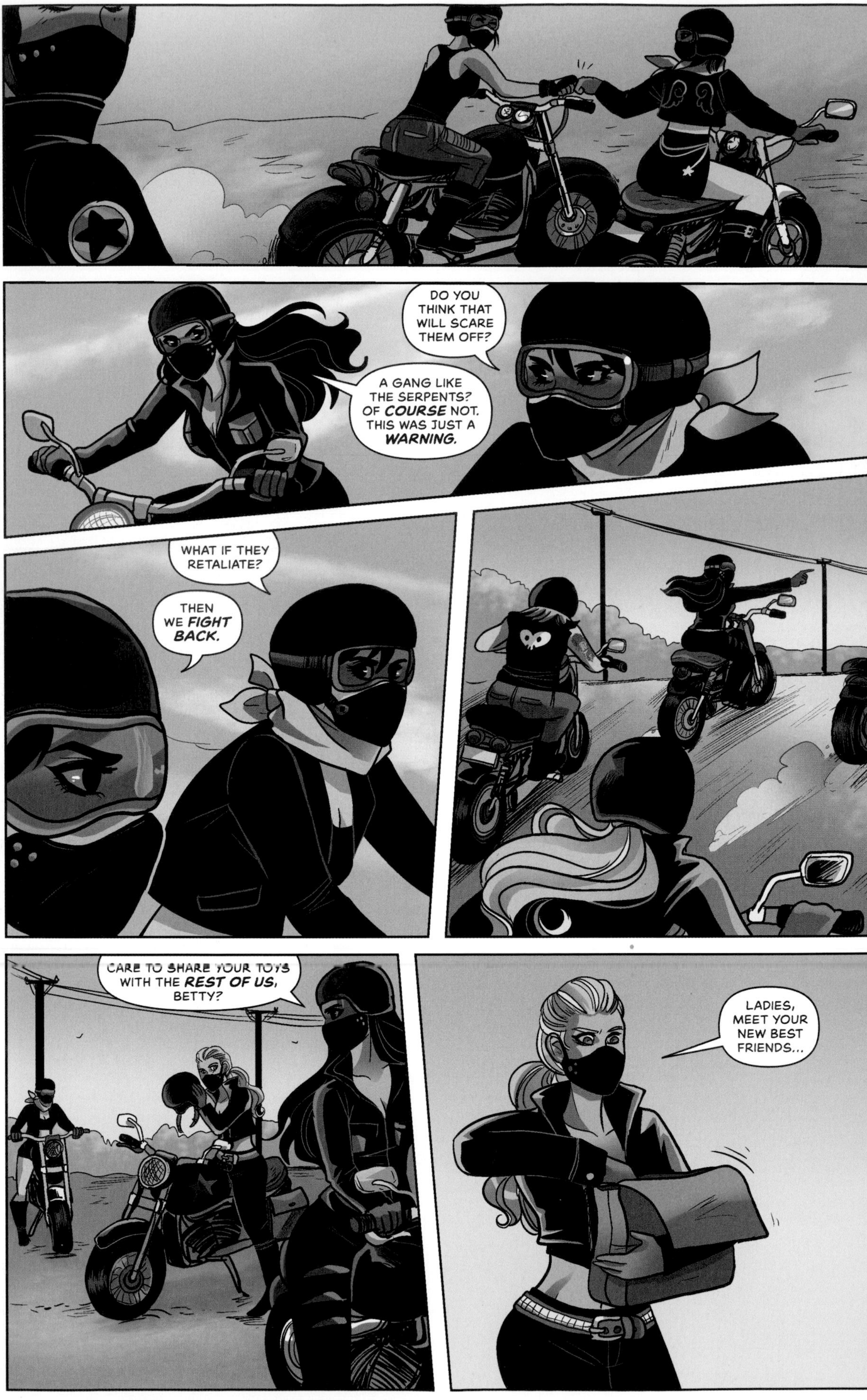
DO YOU THINK THAT WILL SCARE THEM OFF?
A GANG LIKE THE SERPENTS? OF COURSE NOT. THIS WAS JUST A WARNING.
WHAT IF THEY RETALIATE?
THEN WE FIGHT BACK.
CARE TO SHARE YOUR TOYS WITH THE REST OF US, BETTY?
LADIES, MEET YOUR NEW BEST FRIENDS...

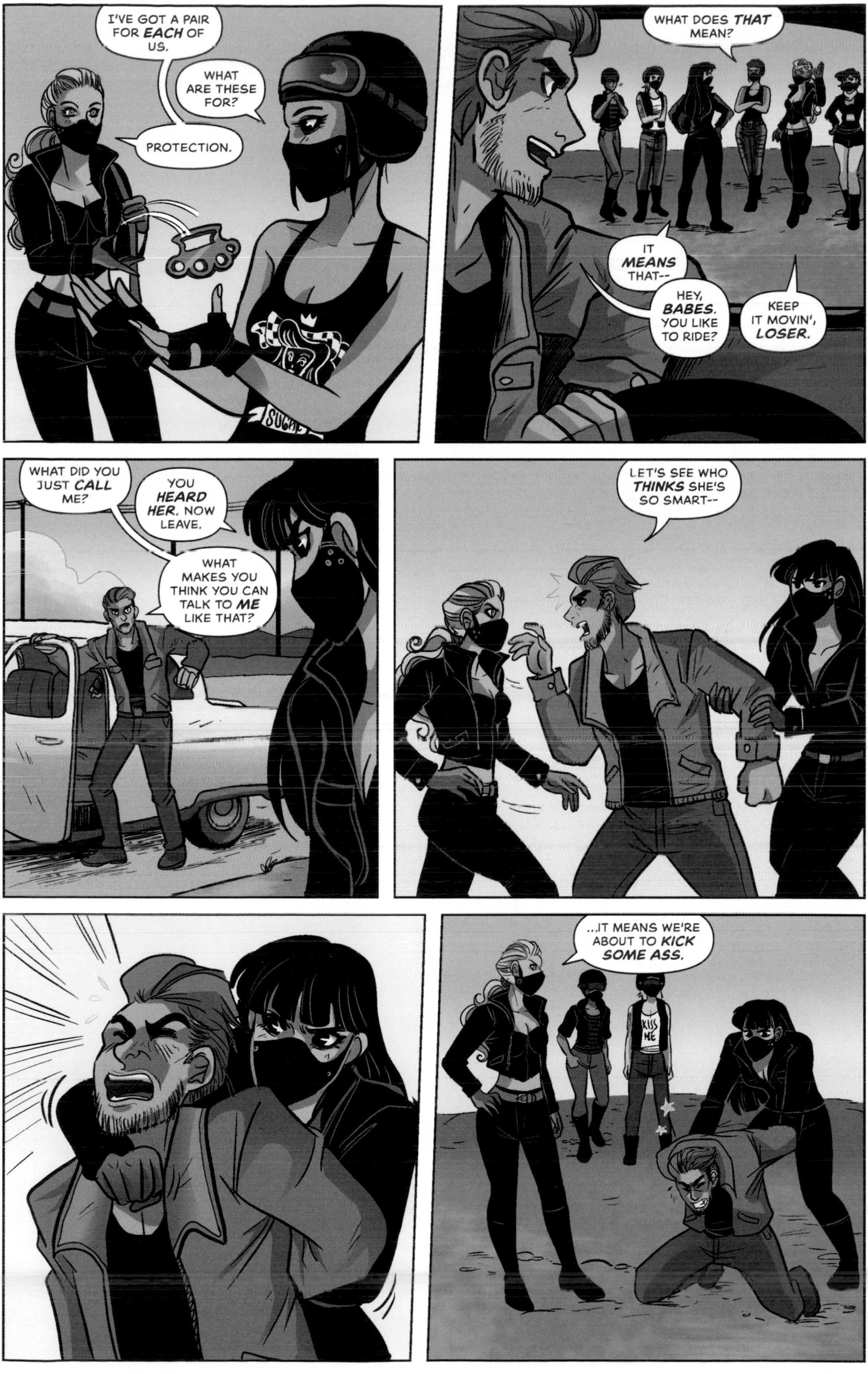

I'VE GOT A PAIR FOR EACH OF US.
WHAT ARE THESE FOR?
PROTECTION.
WHAT DOES THAT MEAN?
IT MEANS THAT--
HEY, BABES. YOU LIKE TO RIDE?
KEEP IT MOVIN', LOSER.
WHAT DID YOU JUST CALL ME?
YOU HEARD HER. NOW LEAVE.
WHAT MAKES YOU THINK YOU CAN TALK TO ME LIKE THAT?
LET'S SEE WHO THINKS SHE'S SO SMART--
...IT MEANS WE'RE ABOUT TO KICK SOME ASS.
KISS ME

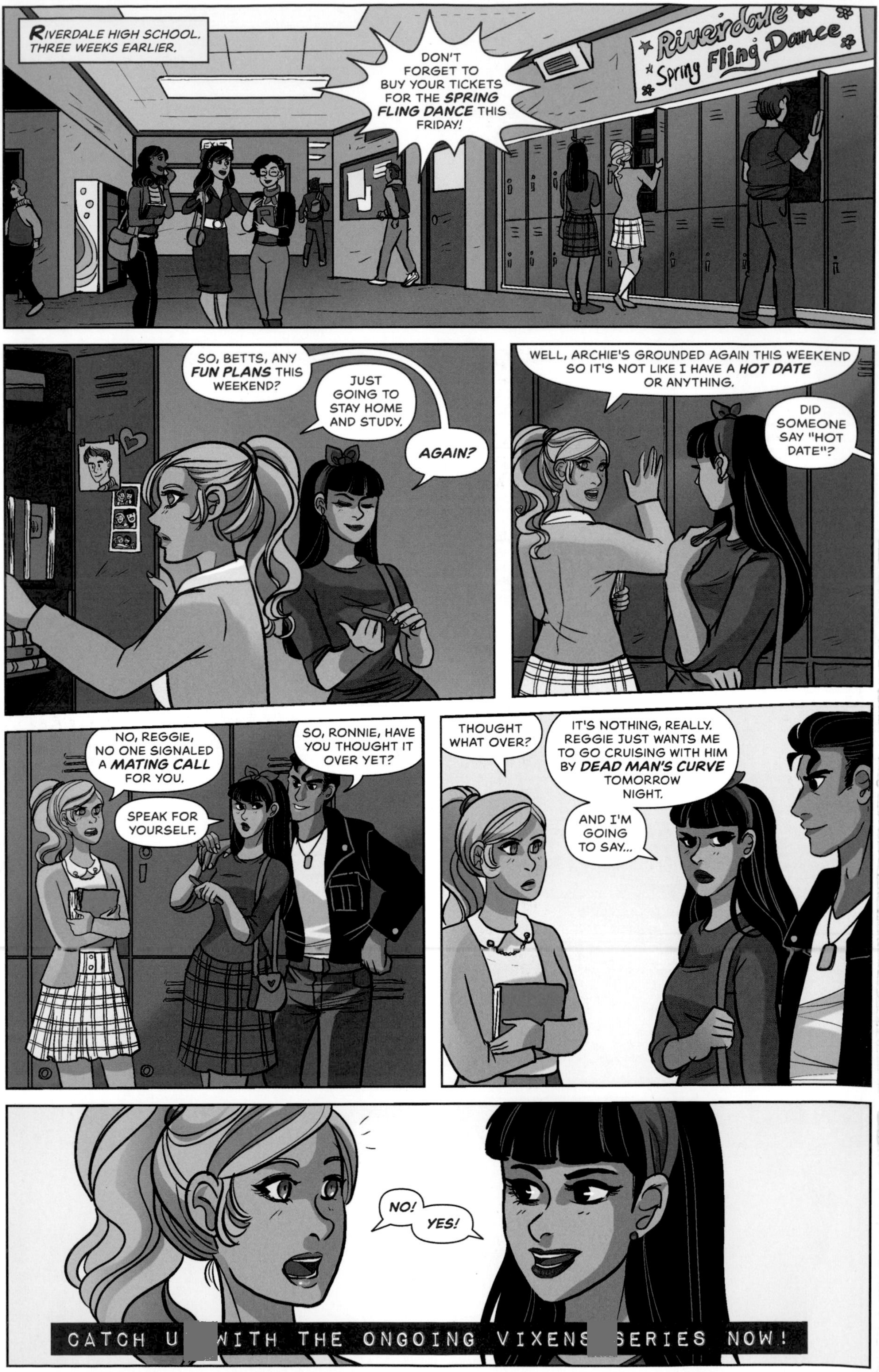

RIVERDALE HIGH SCHOOL. THREE WEEKS EARLIER.
DON'T FORGET TO BUY YOUR TICKETS FOR THE SPRING FLING DANCE THIS FRIDAY!
Riverdale Spring Fling Dance
SO, BETTS, ANY FUN PLANS THIS WEEKEND?
JUST GOING TO STAY HOME AND STUDY.
AGAIN?
WELL, ARCHIE'S GROUNDED AGAIN THIS WEEKEND SO IT'S NOT LIKE I HAVE A HOT DATE OR ANYTHING.
DID SOMEONE SAY "HOT DATE"?
NO, REGGIE, NO ONE SIGNALED A MATING CALL FOR YOU.
SPEAK FOR YOURSELF.
SO, RONNIE, HAVE YOU THOUGHT IT OVER YET?
THOUGHT WHAT OVER?
IT'S NOTHING, REALLY. REGGIE JUST WANTS ME TO GO CRUISING WITH HIM BY DEAD MAN'S CURVE TOMORROW NIGHT.
AND I'M GOING TO SAY...
NO!
YES!
CATCH U[redacted]WITH THE ONGOING VIXENS[redacted]SERIES NOW!